This Land
Is
Your Land

The Upper Yellowstone Falls

This Land Is Your Land

THE STRUGGLE TO SAVE AMERICA'S PUBLIC LANDS

BY

Bernard Shanks

Sierra Club Books · San Francisco

The Sierra Club, founded in 1892 by John Muir, has devoted itself to the study and protection of the earth's scenic and ecological resources—mountains, wetlands, woodlands, wild shores and rivers, deserts and plains. The publishing program of the Sierra Club offers books to the public as a nonprofit educational service in the hope that they may enlarge the public's understanding of the Club's basic concerns. The point of view expressed in each book, however, does not necessarily represent that of the Club. The Sierra Club has some fifty chapters coast to coast, in Canada, Hawaii, and Alaska. For information about how you may participate in its programs to preserve wilderness and the quality of life, please address inquiries to Sierra Club, 530 Bush Street, San Francisco, CA 94108.

LIBRARY OF CONGRESS CATALOGING IN PUBLICATION DATA
Shanks, Bernard.
  This land is your land.

  Bibliography: p.
  Includes index.
  1. United States—Public lands. I. Title.
HD216.S565 1984 333.1'0973 84-5359
ISBN 0-87156-822-5

Jacket design Copyright © 1984 by Lawrence Ratzkin
Book design by Barbara Llewellyn
Printed in the United States of America

10 9 8 7 6 5 4 3 2 1

Dedicated to Arthur C. Shanks,
who instilled in me a sense of history and
introduced me to the West.

Contents

Preface

The federal lands, one-third of the United States, have always been more than just territory. They are a product of convictions embodied through history in an unusual nation founded with a great wealth of land. Their fate is harnessed to the forces of geography and politics; geography dictates the scattering of minerals, water, and scenery. Politics allocates the resources.

The land is now bound by hundreds of laws and countless political pressures, all intertwined with the ethics of the nation, for ultimately the management of the land reflects national values and morality. The public domain shaped the nation more definitively than laws, however, and the land molded generations of people. It shaped me and the ideas in this book, which are the result of more than twenty-five years of intensely personal involvement with the federal lands.

I was raised in the Middle West, where the federal domain long ago passed into corporate and other private hands. As a youth I wandered as a trespasser in fields and along a few polluted streams. As a teenager I traveled West and discovered the freedom of the land when I chased a jackrabbit across the New Mexican desert. Later I rode and hiked into many wilderness areas, astonished that a part of the frontier was left for me. I climbed some of the highest mountains and camped in isolated canyons and valleys of the public domain.

The vision I have of public lands as a welfare system managed for the benefit of an elite group did not come to me swiftly or as a tidy academic theory. It emerged during months of slogging work on forest fires, backcountry trails, and cabins. It came to me during months of splendid isolation on fire lookouts overlooking the expanse of public lands, when I had the gift of time to think and read. This book grew from hundreds of trips and campfires on the public domain from north of the Arctic Circle to the Mexican border.

For several years I was a student of public resources. I also conducted research on the management of public lands, taught public-land policy in universities, and explored the dusty archives of libraries and government offices for insights. I have been a ranger and public-land manager, experiencing first-hand the pressure to compromise the future. I also worked in the industry of politics and have seen public resources doled out as political pork. The reality of the lands' management as I know it contrasts with the myths of "multiple use" of the public lands.

The history of these lands is a story of greed and waste. What is most disturbing is that the practices continue. Today most people think the federal lands are protected by government agencies. That is not the case. The agencies charged with protecting the public trust have a partnership with private developers. The essence of public-land management is to provide an economic subsidy to a handful of people and corporations. The public that owns the land is shortchanged.

It is ironic that as the public gained the leisure and means to enjoy the federal lands, urban life took them farther from both the land and the political allocation of it. Distance isolated most Americans from the daily loss of their resources. Most public activities on the federal lands are guided by rangers, visitor centers, and sanitized information on the "wise use" of public resources. Meanwhile, the historic pattern of exploitation has neither changed nor eased. In recent years it even accelerated; more public resources have been raided for private profit in the 1980s than in any comparable period in history. Yet because of the distance from urban America to the raw development, most people have lost touch with the fate of their lands.

This book returns to the original ideas of the federal lands. It deals with the essential history and problems of public-land management. It has been shaped more by the land than by books or theories or bureaucratic reports.

The federal lands are this nation's most valuable assets, and their great resources are both physical and spiritual. Of all the American freedoms, the opportunity to be on open land is the one I consider most unique and most to be treasured. It is a precious heritage for the future. The land is still shaping me and my son, and I hope it will shape what generations are yet to be born from the earth.

There are many books on the public domain. Some are bureaucratic apologies, some theoretical dissertations, others dry histories. This book is a compendium of sun, sweat, and work on the lands. It is the result of disillusionment, frustration, and anger. It calls for reform to make public-land management more democratic and fair. This hope has little basis in history, but instead arises from miles on the trail and nights around the campfire. This hope comes from the land.

Bernard Shanks
February, 1984

Acknowledgments

Anne Marie Ellis Shanks has been a perfect companion and friend. She has helped and supported me in ways I always appreciate but seldom acknowledge. I also treasure my son Michael, who tolerated my absences while writing. I sincerely thank both of them and promise them more time and attention in the future.

Many conservationists and other friends influenced this book by helping shape my ideas. Certainly no one played a larger role than the remarkable Murie family, who helped guide me along with a whole generation of conservationists. The time I have spent with Ade, Louise, and Marty has been a great gift. Such stalwarts of conservation as Charles Stoddard, Charles Callison, and M. Rupert Cutler have long encouraged my interest in public lands. The field leaders of conservation have always been a source of inspiration and support, most notably Clif Merritt, Bill Cunningham, Dick Carter, and the remarkable Cecil Garland. Finally, California's creative former resources secretary, Huey D. Johnson, has given me and many other people a vision for the public lands. All of these individuals and many others have left their mark on the public domain by protecting portions of it for the future.

I also wish to thank Paul Swatek, who first suggested and supported the idea of this book. He introduced me to Danny Moses, who has been a patient and supportive editor despite many delays. Finally, all who read this book will appreciate the editing skill of Mary Lou Van Deventer, who greatly improved the final manuscript.

America's Ideal Lands

The Heart of the
Nation

As a nation we own lands whose beauty seizes the heart. As Americans, we can stand on our own land at the rim of the Grand Canyon and look into a winter storm, or walk among the geysers of Yellowstone and share the land with grazing elk and bison. On a spring night, with the moon lighting Yosemite Valley, we can listen to the power of a Sierra winter melting.

The allure of the open lands the public owns is a haunting dream, from Assateague Island to the western prow of Point Reyes. Their magic and primal freedom are found along the Yukon River, embodied in a wolf track. Their essence is in the elegant song of a cactus wren as the sun rises over the Sonoran Desert. The people of our nation own the Great Plains, with their smell of short prairie grass after a summer thunderstorm and their fluid music of meadowlarks lifting the eyes and heart to a promising horizon. Beauty is everywhere on the people's lands: in the cool relief of shadows that slide out of the mountains when the sun drops across Nevada's Black Rock Desert; in the labyrinthian redrock canyons of the Colorado Plateau; in the resonant heat of Oregon's stark basalt plains; under a humid blanket of air in the Everglades. The publicly owned lands are the ideal lands of America, the pristine continent from which the nation rose to greatness.

We own them as a people, and the federal government manages them. They are the spiritual heart of this nation, and because of the forces of history and geography, they are also the most evocative territories in the country. The public lands are

3

extremes: the highest peaks, the lowest deserts, the wildest and most exotic regions. They hold relics of the stone age, the spirit of the frontier, and the enchantment found only in the earth's wild heart. They are the most substantial measure of the nation's wealth and an essential source of individual freedom, power, and renewal. They are the most tangible resources for our future generations. Protecting them is a sacred public trust so this generation can provide an endowment to the future.

Public lands are fascinating because they remain largely untamed and primeval. These lands, in a world of asphalt and urbanization, are remnants of a nation once completely wild. They contrast with the attractions of the modern world, in which nature's subtly elegant beauty is shown on a billboard behind some artificial product whose value is measured by its ability to arrest attention. Each area of public lands is distinctive and without comparison; none of them can be replaced by private lands any more than a rainbow can be replaced by McDonald's arches.

Lands used in common by a people were part of the earliest civilizations—Greek, Roman, African, and Asian. Native Americans regarded land not merely as community property, but as elemental wealth held by community tenure. Land was so critical to life that no single generation could be trusted with ownership. Not only American Indians, but people throughout the world who had a direct tie to the earth and its resources considered hunting grounds, grazing regions, and upland watersheds to be held by the community as a trust. The European concept of land as property was totally alien to the Indians. When the Native Americans lost their tribal common lands, they suffered a cultural earthquake that shattered their world.

More than 200 years ago the glint of wildland helped fire the American Revolution. Land was not only a focus of the war, but a weapon to win and a prize for the victors. Revolution won the United States a vast domain, a source of wealth, power, and freedom without equal in the world. When the royal decrees were nullified, the land belonged to the new American nation. Federal land provided the freedom to choose a national goal, the power for manifest destiny, and the wealth to pay the price. It provided cash for Jefferson's great bargain with the French, expanding national boundaries westward with the Louisiana Purchase. It was the raw material that built America.

Public land that could be claimed was a beacon drawing settlers West. It pulled miners to California, farmers to Oregon,
loggers to the forests, and ranchers to the plains. The Marines
marched into Mexico City to seize that country's northern territory; land was the essence of manifest destiny. The drive to
enlarge the national territory and the individual freedom to
claim and settle it dominated Congress for a hundred years.

Then, with the collapse of the frontier, public lands came to
mean more than capital. The country realized that a vital force
in American democracy would be missed. Not only the frontier,
but the hope of land for every citizen was coming to an end;
with it would end a source of strength in the national life and
an important crucible for democracy. At the time Frederick
Jackson Turner explained the loss of the frontier, Theodore
Roosevelt was driving home the essential truth that a nation was
only as strong as its resources. Wasting and destroying natural
resources weaken a nation as surely as the ravages of war. Protecting public resources came to be seen as not only essential
ecologically, but an act of patriotism.

At the beginning of the twentieth century, a major national
social reform—conservation—became the guiding ethic for federal lands. Several historic forces came together at once: geographic limits of the land had been reached; population had
grown; and social change forced a new but imperfect system of
federal land management. At its core was conservation. Conservation was intended to provide a multitude of public values and
benefits and to be democratically applied. But many opportunities remained for private plunder. The science of conservation,
the requirement for national security, and the obligations to
future generations could not defeat the drive for private profit.

Congressional debate reflected fundamental national rifts
concerning the public lands. The conflicts were between aristocratic and democratic philosophies of government, and a corporate and common-citizen approach to economics, always amid
regional tensions. The landed opposed the landless. The West
battled the East. After World War II the hundred-year regional
polarization shifted to an urban-versus-rural conflict. Sharp differences of opinion have persisted in how to time the development of land and resources. Planning has often been argued in
terms of preservation versus development, but more accurately
the debate reflected a contest between using resources today or

conserving them for future generations. Throughout congressional and other political debate, the importance of our common
lands in our current national life has been ignored.

Public lands are far more than territory. They are an artifact
of history, a source of beauty, inspiration, and greed. They are
a durable standard of public wealth, a source of both economic
and personal power. Public lands are part of our national heritage. The finest national gifts we have received and can give to
the future are parks, wildlife refuges, and wild rivers. In contrast, the darkest tales of nineteenth-century American development were woven around the waste, destruction, and theft of
public land and resources.

Seeing the land provides a perspective on the history and the
spiritual geography of our nation. Rusting fragments of pioneer
wagons still sit beside the ruts of trails. The long route the pony
express pounded still traces a path from mountain pass to desert
spring and over the next pass. Camping beside it in the Great
Basin raises an apparition of a small, tough man riding out of
the past with a pounding of hooves and the slap of leather. Old
forts molder in the sun. National parks and monuments recreate
historic scenes from Gettysburg to the Little Big Horn, from the
Everglades swamps to the dry hostility of Death Valley.

Thousands of remote western canyons hold messages of an
even earlier age, left when hunters and warriors etched petroglyphs in the rocks. In the canyons of Utah an ancient grain-
storage bin with dry corn cobs lets anyone grasp more personal
lessons of human survival than any in a museum display. A
broken arrowhead by a desert spring tells volumes about the
skill and life of an earlier warrior. In a world plagued by nuclear
warriors, a broad historical perspective on life, survival, and the
role of human species on the earth is rare. When found, it is to
be cherished.

America's federal lands are one place to find the diversity of
the natural world on a large scale, in contrast to the regimenta-
tion of a cornfield or the monotony of mile upon mile of wheat.
On federal lands big, unconfined wild creatures roam, and humans see them naturally from a distance, not domestically
confined behind a concrete moat or bars. The passion of a wild
peregrine falcon's cry cannot be duplicated by urban pigeons
cooing on courthouse eaves. Public lands provide fleeting

glimpses of a rangy coyote, not a manicured poodle on a leash. These lands have the elegance of wild nature, and they inspire visions and dreams, not just profits and products. They are beautiful because they are wild, open, and free.

One of the greatest benefits public lands provide individuals is physical freedom. In a world ever more crowded and confined, the freedom to roam over big mountains and wide valleys is priceless. Private land often becomes a personal fortress for people threatened by crime, crowds, and urban pressures. It is often closed in. On public lands the open space and human freedom that guided a national destiny and shaped a democratic heritage can still be experienced.

It is in this freedom that American people find their personal share of the public wealth. Using public lands for hiking, sightseeing, and spiritual re-creation is a democratic activity millions of people enjoy every year. Unlike economic development, outdoor activities are not commercial practices. They are the physical and psychological benefits earned by virtue of American citizenship.

The wealth of our lands takes many economic forms, too, however. The people own 740 million acres of land, nearly one-third of the entire nation. The lands also include more than a billion acres of outer-continental shelf, which contains most oil and gas reserves—more than 36 billion barrels of oil and 178 trillion cubic feet of gas. At today's prices, those publicly-owned resources are worth more than $1.3 trillion and are appreciating each year. The nationally-owned coal, oil shale, and other energy resources are worth trillions more. Between 97 and 98 percent of the silver known in the nation comes from land currently or formerly public. Large copper, zinc, gold, and other deposits are under the public domain.

Despite their wealth, however, these mineral lands earn the owners, the American public, no royalties and little rent. Long ago mining and energy companies learned how to gain title to the public minerals, mine the land, and leave the public with a dry husk.

Another source of wealth on the public lands is the grass, the basis of life for native wild animals, wild horses, domestic sheep, goats, and cattle. But its unequal distribution among species tells the problem: most of the grass and forage is claimed by stock raisers at below-market prices to feed domestic livestock, leaving about 10 percent for native wildlife and wild horses. Because of a long history of overgrazing, grass and forage are depleted and soils are eroding. Domestic animals' grazing on public lands in the West is the single most important factor in American desertification. The cattle raised there supply us with only 3 percent of our beef.

Because of the geography of western land, most rain and snow falls on public land. But economics and tradition insist that water, the most precious of western resources, be captured for the profit of private corporations. Not only is the water transferred to private hands, expensive dams and delivery systems are largely paid for by taxpayers. Public lands capture the water, but after thousands of sluices channel it to private hands, only a trickle is left for the people.

There is a conflict between the public that owns the lands and the businesses that capture the resources. Many developers see not the beauty of the land, but the bottom line of a corporate ledger. Others see land in tidy philosophical adages, applying free-market theory and trickle-down economics. Still others see land in political terms as a battleground between environmentalists and business people. The people and corporations who use the lands have always demanded control, but private profit cannot be a substitute for public trust. Public land must have a unique standard of management, a land ethic distinct from private property.

The miner does not see a fragile surface layer of soil, grass, flowers, and herbs, but rather the rock outcrop that hints of secret lodes below—then breaks away the pioneer of lichen, the better to read a story of crystals, minerals, and gold. Land broken and shattered by thousands of earthquakes and countless storms is not a source of a miner's wonder and mystery, and fractured rock, a measure of the earth's inner torments or the invisible strength of frost, is not a riddle. The miracle called soil, the mystical soup of long-dead leaves, grass, flowers, insects, minerals, and moisture is a priceless resource; but it is overburden to the miner, a worthless product hiding El Dorado.

To the cattle ranchers, larkspur is an enemy, not a colorful reminder of a summer day to be pressed into a guidebook. To the stock raisers, the mix of shrubs, plants, and forbs that are a mountain meadow is better replaced with a monoculture. Native plants, having survived the rigors of evolution, serve an array of native wildlife. But the stock raisers consider both wild plants and animals worthless, and they replace the vegetation with a tough grass suited for few species but domestic cattle. Public-land stock raisers see their stock and feel their own tradition but not their debt to all Americans. To them the public lands are their ranch, their territory—not a public trust. Many ranchers, after generations of profiting from federal land, are eager today to take it from public ownership.

When public lands were becoming more and more valuable, the "sagebrush rebellion" emerged. It started with people who had long enjoyed dominion over public land—stock raisers and miners—but soon gained the strange bedfellows of free-market economists, political ideologues, and energy corporations.

Early in the Reagan administration, the "sagebrush rebellion's" agenda changed. The objective was clear: the federal lands were to be sold or leased to private interests in a plan called "privatization." The Reagan administration's program to sell vast tracts of "surplus" public lands and energy leases was nothing but a giant transfer of the American public's wealth, power, and freedom to an aristocratic group. The central objective was not just land, but energy resources.

Energy development in the United States followed much the same pattern as timber and other resources. Private stocks of oil and gas were squandered. On public lands conservation was practiced, and the result is that today these lands contain most remaining reserves of oil, gas, oil shale, tar sands, and geothermal resources. Uranium and coal are also there in vast quantities. The greatest economic wealth of the public lands is energy, not the surface rights.

With the remaining energy resources concentrated on them, these lands naturally became the focus of a major energy boom in the early 1980s during the tenure of Secretary of the Interior James G. Watt. The energy corporations embarked on the greatest exploitation program in American history. Watt launched the largest-ever transfer of public resources into private hands —more than $1 trillion's worth. The total impact will not be known for years, but one point is clear: the transfers cheated the public and robbed future generations.

At first glance the "sagebrush rebellion" and the exploitative tactics of the Reagan-Watt administration seem anachronistic after nearly a century of conservation. But a closer look at history reveals that the themes the "sagebrush rebellion" used to plunder public lands are part of a recurring pattern: "worthless" lands become valuable; economic interests create turmoil; and politicians placate special interests. The result has usually been that today's public and future generations lose wealth, power, and freedom.

Four basic themes, which have been with us since the earliest days of the republic, are a constant source of conflict in public-land policy. The first is regionalism. Public lands have pitted one region against another since the Revolutionary War. Small colonies such as Rhode Island and Maryland were afraid of being dominated by large, wealthy colonies such as Virginia and Georgia, which held large western land claims. After the Revolution the practice of opening federally controlled frontier lands to easy settlement worked against the plantation economy of the South. Attempts to industrialize the urban East were blocked when cheap labor migrated to the frontier for an independent life. The political conflict between various regional forces continued until the Civil War, which brought about the Homestead Act. The act shifted control over public-land policy from the South to the frontier and western states, where it has rested ever since.

The regional opposition persisted through the conservation era at the close of the nineteenth century and the beginning of the twentieth century. It was only when eastern-based ideas on conservation were accepted by some western political leaders that large areas were reserved for parks, wildlife refuges, and forests.

Despite the myth, the West has not been a victim of the East; even in conservation and environmental protection the West has controlled the public lands and its own destiny for over a century. Today the theme of regionalism persists as a tension between urban and rural areas. The sparsely populated western outback essentially dictates public-land policy despite urbanization and the political impacts of reapportionment. Urban areas support the operation and management of the public lands through taxes, but the rural regions, led by a minority of ranchers, miners, water developers, and energy companies, dominate the politics and profits. Every year the taxpayers subsidize the stock raisers, miners, loggers, and energy companies operating on the public domain.

The second theme is the historic contrast between aristocratic and democratic uses of land. Originally conflicts over American land policy arose between the colonists and the English royalty. Soon after the Revolutionary War Thomas Jefferson and Alexander Hamilton emerged as philosophical opponents in debates over federal lands. Hamilton's aristocratic approach favored selling the newly-nationalized land to wealthy speculators and corporations. More democratically, Jefferson and his supporters wanted small land grants with liberal credit for farmers. Even better was the idea of homesteads. The same tensions persisted between the plantation South and the populist West.

Later, when nature's limits were understood and conservation had taken hold in the nineteenth century, public lands essentially became a vast commons. Public land became a territory where all citizens could roam and feel at home on their own estate—their own land. But the economic elitists remained on the public property, and although the lands were purportedly managed for multiple uses, remnants of the old landed aristocracy jealously guarded their traditional profits. The "sagebrush rebels" developed a symbol that was a relic of the western aristocracy steeped in its own mythology of the independent frontier; they captured a macho image reminiscent of the Marlboro Man. They used it to lasso resources for their private profit. The news media, captivated with their own symbols, did not publicize or even understand the opposite side of the conflict—using the land democratically.

A third theme of conflict has been whether to develop the land for economic or social benefits. Economic development has been favored for most of our nation's history. Massive public-land grants were given to a few railroad barons in the nineteenth century. It was not until the 1980 Alaska Lands Act that the amount of land dedicated to national parks and monuments equaled the land given to railroads. More land was given to logging companies than to universities. More land was fraudulently claimed as swamp than was given to all of the war veterans in our history. Despite the "sagebrush rebels'" claims more federal land was granted to states than to homesteaders.

In the 1980s, because a century of conservation has saved

resources and rising energy prices have intensified demand for them, we have more public-land wealth at stake than ever before. The primal conflict remains: whether to use land for widespread social purposes or for private economic development.

Finally, the theme of the sharpest conflict is the newest idea, which is a century old: conservation. Early in the history of public lands, little regard was given to conservation. The fall of the buffalo and the thinning and rapid disappearance of clouds of passenger pigeons made the nation apprehensive. Theodore Roosevelt introduced a new public ethic of conservation. He created most of the national forests, established national monuments the size of parks, and enlarged the park system dramatically. Conservation was a major social reform, but like all reforms, it was not completely successful. An archaic group persisted with an old disregard for exhausting natural resources.

The public had become concerned for future resources after seeing the incredible waste and destruction of its lands. But conservation's protection was left incomplete, permitting the public's lands to be plundered anew. Democratic forces retreated, and economic forces became dominant. Conservation for the future public was sacrificed to present private exploitation.

After decades of conservation, public-land management was sharply skewed toward consumptive practices in the early 1980s. It happened with stunning swiftness on an unrivaled scale. Former Secretary of the Interior James Watt renewed the emphasis on consumption. Within months of taking office, he announced he intended to lease virtually all energy resources on the public lands within five years. It was the most massive transfer of public wealth to private hands in history. If the plan were carried out, it would be the final perverse act of an original American sin, the destruction of public land and erosion of the foundation of national strength. The conflict between conservation and development remains bitter.

All Americans share ownership of the immense resources, both physical and spiritual, available from the public's lands. Western public lands represent this nation's best hope to change from the pattern of wasting land, to demonstrate how the human race can use land in harmony with nature. The past and present abuses of these lands must end, but that will happen only when a public trust in federal land is forged into law and seared into a federal land ethic.

Public-land reform is needed because the dream of conserving public resources was never fully built into the land-management mechanisms. Overgrazing exposes soil to wind and erosion. Productive land is lost to desertification. Renewable resources are sacrificed to economic expedience and the search for minerals, oil, and gas.

Reform is needed because of the scandalous transfer of public wealth to private hands. Energy leasing is one massive problem, but every commercial operator and every economic activity on public lands is subsidized by American taxpayers. Timber harvesting reduces wilderness and wildlife habitat while damaging fishing streams and watersheds. Water developers in the West capture public water with federal dams for private use and profit. Mineral development on public lands, controlled by a law written in 1872, remains a blatant subsidy. Reform is needed to end the giveaway of minerals and other resources.

The lands need a manifesto for the future. They should be managed so all citizens can use them democratically as a national heritage and trust. Conserving them for the future, with healthy native vegetation and wildlife, should be the first priority. If their resources are sold, the price must be fair according to the current market to earn the lands' owners a reasonable return. The revenues, particularly from developing nonrenewable resources, should be used to renew the lands and to develop their renewable resources. This program would be part of a national transition to a steady-state economy, which would derive support from the environment without destroying the diversity that stabilizes life and assures a productive living system for all generations. This is not the direction of current management programs.

In the 1980s the public lands as people have known them during the twentieth century are facing the largest looting in American history. The democratic purposes for which the lands were reserved are endangered. The lands' wealth—and therefore power—is being transferred to a few people and corporations with political clout. The essential American freedom of open land is being diminished. The liberty that comes from public land is fading like a winter sunset.

Land reform is usually the product of epic historic forces and revolutions in the land's use. It is ironic that reforming land management is crucial, because managing public land for the people's benefit is a constant theme of democracy, and abusing the public-land trust is a product of dictatorial instincts. Land reform is generally associated with banana republics, not the United States; yet federal lands here have been seized and looted by powerful economic and political forces, and the public trust is being lost. Nothing less than national reform can restore the values and the resources of federal lands to their rightful owners, the American people.

Writing a manifesto for the public lands will require a perspective that protects the interests of the entire nation over many generations. Public land must be shared with our future citizens; protecting and enhancing it are gifts from this generation to the next. The reform should also end economic subsidies and control by special-interest groups. Non-economic uses of public lands must take precedence over economic activities. Developing renewable resources must be preferred to developing nonrenewable resources. Public values on public land should have priority over private development.

Federal lands are a treasure, not just an amenity or a capital resource. All people of this nation have a basic inalienable right to use and enjoy them. Public lands are a freedom. They are essential to a democratic nation and the spiritual strength of its people.

The beauty of the public's lands and the drama of their history conjure visions of space and openness. The lands draw the eye to the horizon. The sky is clearer there and the horizon wider. Most public lands are in the West, where thin, dry, unpolluted air lets the sun shine brighter and the sky look bluer than anywhere else in the country. Public lands define the region more than literature, art, accent, or cowboy boots. The West of history, movies, myths, and dreams cannot be found in Denver or Los Angeles, but only on the lands the people own. Open land and western space are gifts of the vision and dreams that helped create the nation. Every person, every generation needs to believe in something tangible that is anchored to the past and will extend into the future. Protecting and perpetuating the lands that embody this vision is a trust that was given to this generation; it is a sacred trust in the lands we all own, and we must pass it on to our children.

Lookout Mountain

2

Acquiring the Land

Kachinas danced to the timeless beat of coarse sticks, dry gourds, and brittle shells. Among the ancient symbols of the Hopi world in the smoky and dusty kiva, the hypnotic chant of the masked dancers carried everyone back to a simpler era. The villagers' serious faces broke only when the comic mudhead dancer joked about the alien white in their midst. It was an ancient rite that I was privileged to witness, a link with the Pleistocene. A Native American tribe was renewing its kinship with the earth.

For hours I watched as the clans of the old village Oraibi descended the ladder from the kiva roof, were purified by smoke, and danced in the ancient ceremonial chamber. Abandoned for over a thousand years, cliff dwellings throughout the Southwest had the symbolic earth womb and had felt the chants of many generations of Kachinas. Not only was Oraibi the oldest inhabited American village, but it was also again the site of a timeless ritual. Only hours earlier, the first American orbited the earth.

After the dance, the chants still throbbed in my brain as the Kachinas went back up into the bitter February cold of the Northern Arizona mesa. Soon another clan replaced them. Despite the sterile frost, the ceremony honored the start of another season and the sprouting of the spring beans. As the clans danced, the smoke and dust from the floor clouded my mind, and the chant hypnotized me.

Hours later I emerged from the kiva. The night sky was brittle with cold, and the stars were flinty. The vastness was a shocking contrast to the snug kiva. Soon the chill deposed my imagery and sent me not quite all the way back to my world. I had witnessed an act of faith every bit as impressive as techno- logical prowess and far older than science, a spiritual experi- ence, an ancient link between the Hopis and the land. It was a celebration of the magic fermented by the embryo of the bean and the warming earth. I could almost feel the earth rolling back toward the sun like a great ship caught in a trough half a year deep. A culture and its ancient wisdom of the land had touched me like the first warmth of a spring day.

Land and its life stirs a genetic memory. Land was a human experience long before it became a commodity. It has been the focus of history, war, life and death. It has been symbolically and in reality part of human wealth, power, and freedom. It has also been the subject of mysticism. The American land is no exception. A veneer of urban life and a few generations of com- merce have left us with a sense of isolation from it, but our bones remember, and we are roused from urban tranquility by visions of wild land.

The federal lands, our national commons, give us a window to the past, a tangible liaison with the earth. More than com- merce is possible there. Those lands are a celebration of life larger than our own.

There are problems, however, in our modern system of pub- lic-land ownership and management, and they have their ori- gins in the aristocratic European charters, four centuries old, that brought settlers to the New World. In law and attitude we inherited a Roman view of land. When the Roman legions swept into a frontier region, they appropriated land, for leaders and royalty. They seized common grazing lands shared by pastoral people. Rights to land came only from Rome, the central seat of power. Land was freedom and belonged to the conqueror, the one with power to seize and hold it.

Other peoples did not share such an egocentric view of land. Many close to land had an intimate view, a respect for the soil. Land was not a right of military might, but a gift of the earth. Land was the source of power, not its result. Land and mystical forces made all life possible. Simple ethics required that it be shared. The smallest creature was a product of the gods. Land was a sacred bond with all the past and all the future. It was a gift from antiquity, borrowed from countless generations to come.

But it was the Roman view, carried through French, Spanish, and English land law, that founded this nation's legal convention. The Romans gave land grants for military centers, or *presidia*. Deserving generals were given frontier tracts to fortify, settle, and bring under the influence of the central government. Battle-scarred soldiers were sometimes granted land for their golden years. This was the case with Spanish land grants, some of which still remain valid in the American Southwest. The Continental Congress promised land to soldiers during the American Revolution. Western land helped power our revolution.

A concept embedded deep in English law was that all land and its resources belonged to the king. The king had to dispense land to barons for various personal, economic, and political reasons. The barons might lease land or allow the soil to be worked by tenants, but land ownership was a tangible symbol of a high social class. American land history unfolded using this basic perception, not the mystical view of the American Indian.

On June 24, 1497, John Cabot planted the flag of England on what he believed to be the mainland of China. He carried a land grant from King Henry VII. He had verified the first land claim in America on what was actually the eastern shore of Nova Scotia or Maine. In this manner the European system was first imposed on native Indians.

Other land grants followed Cabot's. In Florida, California, and parts of the Southwest, the Spanish gave large tracts for missionary purposes as well as for military ventures. At other times grants were made for economic colonization, such as to assist in establishing distilleries, grist mills, sawmills, tanneries, and related commercial activities. All came at the expense of the native common-land system.

The European nations that influenced land development in North America also had a tradition of common land with community tenure, and eventually the United States emerged with a public-land system that became a model for democratic countries. The approach was practical, not theoretical. The wealth, power, and freedom once enjoyed by nobility were available for all the people from a vast commons. The native common-land system and the European model developed an American hybrid.

At its core was national security, based on the power of land and its resources.

One of the oldest traditional uses of public land is to provide resources for the military. The British navy and merchant marine exhausted their home-grown timber, then searched abroad. Before the seventeenth century marine timber came from northern and central Europe. A top-rated ship needed a mast forty yards long and forty inches in diameter. The European supply became uncertain because of political unrest. It was discovered that the American white pine made a superior mast, and the first pine masts went eastward across the Atlantic in 1609. Soon the British navy depended on the American colonies.

The crown established the "broad arrow policy," which reserved mast trees on the historic premise that land belonged to the crown. They were marked with three blazes. No one was to cut them. Natural resources were essential weapons of national defense, conservation an ally. But rebellious colonists refused to honor aristocratic control. Broad-arrow trees fell and shook the foundations of an empire. Representatives of the king were sent to America to arrest violators and to assure compliance but had little success.

The colonies had, to a large extent, adopted and directed their own land policies and settlement practices through a sense of independence that came from the frontier. The pattern had been practiced for 160 years. Concerned with autonomous and uncontrolled settlement of royal frontier lands, King George III decreed in 1763 that loyal American subjects should not settle west of the Appalachian Divide. The order, originally planned as a temporary measure, alarmed colonial leaders.

The King's power dwindled as frontier people continued to push west. Rival colonies and land companies continued to settle unallocated western land. King George's proclamation was seen as a fundamental hindrance to freedom and development.

It also failed to conserve the mast trees. One agent of the King estimated that for every mast tree shipped to the mother country, the colonists cut more than 500 for other purposes. Trees suitable for the finest British warship were felled for rustic cabins and barns. Pine marked for royal ships was split to warm New England homes. Trees helped fuel a revolution. The last shipment of mast trees reached England in July 1775, as Jefferson's words of independence fired the minds of frontier settlers.

The Declaration of Independence summarized the complaint against the king: "He has endeavored to prevent the population of these states; for that purpose, obstructing the laws for naturalization of foreigners, refusing to pass others to encourage their migration hither, and raising the conditions of new appropriations of lands." Land as wealth, freedom and, in turn, personal power was one of the linchpins of the American Revolution. Much of the motivation for the American Revolution was undoubtedly selfish and self-serving, not political or philosophical. At its core was land, wild, open, and available, that legally belonged to the king of England. Personal freedom, especially freedom to use frontier land, was an important issue in the Revolution. Adam Smith's *Wealth of Nations* considered the open use of land as one great cause of prosperity in the American colonies.

In 1776 the Continental Congress promised to give land to Hessian soldiers and others in the British Army, should they desert to the colonial side. Crown land was also promised to American soldiers if they enlisted in the revolutionary army. Initially privates were promised 100 acres; up to 500 acres were available for a colonel, and even more for a general. As war continued the ante was upped higher and higher. George Rogers Clark and his men were promised land in the trans-Ohio River Region, if they could wrest it from English control.

The victory at Yorktown brought the first tangible results of the rebellion—land reform. The rebels appropriated and subdivided Tory estates. Other large holdings were sold cheaply or given outright to war veterans.

Revolutionary leaders advocated changes in land laws. Thomas Jefferson, the red-headed genius of the revolutionary government, began the process by drafting the first public-land law. His work was essential because a conflict threatened to tear the colonies apart before any formal union began. The center of the conflict was land: the western lands, wild and unsettled, west of the Appalachian Divide. On one side of the issue were seven colonies that held overlapping and contradictory land claims reaching to the Mississippi River. They were opposed by six colonies without lands. Larger colonies opposed smaller ones, little New England stood against large, rich colonies to the south. Regionalism haunted the arguments.

The conflict lasted for a year and held up the Articles of

Confederation. The smaller eastern states in New England, bound by the ocean or other borders, feared the size and potential economic power of the larger states. Virginia, the wealthiest colony, held the largest land claims, including the present states of West Virginia, Kentucky, Ohio, Indiana, Illinois, Wisconsin, Michigan, and parts of Minnesota and Pennsylvania. Maryland led the smaller states in arguing that western lands were not bound by original imperial charters but by a new, revolutionary pact. It boldly argued that frontier lands were won with the "common blood and treasure of the thirteen colonies." It was suggested that the western territory eventually become free and independent states. Maryland refused to accede to the Articles of Confederation until larger states made some concession.

Finally, in 1780, New York ceded its western lands to the federal government without conditions, starting the federal land system. Soon Congress passed a resolution recommending that the remaining states with western claims relinquish the land to the United States. Part of the resolution provides that public lands should, for their common benefit to the nation, be settled and formed into states. In 1784, Virginia ceded its claims. The remaining states soon followed.

Virginia had magnanimously ceded its vast western claims to secure Maryland's agreement to the Articles of Confederation, but it put two conditions on the gift. First, western public lands were to be considered a common source of wealth for the use and benefit of all the nation's people. Second, the ceded territory would eventually be divided up into states and admitted to the union with standing equal to the original states. This agreement was codified in the Northwest Ordinance, which restricted states' jurisdiction over the public domain. No tax was to be imposed on the public lands, and new states were to abandon their land claims to the federal government. All new states entering the union did so without any legal claim to federal lands.

Although history remains clear, frequently western states with large federal holdings insist the lands should be "returned" to their ownership. They conveniently ignore the sacrifice Virginia and other public-land states made to assure a unified nation. Public lands, won with the common blood and effort of all states, were intended to be used for the common benefit of all people, not just a few. Besides, western states never owned the federal land.

The western land-claim settlement made it possible to ratify the Articles of Confederation and to establish the United States of America. Land, not paper or laws, was the instrument to unite the nation. A body of western territory known as public domain resulted: more than 370,000 square miles, or 236,825,600 acres. It was a vast treasure to a war-torn, debt-ridden nation full of more promise and land than realistic hopes. It was the only tangible source of federal wealth and power. The founding fathers did not take long to begin looking for still more land.

In the spring of 1682 Sieur de La Salle had stood at the mouth of the Mississippi River and declared in the name of King Louis that the entire watershed was part of the French Empire. The territory reached from New Orleans to the northern Rockies in western Montana and became known as Louisiana. In it Jefferson visualized not a French empire, but land for a thousand years of yeoman farmers.

The new nation prospered immediately after the Revolution. Settlers moved west, and by 1802 three new states had been carved out of the western federal territory. The United States had title to frontier lands reaching to the banks of the Mississippi, toward which commerce flowed as the region west of the Appalachian crest developed. Obviously, a trade route down the Mississippi as well as the region's vast resources were vitally important to the United States. Then in October 1802 France closed the port in New Orleans to United States commerce.

President Jefferson dispatched James Monroe to France to negotiate a treaty. Napoleon had been deeply disturbed by losing troops in Santo Domingo. Ambitious and militaristic, he needed to rebuild his army. Land was Napoleon's tool to forge his military power. Jefferson had directed Monroe to buy New Orleans and the mouth of the Mississippi River. Although Monroe was stunned to be offered the entire Louisiana territory, he agreed quickly. The sum of $23 million was agreed upon, which would buy the United States 828,000 square miles, doubling the new nation for four cents an acre.

Despite the great bargain, Jefferson's authority to acquire new territory was constitutionally unclear. New England states opposed the purchase, fearing more southern territory and western influence over national affairs. Jefferson insisted his prerogative to approve a Louisiana purchase was "implied." Later he won from Congress the money to consummate the deal, but only after a bitter fight with New England senators. Regionalism nearly stopped America's greatest land bargain.

Jefferson also hoped to acquire Florida, then claimed by Spain. Meanwhile he sent the first American expedition west of the Mississippi. Meriwether Lewis, his personal secretary, and William Clark, a competent frontiersman, carried out the first official survey of new western public lands. More than two years later they returned, having traveled west to the Pacific shore.

Back in Florida, rapid settlement in nearby Georgia, combined with a weak colonial government, were two pressures on Spain. Some expansion-minded Americans argued that the boundaries of Louisiana included a sizeable chunk of Spanish territory. In 1810, Americans in western Florida declared their independence and requested annexation to the United States. Madison, then President, extended American boundaries east to the Perdido River. The squeeze on Spain continued.

In 1819 President John Quincy Adams and Don Luis de Onis, Spain's envoy, signed a treaty that ceded Florida to the United States. The purchase cost $6.6 million for more than 46 million acres of land, fourteen cents an acre.

The next directions for a growing nation to push were north and west. Many veterans of the American Revolution hoped for a northward annexation of more British territory. Conflicts over the northern boundary of the United States continued for decades. In 1818 a compromise with Great Britain established the boundary at the forty-ninth parallel from Lake of the Woods to the Rocky Mountains. The United States acquired the rich Red River Valley in Minnesota and surrendered a small portion of the Missouri River watershed. Another northern boundary dispute with Britain was settled in 1842. A peaceful treaty arranged the complex border between Canada and the eastern United States, completing the outline of Maine and the northeastern reach of the nation.

In the West, events unfolded rapidly. Empire builders such as Marcus Whitman in Oregon and Stephen F. Austin in Texas had been leading settlers beyond United States borders for years. Other Americans were acquiring Mexican land grants in California. Once Mexico had gained its independence from Spain, it mistakenly encouraged American settlement. Promoters who promised to deliver settlers to Mexican frontier regions were assured imperial estates. "Empresarios," or colony promoters, brought to the Mexican frontier American warriors of manifest destiny in a Trojan horse called colonization. Land was luxuriant fodder for the creature.

By 1830 more than 20,000 settlers from the United States were in Texas territory. Veterans of the American Revolution were still alive, as were Jefferson's land-reform ideas. Mexico soon regretted the generous terms of its settlement plans. The country attempted to outlaw slavery, require membership in the Catholic Church, and centralize its authority. It was asking for trouble. Rebellion was again in the air. First came opposition from Americans, then revolution. War broke out in 1835, and after a year of fighting, Texas became an independent republic.

Rebels petitioned for admission to the union, but countless Congressional debates over slavery held up statehood for a decade. After the revolution, Texas held a vast treasure of land. As a nation it was burdened by debt and used land like cash to pay its bills and reward veterans. Land was quickly sold, granted, traded, and stolen. Eventually Texas joined the union in 1845. Unlike other states with large land claims, Texas remained deeply in debt, and the United States was fairly solvent at the time of its admission. Texas became the only state permitted to retain its public lands, principally because it had been an independent republic. As a state it was even permitted to split into smaller states if it wanted.

Five years later, Texas sold 78.8 million acres of its western and northern lands to the United States for $10 million. These lands included portions of the eventual states of New Mexico, Oklahoma, Wyoming, Colorado, and Kansas. In the process, Texas paid off many debts but unfortunately continued to sell and squander the state land. In the decades ahead, more than 100 million acres were dissipated.

If admitting Texas to the union in 1845 was important for manifest destiny, the following year was, according to historian Bernard DeVoto, a turning point for western expansion and the eventual outcome of public domain. The United States declared war against Mexico over their boundary. Texans had argued over an appropriate border for several years. President Polk had even attempted to purchase California.

During this time, John Fremont made epic journeys across the western wilderness on vague expansionistic missions from Washington. One result was widespread American pressure to push borders west. Originally most settlers in the Northwest were part of the Hudson Bay Company and the British Empire, but the balance of Oregon settlers had begun to shift toward United States citizens as the Oregon Trail opened. Rich and well-watered soil of Oregon and Washington in the Northwest Territory had attracted more settlers than could be controlled by British outposts and the quasi-official Hudson Bay Company. After years of blustering and threats by both sides, Britain and the U.S. reached the Oregon compromise in mid-June 1846. The northern border of the United States was extended along the forty-ninth parallel west to the Pacific. More than 180 million acres were added to the public domain.

The war with Mexico lasted two years. Zachary Taylor won battles in California, securing territory. General Winfield Scott and his army marched into Mexico City and seized the capital in 1847. The result was the Treaty of Guadalupe Hidalgo, signed in 1848. The United States acquired the rich agricultural lands of California just one year before the accidental discovery of gold at Sutter Creek changed the face of California forever. The treaty also granted the present states of Nevada, Utah, Arizona north of the Gila River, New Mexico west of the Rio Grande, and portions of Wyoming and Colorado. It was a vast mineral-rich area, 334.5 million acres.

A few years later America's urge for land cost Mexico still more of its northern territory. Railroads needed the low-lying desert lands south of the Gila River in Arizona for a warm, all-weather route to California. The United States sent James Gadsden, a railroad promoter, to Mexico to negotiate for more territory. Originally Gadsden wanted the Baja Peninsula, Colorado River mouth, and territory more than 100 miles south of the present border. For a time the threat of another war loomed, this time to benefit American railroads, but in 1853 an agreement was reached to exchange nearly 19 million acres of land for $10 million.

The lure of land and the power of manifest destiny had pushed American people across the isolation of the Great Plains and through the mountains and deserts of the West to the Pacific Coast. In eight years, from 1845 to 1853, the territory of the nation had expanded by 781 million acres, nearly 80 percent of it public domain. The nation acquired the maze of Utah canyons, 14,000-foot snow-capped peaks of Colorado, the Grand

Canyon in Arizona, volcanic plains and the rich Willamette Valley in Oregon, and the Central Valley in California. Mountain ranges such as the Sierra, Cascade, Gila, Wasatch, and hundreds of minor ranges in the Great Basin and elsewhere were added to the nation.

Still the drive for land continued.

Although the United States' contiguous boundaries were fixed after the Gadsden Purchase in 1853, William Randolph Hearst, throughout his large newspaper chain, kept up a regular cry for more Mexican territory. The southern region pushed for more slave states in the Caribbean. Still other Americans migrated to Canada and hoped more of the northern lands would fall into the United States orbit, much as Maine had. One by-product of this sentiment and environment was an expansion-minded Secretary of State, William Henry Seward, who bought Alaska.

Alaska was claimed by Vitus Bering in 1728 and had been used by Russian fur traders and fishermen since then. During the Crimean War in the 1850s, however, Russians were afraid Great Britain might seize its Russian-American frontier territory. Military forces and cash were needed to equip an army. Russia offered Alaska for sale to the United States. President Johnson dispatched his Secretary of State to negotiate a treaty for the territory, which was largely unsurveyed and unsettled. He bought it for $7.2 million, or two cents an acre; many people still criticized it as "Seward's Folly."

There is little doubt Seward had more in mind than Alaska when he arranged for its purchase. He hoped to sandwich British Columbia between the Pacific Northwest and Alaska, to have it fall into America's hands. He also looked forward to the annexation of Hawaii and Santo Domingo. But he fell from political grace, retired to his New York home after a world tour, and British Columbia remained British.

Today the great Alaska park, refuge, and wilderness systems have been established in "Seward's Folly," the direct result of settling land claims of the Alaska Native Americans. No discussion of the acquisition of the federal lands would be complete without mentioning the Indian tribal lands that originally embraced nearly all the present United States. Indians moved down from the Bering Strait over a land bridge between Asia and North America many thousands of years ago. They claimed the land by possession, tradition, and moral right. Although in many cases their method of land ownership was far different from that of the Europeans, treaties were imposed upon various tribes by the dominant European culture—first French, then British and Spanish, later American. In later stages of westward expansion, treaties with the Indians provided for tribal reservations to be held in perpetuity. Forever was short.

Repeatedly the American Indian tribes lost their land to the wave of frontier settlement. Dozens of treaties were solemnly signed between various tribes and the United States. The United States broke virtually every treaty, and additional Indian lands were seized, stolen, and transferred from tribal ownership. Land and its resources were the heart of Indian culture; loss of the community land shattered the Indians' world. The foundation of their lives, history, and hopes was swept aside. Entire cultures, rich and unique, died as a result of manifest destiny. Those scattered tribal members who witnessed the demise of their heritage were caustic about the treaties. An old Sioux summarized the government's record in 1891: "They made us many promises, more than I can remember, but they never kept but one; they promised to take our land and they took it."

Indian lands have been taken to create portions of national parks such as Glacier, Canyon de Chelly, and many Alaskan parks. Still other lands, including sacred tribal lands, have been taken for national forests and wildlife refuges. Most Indian lands were lost through homestead settlement and acquisition under various public-land laws. Today, some 100 million acres of private, state, and federal lands are claimed by the first owners' descendants.

A little-known aspect of public-land policy has been to put Corps of Engineers reservoirs and other federal water projects on Indian reservations. Acquisition costs are low, and the Indians' political influence is usually minimal.

Indians have lost large tracts of western lands in every decade during the twentieth century. An equitable and moral settlement of Indian land claims is far from complete. Today, however, some 53 million acres of remaining Indian lands are not regarded as public lands, as they previously were. They are rightfully and legally viewed as tribal lands, with their management and settlement solely a tribal matter. The story of Indian land, yet to be told, is one history more disheartening than the story of America's federal land policy.

Acquisition of public-domain lands was completed with the purchase of Alaska in 1867. The island nation of Hawaii was annexed in 1898; having previously been an independent nation, it yielded no public lands. Numerous American insular possessions have included Puerto Rico, the Virgin Islands, Guam, American Samoa, the Trust Territory of the Pacific Islands, and other islands in the Central Pacific. These territories were administered by the U.S. Department of the Interior, although their actual management and policies are now directed by a complex of treaties and international agreements.

The federal purse has also been used to acquire lands previously in private ownership. Lands originally won by war, treaty, or purchase that have remained in federal ownership are usually referred to as "public domain" lands. Private lands donated or purchased by the United States are called simply "public" or "acquired" lands.

In 1911 Congress delegated to the federal administration the power to purchase lands for national forests. The U.S. Forest Service began to purchase cut-over or burned-over forestlands, most of them in the eastern United States, to protect watersheds. It bought more than 27 million acres in the eastern United States, largely during the Great Depression. The eastern national forests are far from complete, however; large pockets of private land remain.

Still other federal lands were once granted to railroads and were then revested to federal ownership when the railroads failed to meet the terms of their grants. During the 1930s various land laws permitted marginal homesteads to revert to federal ownership and settlers to be compensated for their efforts. Nearly 11 million acres, largely in the northern and western Great Plains, are now in public ownership because of this program.

Purchasing land for military purposes has always been expedient. During World War II the government purchased some 7 million acres of military land. The usual practice during wartime is to condemn private lands and settle on a price negotiated with owners or dictated by courts. Other federal lands are often transferred to the Defense Department. The U.S. Army Corps of Engineers has similar powers to acquire lands for its reservoirs and dams. It has bought 7 million acres, bringing the total military lands to 24 million acres.

Lands are purchased and acquired by gift and donation for national parks, wildlife refuges, and historic sites. Although the bulk of parks and forests are set aside from public-domain lands, public lands in the eastern United States and near urban areas are usually purchased. Still other lands are acquired for federal water projects of the Tennessee Valley Authority and Bureau of Reclamation, and more lands have been needed for post offices, federal buildings, and research laboratories.

The most important land-acquisition program in modern times has been the Federal Land and Water Conservation Fund. Originated in 1964, the program was intended to take revenues from development of the Outer Continental Shelf (OCS), a non-renewable resource, and invest them by buying lands for federal, state, and local park and recreation programs. Sixty percent of the fund was authorized by Congress for state and local governments on a matching basis to provide for badly needed recreation projects. Remaining funds went to the Park Service, Forest Service, and other federal land-management agencies to acquire park and recreation sites. Priority was given to lands near urban areas to help correct the imbalance between public land ownership in rural and urban areas.

Money from the Land and Water Conservation fund helped to establish major urban parks in New York's Gateway National Recreation Area and San Francisco's Golden Gate National Recreation Area, and to acquire portions of the Redwoods National Park, Santa Monica Mountains National Recreation Area above Los Angeles, Indiana Dunes National Lakeshore near Chicago, and Cuyahoga National Recreation Area in Ohio. Many hundreds of other sites were purchased or scheduled for acquisition during the first two decades of the Land and Water Conservation Fund.

Despite this history of rapid acquisition, however, the United States did not wait long before it devised ways of disposing of the lands. First territories, then states, were carved from the public domain. Throughout the era of acquisition there marched a program to transfer federal lands to corporate and private ownership. Reagan administration officials developed plans to sell federal lands to help pay for military debts, reminiscent of Napoleon and the Russian Czar. Reagan's plan for federal land sales is not new; its record lies mired in the unsavory past.

Emigrants Crossing the Plains

3

Disposing of the Land

Yellowstone National Park has more than geysers and tourists—it has an incredible wilderness. It was my good fortune to work in the park's back country for five summers. As a young Park Service employee, I rode on horseback up Pelican Creek Valley early one June day more than twenty years ago. With me rode two others, a veteran employee from Texas and another from Wyoming.

It was a day vital enough to alter a young life. The Absaroka Range loomed ahead, white and bright. The horse drank, nostril-deep in the cold water of Pelican Creek, as cutthroat trout darted into dark pools. The meadows were full of lupine, larkspur, harebell, and Indian paintbrush. I smelled flowers and pine, watched a hawk circling, inhaled bracing mountain air. The day was like a familiar dream unfolding.

During the ride to the Pelican Creek cabin where we would work, I encountered grizzly signs on a muddy trail. Simply seeing the great animal's tracks awoke fears as old as cavemen. When we rode over a sagebrush hill, a band of elk ran for cover in the lodgepole-pine forest. Finally the trail took us to a sweeping vista of mountains, forest, and Pelican Creek Valley. Grazing on a far slope was a small band of buffalo.

We reined in the horses and savored the view. I was stunned, astounded that anything so wild and primitive was still left for me to see. The Texas rider spoke first. "I never stop here that I don't think how pretty this valley would be with my Herefords grazing down there." The Wyoming rider disagreed only with the breed of cattle. I was in the wildest, richest land I had

33

ever seen, in the oldest national park, and my fellow riders visualized a private pasture.

Later I learned the historic weight of their vision. Before the last expansion of the American nation, a complex and often corrupt process transferred public lands to state, corporate, and private ownership. The land seemed limitless; more was always on the western horizon. It was the sole wealth of America, a capital resource to be spent like cash. After the Revolution the new government faced a large war debt and needed financial support. The answer was to sell land.

The young United States faced three major problems: Indians, taxes, and land. Indians were to be left on the poorest lands, and the new nation took the rest. Then, instead of imposing taxes for revenue, the nation sold land. The debate in the Continental Congress over land disposal took more than a year. In 1784 Thomas Jefferson was chair of the land committee, and he wrote a first draft of America's first land ordinance. He often wrote of a democratic and agrarian country in which power would be dispersed, not concentrated. Unfortunately, he left the committee for his ambassadorship in France, and the nation lost an influential voice when formulating its first land policy.

In May of the following year the nation adopted its first land law. The Land Ordinance of 1785 laid a foundation for management and disposal of public lands. It also adopted a rectangular township survey system. To this day the first land law is reflected in every city block, every farm, and every parcel of land carved from the massive public domain.

The ordinance also reflected tensions that persist to this day in American land policy. Jefferson had advocated and emphasized democratic uses and social benefits from public land; Alexander Hamilton favored the corporations. Although the ordinance authorized selling lands, the terms favored wealthy land speculators. Neither the poor nor even the average working family could buy the federal lands. It was the beginning of the polarization between Hamilton and Jefferson over the philosophy of public lands. Who would benefit, corporations or common people?

The ordinance contains rudiments of a democratic policy. It authorized reserving lands for schools, a major advance. A provision also gave land to Revolutionary War veterans in recognition of dubious land grants promised both to Hessians who switched allegiance and to army volunteers. Soon veterans headed west. The frontier swept through the Appalachian passes to flood the Ohio, Tennessee, and Mississippi valleys.

The bill also initiated a reservation system for Indians, which recognized their claims to land. It gave little hint of the abuse to come.

Continuing a colonial policy and ancient European tradition, it reserved a portion of public mineral wealth for the entire nation. As long as people had been civilized, minerals had been regarded as a gift of nature to a nation. Historically, they were not exclusive property of one individual or corporation. Like Indian policy, mineral lands became the focus of widespread larceny and abuse. It continues today.

The 1785 act permitted the disposal of public lands, and the nation clearly chose to use its wealth of land to build a new government. Two years later, during the Constitutional Convention, basic issues of a federal land policy were considered resolved by earlier debates and by the Northwest Ordinance of 1787. Like the ordinance of two years before, the 1787 act was monumental. It provided a method for new states carved from the public domain to join the union, and it laid the basis for equality between states.

After months of debate and two important land laws, the Constitution of the United States encompassed the public lands issue in only twenty-six words in Section 3 of Article IV: "The Congress shall have Power to dispose of and make all needful Rules and Regulations respecting the Territory or other Property belonging to the United States. . . ." Congress had the control. On those few words the entire foundation of a democratic land policy rested. Today those constitutional words resist pseudo-scientific economists and other raiders who would have all lands in private ownership.

Public lands divided the nation into different philosophical camps. The earliest and most persistent rift has been between aristocratic and democratic policies. Conflicts over aristocratic British policies had been a major contributing element in the Revolutionary War. After the war, the conflict was most sharply illustrated by the division between Jefferson and Hamilton. Jefferson favored using public lands for an agrarian nation and the common people. Lands would be granted to states and individuals for a variety of public purposes, but the best use would be to develop a nation of small, independent, self-reliant farmers. Hamilton favored the corporation. Selling lands to liquidate the national debt was his major priority. He favored large blocks sold under terms suited to a corporate world, not to yeoman farmers. By raising broad philosophical questions, Jefferson and Hamilton opened a long and persistent debate over disposition of the public domain. The basic arguments remain today: corporations versus the public as a whole.

It is difficult to imagine, from a perspective of modern urban America, how important public-land issues were to the early government. Rural America was growing. It fermented with ideas and opinions. Federal land was manifest wealth, freedom from aristocratic Europe, and a source of national power. When a federal government began operating in 1789, questions of public lands assumed an extraordinary importance. Frontier representatives demanded pre-emption laws, the right of settlers to claim and purchase land they had broken. Others were more audacious and demanded free land for settlers. Urban representatives opposed such liberalism, fearing a drain on municipal populations. Outmigration would shift power from the settled East to the unruly and somewhat revolutionary frontier.

For one hundred years of American history, Congress spent most of its time and effort dealing with public lands. It debated and passed dozens, then hundreds, and eventually thousands of public-land laws with more complex details than any other policy issue. Today only a handful of scholars understands their scope. Few people appreciate the lands' importance or the fervor of the average citizens two hundred years ago. Still fewer understand how remnants of a landed aristocracy persist on the public domain today. The issues remain essentially unchanged: public and corporate representatives still battle over the wealth, power, and freedom of public lands.

Yet two hundred years ago, lines were drawn sharply and issues were less confused by the myths and traditions. Frontier regions were at odds with older New England states. Regional differences were persistent. An early issue, not sharply in focus and only dimly perceived, was conservation. The abundance of land with a population of fewer than four million people made protection and conservation meaningless. Nevertheless, there were early attempts at conservation—always opposed by developers.

Conservation began modestly in 1799 when the new Congress appropriated 200,000 scarce dollars to buy naval timber reserves, implicitly recognizing that protecting resources was related to national defense. It adopted the ill-fated broad-arrow policy, which had helped lead to the Revolution. Yet it did continue a pattern of naval and military reserves, first protecting oak for masts, keels, and other vital parts of wooden ships. Later, large coal reserves were protected, when the U.S. Navy shifted from sail to steam. Still later, when the navy adopted oil burners, petroleum reserves on public lands were protected.

Military resource reserves were difficult to protect, however. On the southern frontier late in the eighteenth century, raiders took mast trees. In the 1920s, naval reserves were the target of Interior Secretary Albert Fall's greed. Millions of barrels of military oil flowed to Interior, then to private hands. In the early 1980s, Secretary Watt in the Reagan administration plundered the naval reserves by leasing them at outrageously low prices to permit corporate profit. He was part of an old and wasteful tradition.

But the naval reserves were an aberration in our early history. The predominant theme was not conservation, but exploitation and development. There appeared to be no end to natural resources. For decades this attitude reigned. The vast eastern forests seemed endless; they blocked the sun and broke plows and the backs of men and women who tried to clear them. It was not understood that trees held soil in place, and soil held water, keeping rivers within their banks. Decades later the forests had fallen to the ax and the injudicious use of forest fires to clear the land. Soil was turned by wooden plows, and thin crops grew in the place of a dense forest canopy. Rains fell on exposed soil, and humus a thousand years old washed into streams, choking salmon in their timeless cycle of renewal. Clearing the eastern forests launched a crescendo of destructive and wasteful events.

The frontier pushed westward. After the dense eastern forests gave way to the ax and plow, the frontier rolled onto the Great Plains. Suddenly the problem of virgin land was different. Prairie sod was tough and held together a complex ecology of grasses, forbs, and flowers. The pioneers' wooden plows splintered. But underneath the soil was richer and in a larger tract than anywhere else on earth.

Civilizations had been founded on fertile but narrow banks

of the Nile, Tigres, and Euphrates rivers. On the North American continent, the prairie was hundreds of miles wide, and the sea of grassland hid a rich lode of soil. Lust for land proved tougher than prairie sod. New steel plows cut the mat of grass and roots, rolling its black side to the sun. For the first time since glaciers retreated, the Great Plains were dark as ravens.

But the subtle community of flower and grass that had built it was gone, replaced by the simplicity of a field of corn or beans. Native grasses had harbored a complex world of insects in a protracted struggle for dominance, neither side ever gaining supremacy. Balance is a guiding philosophy of nature; along with complexity, it provides stability. The simple ecology of a farmer's field brought the demise of some predators and a rise of those that fed on specific plants. Other creatures were carried into this new and simple environment from foreign lands. The land, unlocked by the steel plow, was theirs to conquer and to change more than glacial scour had done.

Virgin forests held a complex of birds that had evolved into specific niches since the ice retreated. Passenger pigeons darkened the sky when they passed. They fed thousands of people; pigeon feathers filled mattresses and pillows. As the hardwood forests that covered land and protected pigeons were exhausted, no one complained. Waste was not against any law; it was fashionable. The complexities of pigeon or insect, soil or water were beyond the comprehension of most people, and certainly of politicians who crafted land law. But lessons were everywhere. No pigeons returned to roost.

Land was the basis of wealth and an object of waste. It was used to carve a destiny from a continent. Lessons of time and history remain hidden by today's freeze-frame view of a complex and dynamic process. Only a few scenes are clear. The doddering post-office pigeon is a sad reminder of passenger pigeons, whose flocks hid the sun. Thin soil annually hand-fed with fertilizer and chemicals is a poor replacement for the wealth of a dark prairie sod. A channelized stream, gloomy with sediment and rank with chemicals, holds only carp instead of the clear-water bass and pike of an earlier era. The land's gifts have been wasted.

Development and growth were national catchwords. Arguments were not whether to develop, but how. Who would benefit, farmer or corporation? First it was the corporation.

The ordinance of 1785 had been unfavorable to genuine settlers. Hamiltonian policies required cash to purchase public land. A minimum purchase of 640 acres at a price of one dollar an acre had been required. Credit was not available. Few immigrants or settlers could afford the purchase. Instead, land speculators and corporations bought large tracts and sold them at inflated prices and interest rates to settlers. Developers even prevailed upon Congress for many years to keep settlers from directly acquiring federal lands.

The threat of a frontier rebellion was never far from the minds of early representatives. The pioneers on the edge of civilization had a well-earned reputation for independent and radical views. As a result, various amendments were made in land laws during the early 1800s. First, Congress offered credit to purchase land. It reduced the minimum plot to a more reasonable 160 acres, allowing farmers to buy. But as land developers gained political power, the price was raised. Settlers fell behind in their payments. In 1820 the government returned to selling to highest bidders for cash; frontier discontent rose as sales fell.

Pre-emption became a political battle cry from the west. Throughout the early decades of American history, there were always pioneers who pushed the frontier's limits. They leap-frogged settlements and carved out homes from the wilderness. Life was risky for them. They faced a hostile environment but created their homes and livelihoods from raw material. Life was also perilous for the land speculator or government agent who eventually arrived with civilization. Sometimes squatters could be forceably evicted from lands they had settled. Sometimes they were offered a chance to purchase land they had cleared and farmed, the same ground that held their homes, crops, and often graves of their families. It was a tense time for agents of progress to move independent settlers. Sometimes settlers might push on west, sometimes they might choose to fight. Always they argued for a right of pre-emption.

Pre-emption was an official pardon to the squatter for illegal settlement. It meant a preferential right to buy land carved from the wilderness. It was seen as a moral right, a concession of the government or land companies to recognize the courage and labor of frontierspeople and was a powerful motivation for settlers, making public-land policy a political powder keg. To sever a family from land often took more power than could be marshaled from a fresh wave of civilization.

Land companies and corporations succeeding on the frontier at the expense of settlers was a source of tension and argument for a long time. The issue plagued individual states and the Continental Congress and was clouded because many early colonial leaders were land speculators. So heated were land issues that during some debates in the Continental Congress, members demanded an ethical statement. Those involved in public-land issues were required to declare whether they had ties to land companies. Speculators could not be trusted to represent the public. Richard Henry Lee contemptuously referred to them as "land mongers."

Despite the influence of commerce, the land-reform crusade that began with Jefferson continued to be pushed by agrarian forces in the South and West and in 1830 achieved a measure of relief for the frontier. Congress authorized a one-year trial of pre-emption sales. The law was signed by Andrew Jackson, the first frontier president. It polarized West and East. Thomas Hart Benton, a pro-development senator from Missouri, continued to challenge the East to overcome its selfishness, myopia, and provincial attitudes toward hardy settlers. Daniel Webster, a leader of more settled New England territory, opposed pre-emption. Public land became the major sectional issue of this era. Pre-emption laws were frequently passed but, like all public-land laws, were subject to widespread abuse. It was not always a poor settler who profited.

Pre-emption was more than a triumph for settlers; it was a victory for a region. After this battle the West never again lost control over the public lands. Other regional issues would emerge, but public land became the unique political turf of western states. The East was placed in a less powerful role to influence legislation and policy, where it remains today.

Next the South and West split. They had joined forces to encourage pre-emption, but soon western leaders were pushing for free land, with no cash payments for actual settlers. This proposal divided West and South because of fundamental differences in their economies and values. Southern plantation owners feared competition from small farmers, who demanded open and free land. The issue, like pre-emption, took years to resolve. Again the West won.

Civil war broke the deadlock in more ways than one. With southern delegations removed from Congress, the Homestead Act passed overwhelmingly on May 20, 1862. It was signed into law by Abraham Lincoln, another product of the western frontier. The act permitted any person, citizen or not, to settle on 160 acres of land and either purchase land at a minimum price of $1.25 per acre or acquire title free after five years of residence and cultivation. It was the most progressive land law in history. It attracted settlers from throughout the world to the public lands. All one had to do was clear land and build a home, and prosperity would be found. Settlers came by the thousands, and millions of acres of land were transferred to them. Yeoman farmers shared in the wealth of land. Jefferson's ideal agrarian model seemed within reach. Superficially, it appeared that preemption and the Homestead Act would put an end to conflicts over who was to benefit—corporation or common citizen. That was not the case.

The Homestead Act was aptly called by Horace Greeley "a magnificent national democratic triumph—a bold but noble promise." Lincoln felt its essential point was that capital to purchase land was no longer superior to the labor required to conquer wilderness. Yet in the years before and after the Homestead Act, Congress continued to indulge corporations and aristocratic interests. By 1860 it had given 27.8 million acres to railroad corporations. By the end of Lincoln's administration, railroads received another 74.4 million acres. Only 3.4 million acres of land had been claimed under the Homestead Act.

Large grants had been given for tanneries, distilleries, grist mills, and sawmills before any were given to ordinary settlers. Mineral lands had already been stolen and dissipated from public lands for decades. Taking timber from public lands was not considered a crime but an inalienable right. Frontier congressmen, like their western counterparts today, eloquently defended the right of loggers to take public resources. The General Land Office Commissioner in 1855, John Wilson, attempted to prosecute loggers, sawmill owners, and companies that were stealing timber from the public lands. His field agents seized stolen timber. Protests and riots broke out in Great Lakes logging towns. Wilson was fired as commissioner and assigned to negotiate Indian treaties in the West.

The government earned little more from minerals than from timber. The earliest land charters granted by the kings of England, France, and Spain carried a provision for mineral royalties on gold, silver, copper, and other precious minerals. The tradition dated back to the Greek and Roman governments and continued through the Middle Ages in Europe. The wealth of minerals was considered a gift of nature, but a portion of it was to be returned to the king or, in a democracy, to the public. The concept of royalties for minerals was incorporated into the first public-land law Congress passed. But the substantial mineral wealth of public lands earned little revenue for the public treasury.

The Mesabi Range in Minnesota, rich in iron, passed into corporate ownership with little compensation to the public. Although all mineral lands were to be reserved from public entry, the government sold the Mesabi Range at a minimum price and never received any royalty. If it had kept Great Lakes mineral lands, it would have received more than $1 billion in royalties. In 1852, the federal government gave Michigan 750,-000 acres to aid in construction of the Soo Canal. The canal company selected lands including the Calument Lode, which became the foundation for the Calument and Hecla Consolidated Copper Company empire. The government had neither the will nor the resources to stop the looting.

On the western mining frontier, the leasing and royalty systems completely collapsed. The California gold rush brought a stampede into the Sierra foothills. Placer lodes were rapidly sifted and depleted, and by the late 1850s the rush was largely played out. A military governor of California recommended a portion of gold be given to the public treasury, but no one attempted to claim a public share of the gold rush, although miners were trespassers on public land. By force of numbers and with the righteous indignation of bandits, they made their own rules and regulations.

In recognition of western mining conditions, Congress passed a new mining law in 1866. It was amended in 1872. Lands that looked promising for mining were to be claimed free from public lands. If mining was shown to be feasible, then the land could be purchased for $2.50 an acre. The 1872 Mining Act ended nearly 300 years of charging royalties for minerals on the American continent, a policy that had required miners to give the public a share of income from nature's mineral gift. The strange law remains in effect today.

Occasionally investigations were ordered into public-land scams. In 1874 the California legislature was concerned with federal land fraud and corruption. It asked for a report, which focused on swamp and "overflow" lands. The report concluded, ". . . through the connivance of parties, surveyors were appointed who segregated lands as swamp, which were not so in fact . . . the loose laws of the State lands have enabled wealthy parties to obtain much of it under circumstances which, in some countries, where laws were more rigid and terms less refined, would be termed fraudulent, but we can designate it as keen foresight and wise (for the land grabbers) construction of loose, unwholesome laws."

The case of the "Inyo Grab" was cited as typical. Josiah Earle was a registrar in the General Land Office at Independence, California, in Inyo County. He helped apply for 133,000 acres, which included 12,000 acres settled by some of the oldest residents of the county. These lands on the lee side of the Sierra, sold as swamplands, are dry. Steep mountains to the west wring out winter storms and capture most of the moisture. All of the valleys to the east are arid and desert, as is the Owens Valley. The legislature's report accurately describes the lands as dry ". . . as they unquestionably are, as there can be no crops produced thereon without extensive and constant irrigation." Unknown to legitimate settlers, the county surveyor signed applications for Earle stating there were no residents or claimants on the land. The federal government sold the land as uninhabited swamp. The California Committee on Swamp and Overflowed Lands and Land Monopoly filed a report but could offer no "cure for the gigantic evils which have grown out of the reckless land policy of the government. . . . "

It was not until 1871 that Congress appropriated any money to enforce various laws protecting timber. But even at 1871 prices the $5000 appropriation did not go far. By 1877, Secretary of Agriculture Watts had asked Dr. Franklin B. Hough, an early conservationist, to write the first *Report Upon Forestry*. In his report to the 54th Congress, Hough pointed out that trespassers were stealing entire forests. The longstanding timber subsidy was mentioned in an 1874 report. "The produce of these lands is of universal use, and forms the staple of commerce of no inconsiderable portion of the nation. The difference between the government price [for timber] and the actual price thereof is large, yet Congress provides that these lands shall be disposed of under the pre-emption laws at $1.25 per acre. . . ." In 1875 still another report says: "A national calamity is being rapidly and surely brought upon the country by the useless destruction of forests." At long last the concept that a nation is as strong as its resources was slowly emerging from the waste and destruction.

Carl Schurz, secretary of the interior under President Rutherford Hayes, sounded a warning on depredations of timber. He sent his agents into the field to prosecute the robbers. Three months later, more fines had been levied for timber trespass than in the previous twenty years. Timber-state congressmen accused Schurz of introducing "Prussian methods" into democratic America. Congress cut Interior Department appropriations, timber inspectors were laid off, and public forestland remained unprotected. Schurz lost a battle and became an early casualty of the war for conservation. But he helped start a movement and left his mark as the first secretary of the interior to carry a banner for the public at large instead of for commercial interests.

With the exhaustion of timber resources in the Great Lakes and the decimation of hardwood forests in the South, the logging frontier moved west. California and Oregon, with their massive forests and high-value timber such as redwood and douglas fir, were obvious targets. Miners required large amounts of timber for their burrows. Loggers were eager to comply. Before long, the lovely Tahoe Basin was stripped of its timber to support Virginia City's mines. By 1885 William Andrew Jackson Sparks became commissioner of the General Land Office and vowed to prosecute the "bold, defiant, persistent depredators on the public domain." He found that 100,000 acres of valuable redwood were illegally claimed in California's North-Coast Humboldt County. He also found it impossible to stop the theft.

Others looked at earlier civilizations and feared for America's future. Dr. Henry N. Bolander wrote for the California Academy of Science in 1865, "It remains to be seen whether we shall be benefitted or not by the horrible experience such countries as Asia Minor, Greece, Spain and France have made by having barbarously destroyed their woods and forests." Bolander saw the only hope in governmental action and predicted disaster. "If the redwoods are destroyed—and they necessarily will be if not protected by a wise action of our government. . . ."

The beauty of the redwoods is visible not only through our eyes today, but also through those of one hundred years ago. Franklin Hough wrote:

A redwood forest is described as grand beyond power of appreciation to one who has not witnessed the dense masses of fog come rolling in from the Pacific, creeping through the foliage, covering the hilltops, flowing down the opposite slopes, and filling the canyons until hill and valley are wrapped in dripping mist, or as the process is reversed in early light of mornings, as these fogs melt away and reveal the forests, in all their grandeur of dimensions and distance stretching away until lost to view on the far off horizon.

The beauty and power of America's resources stirred more than greed in some citizens, yet a hundred years passed before a substantial stand of redwoods was protected as a national park. Even then the park's lands were already logged in many areas.

Using federal lands to encourage development and private enterprise began early. It was believed that granting land for canals, roads, and other projects—helping build the national infrastructure—would add to the value of adjacent federal lands. Increased value would be reflected in higher prices and more revenue for the U.S. treasury. This was not the case. The best lands went to development companies. The poorest lands remained in federal hands. The public lost wealth.

Five percent of the revenues from selling certain public lands was earmarked for internal improvements. In 1806 such funds helped build the Cumberland or National Road from Cumberland, Maryland, to the Ohio River. By 1827 Congress began granting land to companies that would develop western regions by building such canals as the Erie Canal. Within two decades major canals were begun in Indiana, Illinois, and Ohio, as well as other midwestern states. Then came a depression, the Civil War, and the western railroads. Canals faded as a means of commerce and transportation.

After 1835 Congress granted free rights-of-way across the public lands in the East, Midwest, and South for railroads. Demand for similar but larger grants within western states was sometimes opposed; one region feared that another would gain an economic advantage. The first large land grants, for construction of the Illinois Central Railroad, were made in 1850. As a concession to the South, the route reached from Mobile, Alabama, to Chicago, Illinois. The railroad was also granted alternate sections on each side of the railroad. Following an historic pattern, land-grant subsidies for railroads became more and more generous.

Not surprisingly, railroads became major land speculators and developers. Sometimes intended railroads were never built. The corporate objective was to secure public land with a generous congressional grant, then sell the land. As the frontier pushed westward into the harsh plains, railroads attracted settlers from Europe with false promises about fertility of far western soils and prospects for farms. Dozens of salesmen in Europe attracted settlers to the West, often providing free ship passage and train tickets to frontier stations.

The Northern Pacific Railroad was constructed across the Northern Great Plains and Rockies with the help of a federal subsidy of 58 million acres. The grant cut a swath 120 miles wide from Minnesota to Puget Sound. For each mile of railroad constructed, the company received 25,600 acres of land, enough to make hundreds of family farms. Total railroad land grants exceeded the size of Germany, Holland, and Belgium together and were larger than any individual European country except Russia. Little wonder European immigrants flocked westward at the invitation of the railroads.

The total lands granted to railroads and other corporations by the federal government were approximately 223 million acres. Because many railroads did not complete their lines or abandoned them after a period of time, more than 43 million acres were eventually seized and returned to public ownership or sold. However, the finest farm lands and richest mineral lands had passed to private ownership through the various development corporations. The public was usually left with western grazing and desert land that had little value at the time. Also, the railroads often succeeded in ousting the legitimate settler who arrived before the railroad, especially if the land was fertile.

But land grants did not insure success. Northern Pacific's Jay Cooke received a 58-million-acre subsidy for his Northern Pacific Railroad empire, but his company went bankrupt. Cooke's competitor, James J. Hill, built the Great Northern Railway across the Great Plains and northern Rockies parallel to the Northern Pacific route. It was the most successful transcontinental line and was built without an acre of federal land. Hill was so successful he eventually gained substantial control of the Northern Pacific Railroad and its land grant.

The 1888 Democratic Party platform demanded that 100 million acres of railroad land be returned to authentic homesteaders because of fraudulent corporate claims. Phony grants were seldom returned to public ownership. But Republican Benjamin Harrison won the presidency, and the lands were not returned. As a result, even today the largest landowners in California and other western states are railroad companies. Only 4 million acres were given for road construction and another 4 million for canals. The railroads were the most successful looters of the public domain until they were surpassed by energy companies in the 1970s and '80s.

Early exploiters needed to be creative in acquiring public lands. Abusing public grazing lands was one technique. No legislation provided for livestock grazing land to be disposed of until the Stockraising Homestead Act passed Congress in 1916. Yet for many decades western stock owners had acquired valuable rangelands. Most western rangelands had little surface water and few streams or springs. Ranchers who controlled water dominated the outlying, dry public land. Controlling the land was simple. Using the Homestead Act and other land laws designed for farmers, ranchers required cowboys to serve as "dummy entrymen." At the local land office, cowboys claimed long, narrow parcels of land bordering streams. As a condition of their employment, they turned the property over to the main ranch owner, sometimes for a fee, sometimes only for the wages they had earned. Meanwhile, the ranchers' control was expanded. Vast cattle ranches emerged from counterfeit claims and the rubble of broken public land laws. Contrary to myth, western ranch tradition was not the courtly morality of the Virginian, but lawlessness and defiance of public-land law.

The control of the western springs and streams permitted wholesale trespassing of livestock on the public lands. The niche once filled by hordes of buffalo was commandeered by stockraisers' cattle and sheep. As rangeland became overgrazed, the land's ability to support life decreased. Illegal fences sprang up throughout the West as cattle ranchers tried to secure their claims and keep out settlers and sheepherders. The Department of the Interior had little success removing the fences. Grazing remained completely uncontrolled on the public domain until 1934. Only minimal grazing controls exist even today, and ranchers enjoy a juicy subsidy as their livestock fatten on public lands.

Besides abusing grazing land, another simple way to acquire land was to abuse Indian treaties. Initially, individual Indians received land grants, which were acquired quickly by whites. Still other Indian lands were transferred to whites after Congress declared them "surplus" to the needs of Native Americans. If any citizen's property had been termed "surplus," it would have been called larceny; Indians, however, were not citizens then. Settlers did complain, but only when several treaties permitted the sale of six entire Indian reservations, including 8 million acres of the Osage Reservation in Kansas, to railroads. That was too much for independent frontierspeople. It was one thing to steal from Indians but quite another for railroads to steal Indian land from white settlers. A major change came in 1871. A new law prohibited secret treaties. Before, private treaties were often known to only a few corporate and congressional insiders.

More openly, in 1874 gold miners invaded Sioux lands in the Black Hills, led by the U.S. Army's Seventh Cavalry and George Armstrong Custer. Indian resentment over this foray led to a rendezvous with Custer at the Little Big Horn. But the Indians' victory was only temporary; Custer's hair was a small reward. Indians were forced to surrender not only their common hunting grounds, but also sacred mountains and ancient burial grounds. American treaties were worthless. Indians lost more than 100 million acres of reservation lands granted by treaties with the United States.

Indian-land policy degenerated dramatically in 1887 with the Dawes Act, which accelerated the theft of Indian land. The act's ostensible purpose was to promote the assimilation of Native Americans into the larger culture. Soon 26 million acres were transferred to corporate or private ownership. Tribe after tribe lost the majority of its land. "Surplus" Indian lands in Oklahoma were opened to whites in a classic land rush in 1889; more than 50,000 people participated. Tens of thousands of settlers rushed for Indian lands in 1891, 1892, 1893, 1895, and 1901.

Whites invaded reservations, repeatedly provoking battles and further loss of Indian land. Land rushes made colorful art and history, but to Native Americans they were neither honorable nor honest.

By the 1880s it was a regular practice in the West for cattle ranchers to graze their livestock in trespass on Indian reservations. In most cases this led to a reduction of the reservation's size. Some Indian agents tried to enforce laws, but western juries were averse to convicting their fellow ranchers, often local political leaders.

The disastrous winter of 1886–1887 decimated herds and led to more poaching of Indian lands. The Blackfoot reservation, which reached from north of the Missouri River to the Canadian border, became a major source of illegal forage. Cattle ranchers pushed surviving herds across the Missouri and helped themselves to Indian grass. A few years later the Blackfoot tribe lost millions of acres north of the Missouri by treaty. It was more formal, if not more ethical, than trespassing cattle. The Blackfoot treaty followed the usual pattern: by treaty, Indians were first given land thought to be worthless, but once it became valuable, it was transferred to private ownership.

Indian reservations have remained prime targets for land speculators and schemers. Even in the 1950s and 1960s, large chunks of Indian lands along the Missouri River were drowned by reservoirs built by the U.S. Army Corps of Engineers. Some tribes had lived along the Missouri in perfect harmony with river rhythms and resources since the last ice age. Mandan villagers welcomed the first American expedition coming upriver in 1804. Lewis and Clark, exploring the Louisiana Purchase, spent their first winter in the comfort of Mandan lodges. This area and 155,000 acres of the most fertile land in western North Dakota, including old forts, sacred burial grounds, and ancient villages, lie under water behind Fort Garrison Dam. One final insult remained. Army engineers named the reservoir flooding the Indian reservation Lake Sacajawea. She was not even a member of a Missouri River tribe, but was from the Shoshone tribe to the west.

Today's Indians battle the Army Corps of Engineers instead of the Seventh Cavalry. They understand clearly that their reservation land today is less than a third the size it once was. The rest of the public lands have followed the same pattern: once they have been found to be valuable, they have ended in private ownership.

There is no doubt the founding fathers wanted to use western cession lands and the Louisiana Purchase to encourage development and to form new states. As the frontier moved west the United States became more and more generous in its land grants. First it gave one section for schools per township, or one square mile out of every thirty-six. Later the size doubled, and still later it doubled again to four sections per township, or four square miles out of every thirty-six. Finally, with the admission of Alaska, Congress outdid itself in generosity.

The State of Alaska in 1959 received a guarantee to nearly one-third of the federal lands within its boundary, more than 100 million acres. Carefully selecting the most valuable mineral and oil lands, Alaska was overwhelmed by the wealth. By the early 1980s the state had virtually abolished taxes and was dreaming up innovative ways to spend the money from its oil, gas, and mineral resources previously held in federal ownership.

Eastern states were not as fortunate. The first two states admitted to the union after the Revolution were Vermont and Kentucky. They had no federal lands within their boundaries. Tennessee had a complicated agreement with North Carolina but received some remaining public lands. Only with the State of Ohio did the normal pattern begin, and it persisted for the admission of more than thirty states.

Only three states were admitted after this period without public lands. The first was Maine, which had been part of Massachusetts and therefore held no federal lands. The second was Texas, which had won its independence from Mexico in 1836 but was not immediately admitted to the Union because of the slavery issue. Ten years of independence left Texas debt-ridden. Upon admission, it was not required to cede its lands; instead, the United States purchased part of its northern lands. Texas went on to squander its hundred-million-acre state heritage. The third state was Hawaii, also an independent republic prior to statehood.

The remaining states received various amounts of federal lands on admission to statehood and through various acts of Congress. California received 8.8 million acres, one of the largest grants. Today 8 million acres have passed to private hands, and remaining land contributes some revenue to the state school fund. If California had rented the 8 million acres instead of selling them, it would reap large benefits today and in the future.

Nevada, long an antagonist of the federal government over the amount of federal land within its boundaries, provides another pathetic example of state land management. Nevada was admitted to statehood in 1864 and received two sections, numbered 16 and 36, per township. As a result it acquired mountain tops, desert valleys, and isolated tracts essentially useless. Later it petitioned Congress to reduce the total acreage but to let it select the limited amount of land suitable for irrigation, mining, and other commercial activities. Congress generously granted the request. The state promptly set out to dispose of these lands, often to people with important political connections. As recently as the 1960s Nevada was given a large parcel of land for a state park at Lake Tahoe from the estate of conservationist George Whittell. A choice parcel ended up in the hands of a prominent state politician. It remains in private hands today, an idyllic private inholding in Nevada's premier state park.

New Mexico, Idaho, Utah, and other western states followed similar patterns. The lands in state ownership today were not held out of any sense of public trust; they simply lacked economic value. The most valuable lands for mining, agriculture, and water development passed to private ownership long ago. The remaining state land has been considered essentially worthless until recent years, and it could not be sold or looted. But as the lands grew valuable, they then became the object of private developers.

One of the major reasons lands in the western states are misused is that policy goals encourage abuse. Most western states require land managers to maximize economic returns from their lands for local school systems. Such a policy is not multiple use; it is similar to a commercial enterprise, and with such a simple economic goal, it is opposed to the long-term interests of society. Because of the economics of resource development, such a policy assures that nonrenewable resources will be depleted, and renewable ones will become nonrenewable. Energy resources, especially, are given a priority in development. It is not conservation policy. It does not serve future generations. It violates the ethic of public trust.

Other grants were given to states to reclaim swampland, a

notorious mechanism of fraud and deception. A total of 65 million acres were transferred from federal ownership by this method. Grants were given for state universities, agricultural colleges, mental hospitals, penitentiaries, fish hatcheries, poor farms, miners' hospitals, and many other uses.

There is little doubt that these grants often served valuable, even essential purposes to initiate development. More than 77 million acres were granted for schools and 21 million acres for universities and technical schools. But this amount is less than half the size of railroad grants. The states used their grants for desert reclamation, railroad grants, and other projects that usually favored corporations, the wealthy, and people with political connections.

The public-land states received more than 400 million acres directly from the federal government. The cessions made by Virginia and the first colonies favored the entire nation, but eastern states were given only small federal land grants. In contrast, the federal government has been generous with western states and even foolish with Alaskan land and resources. Yet western states persist in the myth they have been ill-treated by federal land grants.

Before the close of the nineteenth century, most grants had been made, and they went to railroads, states, and land speculators. Only a fraction of homestead land went to genuine settlers. Most went to ranchers, speculators, and developers. Developers alone bought 100 million acres directly. Another 100 million acres had been taken from Indian reservations; most ended up with a few large landowners. In all, more than a half-billion acres of public land had gone to corporations and large land developers. The foundation of such companies as Burlington Northern, Weyerhaeuser, Southern Pacific, Anaconda, and ARCO rests on public lands.

This transfer of public lands to private ownership happened in a nation that boasted of its generous and democratic land policy, which had drawn the poor and downtrodden from around the world. But princely estates had gone to railroad magnates, cattle kings, mining barons, and lumber monarchs at the expense of public wealth, individual freedom, and the power of common people.

Farsighted people had been warning of the consequences of unrestrained greed for decades. It was time for a major reform in American land law; a revolution was needed in the nation's attitude toward its heritage. It was time to recognize that a nation's strength and defense were directly tied to its resources. Teddy Roosevelt rose to start public land reform, but he, like Jefferson, fell short of his goal.

The Catskills: Sunrise from South Mountain

4

The Dawn of a
Conservation Ethic

The conservation movement, like a river, had many beginnings. No doubt there were hunters who watched the fall of buffalo and saw more than prairie dust stirred by their collapse. The scope of the butchery and the rotting carcasses offended some minds as well as nostrils. Certainly one was George Bird Grinnell, who sat in front of his fireplace in 1892, as he wrote for *Scribners' Magazine,* with a pair of bleached buffalo skulls on either side of his fireplace. Late at night he would muse and dream: ". . . they take life before my eyes. The matted brown hair again clothes the dry bone, and in the empty orbits the wild eyes gleam. Above me curves the blue arch; away on every hand stretches the yellow prairie, and scattered near and far are the dark forms of buffalo." The buffalo of Grinnell's dreams had only recently fallen, but they were the quintessential wild American animal that could be considered a resource on the hoof. Grinnell's words were but a trickle in a great river that swept the idea of conservation into the national consciousness.

Conservation was a major social reform in American history. As a political movement it had its basis in science and included both a businesslike efficiency and a conservative, rational response to the rapid loss of natural resources. Forests, soils, fisheries, and wildlife had been recklessly and frighteningly depleted. Vast oak and hardwood forests facing early pioneers seemed limitless, but they fell. The prairie sod was deep, rich, and tough, but the steel plow peeled the land. Sixty million buffalo on the Great Plains were a vast national resource. Hun-

dreds of generations of Native Americans had lived off the
beasts; still, the population had thrived. Technology had made
a quantum leap from the Osage bow to the rifle, however, and
a great national asset fell before the long reach of Sharp's rifle.
Technology, population growth, and greed were enemies of the
American land and its resources.

Conservation was a major philosophical response to environmental destruction and a recognition that economic and social
goals implicit in the first American land laws had not been
attained. Corporations had triumphed over the common people,
and the wealth of land had been squandered. Decades of study
and debate preceded major shifts in policy. Programs were
tried, experiments were planned, and tentative reforms were
attempted. The goal was to manage the public land more democratically and to sustain productivity for future generations. But
some reforms offended public-land developers.

The long pilgrimage to conservation began when the first
pioneers who pushed into American wilderness were accompanied by a few people who traveled to study, to learn, and to
write about what they saw of the natural world. William Bar-
tram traveled in the wildernesses of the East and South. He
harvested only plants and flowers but sowed wonder and curios-
ity in thousands of people who came after him. His book *Travels*
became a naturalist's classic, and its descriptions of wild scenery
influenced literature and art for decades.

John James Audubon traveled through the South and Midwest and up the Missouri River during the early 1830s. His
portraits, *The Birds of America*, revealed the beauty of America's
wild creatures. Audubon did not establish, but later influenced,
one of the premier North American conservation organizations,
the National Audubon Society.

Philosophically, transcendentalism was a foundation for conservation. This school of thought, led by Ralph Waldo Emerson,
said that there is a reality beyond the world we experience; that
everything we know is infused with it; that intuitive or spiritual
perceptions are the superior way to discover it; and that the
natural world is an allegory of the transcending truth and moral
law. Henry David Thoreau became prominent in this school of
thought, but only after the waste and destruction of resources
had been comprehended. Thoreau wrote both of the natural
world and of the strife of living in a material world. A half-

century before conservation became a major political and social movement, he began one lecture with, "I wish to speak a word for nature, for absolute freedom and wildness, as contrasted with a freedom and culture merely civil, to regard man as an inhabitant, or a part and parcel of nature, rather than a member of society." He reached into the spirit with his cry, "Give me the ocean, the desert, or the wilderness!"

If Thoreau was the poet of wilderness and conservation, then George Perkins Marsh was the scientist, an exceptional linguist and scholar. He traveled throughout Europe and the Middle East, reading historic accounts and the land. They told him a dismal story that was revolutionary at the time. Humanity had degraded land, often with disastrous consequences. Published in 1864, his book *Man and Nature, Physical Geography as Modified by Human Action* became the first environmental text. Marsh was the first to say that the condition of the land is reflected in the strength of the nation. Deforestation has disastrous impacts for land, water—and civilization. Drawing on dramatic examples since the beginning of civilization, Marsh reached a shocking conclusion. Eventually the United States, if it continued to waste its resources, would degrade its land. After this degradation, the nation could decline. Like Thoreau, Marsh never lived to see his ideas accepted. But slowly Americans began to develop a sense of responsibility for land.

Conservation's momentum increased as the end of the frontier approached. Two forces were dominant in the western territory. The first was the frontier mentality that depended on exhausting resources. The frontier was the cornucopia called western expansion. It was intended to be democratic, but instead corporate railroads and energy businesses succeeded while family farms failed. The public supported conservation as the nation plundered its resources. As long as waste was profitable, it continued, and conservation-oriented policies were not put into effect until resources were left degenerated and degraded.

The second major force was western aridity. Most of the nation is well watered and suitable for agriculture, and soils are deep and dark. Not in the West. The dominant force in the West is aridity. Water is the single most limiting factor, a fact well known to scientists but ignored by many other people. The greenness of Salt Lake City, the trees of Los Angeles, and the lawns of Denver are artificial, made possible only by elaborate dams, irrigation ditches, and water-delivery systems. The air is dry; most of the lowlands where cities lie do not receive summer rain to support crops, lawns, or trees. Summer greenness grows from winter snow that is stored in the mountains and released by the rhythmic pulse of sprinklers.

Early pioneers did not understand the limitations of the West. The transition to aridity across the Great Plains is subtle. It took decades of crop failure to drive home the differences between humid East and arid West. Even today the transformation comes slowly to consciousness. Headed west, one is clearly in the humid region when crossing the eastern borders of the Dakotas, Nebraska, Kansas, or Texas. By the western borders, it's the West. The farms and towns are farther apart, there are few crops without irrigation, even the sky is clearer and bluer. To the east the sky is hazy, the horizon blurry. In the West the horizon is sharper, the sun hotter, the faces of people who work outdoors more bronzed.

Crossing the frontier into the arid West created an upheaval in the lives of tens of thousands of settlers. Agricultural practices successful in the East failed.

At first agricultural "scientists" from western colleges theorized and promised that "rain would follow the plow." Somehow, in an unknown chemical process, exposing black soil to hot sun would precipitate abundant rain. This foolishly optimistic agricultural theory persisted in some circles until well into the twentieth century.

A related pseudo-scientific argument explained the insufficient rains of the Great Plains by its lack of trees. Once trees were planted, their branches would snare more moisture from the passing clouds, and crops would prosper. An entire aforestation program emerged, evolved, and grew. Its remnants can be seen to this day on any drive across the Great Plains. The splendid sweep of the plains is broken by trees and shelterbelts intended to snatch rain from arid winds.

But rains did not come often enough or long enough. Thousands of settlers broke land only to have the land and its climate break them. More of the West stayed in federal ownership because of western aridity than because of the politics of conservation. Arid geography was the nation's best conservationist.

A one-armed geologist and Civil War veteran named John Wesley Powell first articulated the West's limits and what land reforms would bring public-land law into balance with the resource. He was ignored for many decades. He first gained fame by his adventure exploring the Colorado River and Grand Canyon. In 1878 he issued a government report, based on his travels, titled *Report on the Lands of the Arid Region of the United States.* In it, he called for people to recognize that the West's resources were limited and the region was suited for only limited agriculture. The simple reason was that the water for irrigation was severely limited. He argued for fundamental changes in land laws and for federal assistance to build substantial water projects.

Finally, the year Powell died and long after he had lost favor and influence in Washington, Congress passed legislation to establish the Bureau of Reclamation and federal water developments. It was the first uniquely western institution. Like many conservation-related ideas of that era, reclamation was later perverted into a program that benefited only a few individuals and corporate farms. The Bureau of Reclamation later turned Powell's and Jefferson's agrarian dream into corporate welfare farms.

When the idea of conservation took hold, people saw that more than water was limited. Forests were, too. The limit of eastern forests had been reached dramatically; the logging ended first in the Northeast, then in the Great Lakes states, and finally in the South. Only the Pacific Northwest was left, so the industry moved to that region. It was obvious the last frontier of logging was limited to western mountains; the valleys, plateaus, and deserts would never produce timber.

Timber was technically protected under many early laws. Enforcement was non-existent, however, and was not a realistic deterrent to stealing public timber. After the Civil War more and more people warned that eventually American forests would be destroyed. As the frontier moved west, some scientists realized that removing the forest cover caused floods and loss of soil. They realized that forests must be protected to assure water for irrigation. Additionally, the myth advocated by western colleges that trees helped bring rain served forest conservation well. The West was arid enough without cutting the few forests and turning everything to desert.

A few German- and Austrian-trained foresters, such as Bernhard Fernow, provided leadership and understanding of what scientific forestry was about: producing a continued supply of timber—a sustained yield. The role of science in forest conservation was obvious, and the American Association for the Advancement of Science took an early and active interest. Science, education, and government responsibility for the future were all considered essential to forest protection. A recognition of how important forests were to the national welfare was obvious in early reports and history. In 1875 the American Forestry Association was formed; it was an early conservation organization bent on protecting forest land, and it still is alive today. It was an early private, nonprofit organization that played a leading role in conservation. Its establishment was also an early indication that when economic interests are at stake, governmental agencies will not defend the public trust without the prodding of independent and organized citizens.

In 1877 Franklin Hough completed his monumental *Report Upon Forestry*, a one-volume comprehensive look at forestry in the United States. It included an outline of the European model of forestry and a blueprint of what was needed to correct problems on American forestlands. In 1882, Hough followed up with *The Elements of Forestry*. Forestry as a discipline had both a comprehensive report and a basic textbook. Managers of the other public-land resources—wildlife, parks, minerals, water, and range—did not have a comprehensive view of their fields until well into the twentieth century. Forestry made the most auspicious beginning, and the profession dominated conservation for decades.

Prussian-trained Bernhard Fernow became the first chief of the new Division of Forestry in 1886. Working within the Department of the Interior, Fernow, a scientist, helped originate research and develop a scientific basis for American forestry. The German forestry schools also trained Carl Schurz, a secretary of the interior, as well as Gifford Pinchot and Henry Graves, the first and second chiefs of the Forest Service. They gave the discipline an authoritarian cast and a professional stature.

The call for forest reserves carved from public lands came early. The first legislation, introduced in 1876, recognized ties between forest and watersheds. Its purpose was "for the preservation of the forests of the national domain adjacent to the sources of navigable rivers and other streams of the United

States." It was defeated. By the time the Forest Reserve Act finally passed Congress fifteen years later, more than 200 forestry bills had been introduced but had failed to pass. Congress built a foundation of conservation slowly.

The Forest Reserve Act of 1891 became the basis of the national forest system. Most of the law amended general land laws, but the final section, 24, was a wonderful congressional misunderstanding. It gave the president authority to designate portions of public domain as forest reserves—now called national forests. Although John Muir, Bernhard Fernow, and others had promoted similar ideas for decades, historians do not know who wrote Section 24; they know only its product: more than 190 million acres of public forestland.

President Harrison proclaimed the first forest reserve less than a month after the act passed. He established Yellowstone Forest Reservation adjacent to the national park. Other reserves were to be proclaimed in the next few years. Local residents initiated most of them to protect watersheds and forestlands from destruction not only by harvesting timber, but also by overgrazing livestock. Western agricultural interests had a stake in protecting mountain forests.

President Cleveland celebrated Washington's birthday in 1897 by creating thirteen new forest reserves totalling more than 21 million acres. Unfortunately, the reserves' boundaries were poorly drawn, and opposition grew because the reservations conflicted with towns and included land suitable for agriculture and mining. Conservation was growing stronger at the close of the century but was still too weak to directly confront the land developers; it was intended for public lands regarded as worthless.

Originally, the Department of the Interior administered all public lands. Various chores concerned with disposal or protection of forestlands, like hundreds of other public-lands matters, were delegated to Interior officials. The department was oriented toward disposal, and during its early history, it earned the reputation of being neither efficient nor totally honest. It was politically powerless to keep loggers from stealing timber or stock raisers from destroying western rangelands, yet it was legally charged with the lands' protection.

From his post in the Agriculture Department, Fernow helped establish the original forest reserves. He wrote the first policies for their protection and management. But in 1898, after twelve years as head of the Forestry Bureau, Fernow decided to step down and accept a position at Cornell, where he organized the first academic forestry program in the United States.

He was followed by a master politician, Gifford Pinchot, who later forged political alliances with universities and commercial foresters, making the United States Forest Service one of the most successful bureaucracies in the government. It also resulted in decades of competition and conflict between two federal departments, Interior and Agriculture.

Pinchot became the Chief of the Forestry Division, which was concerned with education, limited research, and a type of extension work. Forestry was in the Department of Agriculture, but the forest reserves were located in the Department of the Interior and were managed by the General Land Office. Pinchot, always the master manipulator, worked with private forestry groups and within the administration to arrange for the forest reserves be transferred to Agriculture, where trees could be treated like any other crop. After seven years he was successful. Pinchot was free to develop the professional agency he envisioned, the Forest Service. It was the first professional conservation agency.

During the administration of Theodore Roosevelt, Pinchot helped create some of the most tangible products of the conservation era. Roosevelt's conservation program was founded on reservations within the public domain. When McKinley was assassinated there were forty-one forests containing 46.4 million acres. In seven and one-half years as president, Roosevelt added 148 million acres to the forest reserves. In addition, he withdrew from private exploitation 80 million acres of public land rich in coal and 4 million acres of oil land. He also protected several million acres as national monuments and began the wildlife refuge system—all from the public domain.

Congress resented the display of presidential authority, especially on behalf of conservation. Roosevelt had withdrawn large tracts for national monuments and forests. Congress then amended the Forest Reserve Act of 1891 to prohibit forest withdrawals. To assure its passage, its sponsors attached it to the 1907 Department of Agriculture Appropriation Bill. Pinchot and Roosevelt stayed up late poring over primitive maps of western mountain ranges. On the final day before signing the bill that abolished his power, Roosevelt reserved another 16 million acres of national forests. It was an act of defiance; still, three-quarters of a century later, millions of people are enjoying the public forests reserved at the last moment under the 1891 act.

Teddy Roosevelt understood the western wilderness and why it needed careful management, not only as national forests, but also as parks. He had camped and traveled on both mountains and plains. He also knew Yellowstone National Park and the headwaters of the Yellowstone and Snake Rivers in Wyoming. It is high country, largely volcanic plateau and heavy lodgepole pine forests that are closed by snow much of the year. Although it was traversed and explored by trappers early in the nineteenth century, it remained largely a land of mystery, hot springs, and geysers through most of the frontier era.

The Washburn-Lanford-Doane surveying expedition in 1870 found the exotic country too high and remote for agriculture and geologically unlikely to be a major mining area. The explorers began to consider alternatives to settlement and development. Leaders from Montana advocated a park on a scale never before considered. They traveled east to sell the idea to Congress, and in March 1872 President Grant signed into law the Yellowstone National Park bill, reserving a block of land almost 60 miles on each border encompassing 3500 square miles. The bill's language was extraordinary, given the history of public lands. Yellowstone was "reserved and dedicated and set apart as a public park or pleasuring-ground for benefit and enjoyment of the people." The act went on to require that the secretary of the interior "provide for the preservation, from injury or spoilation, of all timber, mineral deposits, natural curiosities, or wonders within said park, and their retention in their natural condition." The rush to exhaust the public lands paused for the first time.

The early Yellowstone had little legal protection, but the idea of a public park reserved for future generations had inherent power. John Muir and others prevailed on Congress to add more parks—Yosemite, Sequoia, and General Grant (now part of Sequoia) in California. Local residents who understood the practical economic benefits of parks and tourism supported park status for other natural areas. Pride in the spectacular features of American land and a desire to preserve the frontier for the future guided many early efforts.

The idea of protecting land as a cultural heritage also began in the West. Ten years after General Custer led his troops into history in 1876 on the banks of Montana's Little Bighorn, the bloody ridge was set aside as a national cemetery. Civil War battlefields were protected later in the nineteenth century—Antietam; Chickamauga and Chattanooga; Shiloh; Gettysburg; and Vicksburg. All were managed by the War Department, and so were the early national parks. From 1886 until the establishment of the National Park Service in 1916, U.S. Cavalry stood between the public trust in national parks and the forces of greed.

Early in Roosevelt's administration a cavalry scout caught a well-known poacher, Ed Howell, skinning a buffalo in Yellowstone Park's Pelican Valley. Four other bison lay nearby, close to the hot springs and open ground where the animals wintered. The scout soon found heads and hides of six other bison. The deep snows of Pelican Valley and the concentration of bison near the springs made poaching easy. Ed Howell had ambushed the last wild buffalo herd in America.

Through photographs and articles in magazines, including *Field and Stream,* Howell's poaching gained national attention. One friend wrote the park superintendent that "Roosevelt says you made the greatest mistake of your life in not accidentally having that scoundrel [Howell] killed and he speaks as if he would have shot him on the spot." The buffalo were on the verge of going the route of the passenger pigeon. No law prevented the decimation, even in the park. The poacher was released, but the nation protested the destruction.

With Roosevelt's help, Congress passed legislation to protect all park wildlife. Yellowstone's remaining buffalo were rounded up and raised like cattle for decades. Surplus animals were shipped around the country to start new herds. When the herds were firmly established, the park's buffalo ranch closed down, and the shaggy bison returned to the wild. Pelican Valley remains a wilderness, and every winter the largest wild buffalo herd in the world still seeks the warmth of the park's springs as well as protection from poachers.

American concern expanded to prehistoric Indian sites in the Southwest. Presidential executive orders protected the Casa Grande ruin outside Phoenix. Mesa Verde became a national park in 1906, but thousands of Indian ruins, a vital link to the history of America, remained unprotected.

In 1906 Congress passed the Lacey Act, named for an Iowa Congressman with the vision of a genius; it eventually became known as the Antiquities Act. It was a simple bill permitting the president to withdraw from development those public lands with historic or scientific interest. Congressman Lacey, one of the great conservationists of his day, fought to protect Indian ruins and to establish Mesa Verde and Bandolier national parks. He helped save the buffalo from extinction and he later fought to protect forest reserves and to conserve public-domain land in general. Overshadowed today by Roosevelt's conservation record, Lacey remains Iowa's greatest gift to the nation's land and resources.

Some of the finest conservation legislation emerges when Congress does not realize what it is doing. When Lacey's Antiquities Act passed, there was little doubt Congress had intended it to apply to sites such as cliff dwellings and other small "monuments." The key to the act was that the executive could protect lands without waiting for Congress to act. For six years Congress considered limiting sites to 320 and 640 acres, but fortunately, no limits were in the final provision.

Teddy Roosevelt gave "monument" a new definition. It did not take him long. The Antiquities Act had a loophole, and Roosevelt was not afraid to charge through it.

Roosevelt's great conservation vision was born in pain. In June 1884, along the little Missouri River in the Dakotas where he had a ranch, young Roosevelt rode. Buffalo could still be found, but Roosevelt was looking for something else. His wife had died the winter before, and he rode alone and camped alone in the empty space of the plains. A meadowlark caught his ear with its rich and bubbling sound, "a cadence of wild sadness, inexpressibly touching." It was ". . . laden with a hundred memories and associations; with the sight of dim hills reddening in the dawn; with the breath of cool morning winds blowing across lonely plains; with the scent of flowers on the sunlit prairie." He found not just the song of a meadowlark, but a purpose much larger than himself. Twenty years later he began to save more of the western wildlands than any other man.

In September 1906 Roosevelt first used the Antiquities Act and withdrew Devil's Tower National Monument in eastern Wyoming from development. Three months later he withdrew three areas, Petrified Forest, Montezuma Castle, and El Morro, and the following year he reserved Chaco Canyon, Lassen Peak, Gila Cliff Dwelling, and Tonto National Monument. All these areas became closed to miners and private development. In 1908 Roosevelt protected Muir Woods. A few days later, frustrated with the delays in Congress over the question of park status, Roosevelt withdrew Grand Canyon as a national monument. Warming to his task, Roosevelt then protected Jewel Cave in South Dakota, Natural Bridges in Utah, Lewis and Clark Cavern in Montana, and Tumacacori Mission in Arizona. Trees, caves, old missions, great canyons, and cliff dwellings all fit Roosevelt's definition of a "monument." His vision became a great gift to the future.

Succeeding presidents continued the pattern. President Wilson in 1918 proclaimed Katmai National Monument in Alaska; at 2.7 million acres, it was larger than Yellowstone Park. President Carter gave the Antiquities Act its greatest test by reserving 56 million acres in 1978 to protect potential parklands in Alaska, pending congressional settlement of Alaska lands legislation.

Many monuments protected by presidential action have been changed by acts of Congress to become national parks. In 1933 all national monuments were transferred to the jurisdiction of the National Park Service. Today the administration of parks and monuments is virtually indistinguishable. National parks are created by an act of Congress; national monuments are reserved by presidential proclamation—using authority delegated by Congressman Lacey's Antiquities Act.

The final type of reservation created in the Roosevelt Era was the wildlife reserve. In Roman times, the legal institutions regarded animals in their wild state as like the air or water—they belonged to everyone and no one. Economically they were "fugitive" resources, that is, capable of running away, and became the property of those who captured them. But when the feudal system emerged in Europe and England, where much American law originated, commoners were prohibited from capturing the king's deer or salmon. On the eve of the American Revolution, parliament and the king controlled wildlife. In the United States, this authority belonged to the states, and state jurisdiction over wildlife is today a central tenet of wildlife managers. It has been constantly eroded by various court decisions but remains a major block to a comprehensive public-land wildlife program.

Early federal wildlife conservation focused on areas where the federal government had clear authority, such as negotiating wildlife conservation treaties with other countries and regulating interstate traffic in furs and commercial aspects of hunting and fishing. Then, with the realization that wildlife could only be conserved by protecting habitat and not just the bodies of the animals themselves, a new era of federal wildlife conservation began.

Obviously the federal lands offered the largest opportunity to conserve wildlife. But most reservations were established primarily for power sites, timber, water, and recreation. Wildlife was only a secondary factor. Private refuges had been purchased for many decades, but it took Theodore Roosevelt to expand the concept to federal lands.

Pelican Island off the east coast of Florida was well known to ornithologists by the turn of the century as a nesting site for brown pelicans. Although the birds were hardly trophies in the usual sense, people shot them to see a big, slow bird drop. The scholarly American Ornithologists Union became concerned about their declining numbers and recommended to President Roosevelt that the island be set aside for a federal wildlife refuge. Unfortunately, there was no precedent for a wildlife refuge and no definitive legislation to give this authority to the chief executive. With his characteristic boldness, Roosevelt signed an executive order creating the Pelican Island Refuge, the nation's first. Most refuges established since then have been created administratively, not legislatively.

At the close of Roosevelt's administration wildlife refuges had made only a modest beginning, although one purpose of parks and monuments was also undoubtedly to provide wildlife refuges. Indeed, early park rangers diligently hunted down and shot every wolf, mountain lion, and coyote they could find under the misguided conception that they were protecting "desirable" species such as deer and elk. Of all activities on the public lands, protecting wildlife has had the most difficult time establishing its own niche.

At the end of Roosevelt's administration, now regarded as the golden age of conservation, progress in public-land policy was impressive. The national park system had begun; the Antiquities Act was in place; public land had been withdrawn from development to protect water and energy resources; more than 190 million acres of national forests had been established; and wildlife refuges had been established. Finally, after three centuries of being exploited, the public lands were being protected with institutional mechanisms. Yet, as the golden age was fading, the gains were being compromised.

The first parks and natural areas immediately ran into opposing economic and political forces. Opposition was always present and was quick to split the conservation movement. One branch of conservation favored protecting land for its own sake and rested its arguments on philosophy and even the broad cultural influences of art, poetry, and literature. The other branch was led by foresters, who were utilitarian, not aesthetic or intuitive. More than any other resource, forests became the focus of controversy within conservation, and the two camps became polarized.

The practice of forestry was tied to its applied, Teutonic roots and was conceived of as only a modification of the waste and destruction of an uncontrolled free-market development of resources. To the early foresters, the free-market pattern was wasteful because it did not provide future crops. But establishing national parks and wildland preserves was even more wasteful because it permitted only the appreciation of nature and not its harvest.

The two movements diverged early, one branch led by John Muir, the other by Gifford Pinchot. One had its roots in philosophy, the other in economics. One group favored parks and wildlife refuges, the other national forests and multiple-use lands. One group saw the land's wealth in its beauty and its gift to the next generation, whereas the other saw wealth as tangible and useable resources. Muir's followers saw power in the land's capacity to inspire people and in the opportunities it offered for individual growth and development. Foresters saw power in products, the result of humans applying technology to provide useful resources and national strength. One faction was convinced the land must be shared between the natural and human world and that its administration was part of a democratic social contract with citizens. These people were often branded "preservationists" and criticized as impractical and quasi-religious. The other group saw the freedom land offered more as a freedom from shortages of resources. They seized the term "conservationists" and were later captured by exploitative industries, which mouthed the principles of conservation while whetting their appetites for public resources.

The pattern has persisted. Industry helped split the conservation community as soon as conservation gained its most impressive victories. The same attempt was made in the 1980s, when Interior Secretary Watt set out to split environmentalists. Decades ago industry helped western politicians tighten their influence over public-land laws. In the 1980s international energy corporations helped Reagan and Watt in their political battles. Key congressional committees that controlled both money and policies for the public lands were controlled by western politicians. Roosevelt and Pinchot had convinced western political leaders that conservation was the wisest policy from a traditional business perspective, but compromise of the public trust had already begun. Business on the public lands was protected, not prohibited. The changes modified the methods individuals used to acquire public wealth but failed to stop the transfer of public resources to private banks.

Conservation, for all its popular and progressive appeal, was basically a conservative tradition. It supported using and developing resources, but at its core it retained an apprehension about the future. Saving resources, land, and public wealth for future use and development was as fundamentally conservative as the thinking of a small-town banker. It is not surprising development groups, selfish and shortsighted, were constantly opposed.

The status of commerce at the close of the Roosevelt era is worth summarizing. The mining industry was most successful. For 250 years minerals had been regarded as nature's bounty to the public, and exploiters paid royalties to the government representing the society at large. The first American land law included this requirement. The California gold rush, a stampede of greed, overwhelmed the federal government's ability to enforce its mining policy. Then the concept of the public interest in minerals was lost in the mining laws of 1866 and 1872. With a few exceptions public lands remained open to mineral development, not only as the dominant use, but essentially as a free one. Those who found the wealth belonging to the nation were not asked to share even a small portion.

Ranchers spent much of the Roosevelt era fighting each other and sheep herders for control of the limited western rangelands. Those who controlled the water controlled the surrounding dry land. The Desert Land Act and other laws designed for the small family homesteader were subverted by the western stock raisers, particularly cattle ranchers. Their success was large, usually dependent on fraud, dishonesty, and dummy entry people. Conservation, especially the creation of national forests, changed their ways of doing business and threatened them. Before long they turned the new laws to their advantage: the national forests were opened to cattle-grazing, but sheep-grazing was tightly restricted.

The timber industry accommodated conservation. Not the entire industry was sympathetic, but many companies, especially those with large private land holdings, supported the Forest Service. The political process and management of the public lands could be manipulated to their advantage, and before long the large companies helped guide federal policy.

Most of the moisture on the western lands fell on the public lands in the mountains. The Bureau of Reclamation was established in 1902 to help small farmers by developing irrigation projects, which were intended to be paid for by their users. Instead, federal water soon benefited corporate farms and was heavily subsidized by the taxpayer.

At the close of the Roosevelt administration, therefore, the public had obviously gained on the public lands, but at the same time, most of the new conservation policies were already being compromised. In addition, the conservation movement itself was changing. It was young and was considered an idealistic wave of the future, but it did not successfully cope with free-market forces, nor was it reconciled with preservationists. While 25 percent of the lands in western states had been reserved for the public, over half the homestead acreage had yet to be allocated, and another frenzied wave of development was about to sweep the West, exhausting the frontier dream.

The basic principles of scientific land management and economic efficiency had been articulated and were included in the national system of values. Virtually everyone claimed to be a conservationist—but the definition was elastic. Conservation agencies were captured by the developers they were intended to regulate. Subsidized commercial activity continued on most public lands, including forests, parks, monuments, and refuges. Conservation made the first attempt in public-land policy at defining the public trust, but it was co-opted and diverted. Nevertheless, its roots are in a golden, optimistic age.

Buffalo Skinning

5

The Persistence
of Greed

Albert Fall was a colorful, flamboyant character from the Old West. He became a miner, rancher, U.S. senator, and in 1921 the secretary of the interior. He had faced gunmen on the frontier, had gambled in high stakes poker, and had come to Washington with both confidence and a wide-brimmed black Stetson. He opposed government meddling in business affairs, his own or those on the public lands. One reason was that he was a crook.

Shortly before Fall became secretary of the interior, Congress passed the Mineral Leasing Act of 1920 giving the secretary authority to sell public-land energy resources through a leasing system. Fall quickly went to work. First he quietly gained control of the naval petroleum reserves. The next year he secretly leased the Teapot Dome oil reserve in Wyoming and part of California's Elk Hills petroleum reserve for a $200,000 cash bribe. The oil from each reserve was worth in excess of $100 million. As a land contract, it could not be cancelled without just compensation and a complex legal process. The lease was a new route to public-land wealth; instead of gaining full title to the land, corporations acquired the most valuable resources, the oil, gas, and minerals.

Albert Fall eventually went to jail and earned a black place in public-land history, but the mechanism of mineral leasing remained in place, a dagger at the heart of conservation. It was the weapon James Watt dusted off to use on a scale even Albert Fall would never have dreamed possible.

Leasing public-land energy was only one of the new disposal

techniques to emerge in the post-conservation era. It proved to be the most efficient way to transfer public wealth to private hands.

Most of the states west of the hundredth meridian, the demarcation between arid West and humid East, remained in public ownership because of the harsh land and climate. Public-land laws permitted settlement, but the laws of economics did not. The meager water on the public domain had been fought over and claimed or stolen by stock ranchers. Homesteaders who ventured into the parched domain earned more than the epithet "nester": the wages of their audacity and belief in democratic land laws earned them threats, hatred, and sometimes grief and death at the hands of ranchers. Land laws had never bound the stock raisers' dreams of manifest destiny over the western rangeland. Neither would the nesters.

But the final surge of western development by the homesteader entailed more than the fight between common sodbuster and cattle baron. It brought agricultural revolution. Land-grant colleges had touted the benefits of plowing the prairie and the theory that "rain follows the plow" for decades. More realistic agriculturalists understood the cycle of winter snows, spring rains, and dry summers. Agriculture was adapted to meet the rigorous demands of the climate. Hardy breeds of wheat, barley, and other grain crops were developed. Some types of winter wheat, planted in the fall, sprouted and then rested dormant under the winter snow to grow rapidly in the spring and ripen early in the summer. Other kinds of grain were planted in the early spring, when the soil was warming and spring rains usually kept the ground moist and fertile. Roots raced toward the falling water table. Sometimes they didn't make it, and the sun and air dried the plants out. Other times a passing summer storm cooled the soil for a day or two longer, and the grain matured. With new species of spring wheat, the confines of climate were overcome and rich grain ripened.

Another innovation was tried. Farmers planted alternate strips of land each year; the remaining land was kept plowed and free of vegetation. The fallow strips stored and insulated moisture from the blazing summer sun. The next year the pattern was reversed. Two years of moisture could grow one hardy grain crop without irrigation. As a result of this technique, millions of acres of public land in the western plains rolled under the plow.

Agricultural adaptations to the aridity helped precipitate the final land rush in the West, and other factors also helped. World War I had disrupted farming throughout Europe. Grain prices reached record levels between 1910 and 1920. As an accident of history, the cyclic moisture on the Great Plains also reached a high point, and several successive years of above-average rainfall raised expectations for Great Plains agriculture.

Two major institutional changes boosted the boom. First came the Enlarged Homestead Act in 1909, which permitted doubling the size of homesteads for dry-land farmers. In 1916 the original Homestead Act was changed again to adapt to western conditions; the Stockraising Homestead Act doubled the size of homesteads again, to 640 acres. These changes combined with a major setback to conservation in 1906, which had opened the national forests to homesteading. A land boom was on.

When the boom collapsed during the Great Depression in the 1930s, the western land was exhausted and broken. High prices, above-average rainfall, war, and the gift of virgin soil had not lasted. Dry figures tell the tale. From the passage of the Homestead Act during Lincoln's administration until 1900, 78 million acres had passed into homesteaders' ownership. Four times that area, a total of 328 million acres, was claimed in the first decades of the twentieth century. The population in western counties soared for a few years. Homestead shacks and homes dotted the plains. The cattle ranchers were driven back to the mountains and badlands. But moisture was not restored, nor would passing bison fertilize the lean sod. Farm prices dropped. A cycle of drought returned. Homesteaders first took part-time jobs back home or in cities and eventually sold their homesteads to nearby ranchers for pasture or simply forfeited their land claims. Population dropped in western counties and continued to drop for fifty years as the economics of agriculture favored more mechanization and bigger farms operated by fewer people.

Today many counties on the western plains have only one-fifth the 1920 population. Four out of five people left; their homesteads and shacks are now cold and isolated. The land was reseeded or farmed by giant machines instead of homesteaders and their simple plows.

Long before the homesteaders gave up, westerners had accepted conservation but had compromised and altered it to favor not the nation or future generations, but the few who earned a living from public resources. The first challenge to conservation's gains came, as might be expected, from people who had enjoyed an aristocratic privilege on western lands. Stock ranchers were angered by the first forest reservations. Foresters and Pinchot had assured them that conservation meant domestic livestock could use rangelands. Pinchot, always a shrewd political tactician, split stockraisers' opposition by capitalizing on the old antagonism between sheep herders and cattle ranchers. Sheep herders and migratory grazing animals were driven off many forests to protect both watersheds and timber, two major purposes for forest reserves.

Privileges were reserved in many other ways, too. The Forest Service built and leased summer homes near scenic canyons, lakes, and rivers in western forests. For a low fee and a long-term lease, cabins and homes were built on choice recreation spots. They remain in many western areas, preempting public use.

Private interests gained control of public water, too. The federal government, during the conservation era, protected many water-development sites from various power-development proposals. After the conservation era, however, choice power sites on public lands were transferred by lease to a few corporations. By 1920, 90 percent of the available power sites on western public-domain lands had been developed by twenty-eight corporations. Six major companies held 56 percent of the sites. A pattern of corporate control of public resources had begun.

The Reclamation Act of 1902 was clearly established to develop small family farms in the arid West. Debate over details of the act involved acreage limitations and fears the program would benefit large corporations. Originally federal dams and water projects were to be self-supporting; farmers would buy water to grow their crops, and the entire cost of a project plus interest would be repaid the taxpayer. Before long, however, it was obvious reclamation projects would not be self-supporting. Taxpayer support was needed.

By the time the Reclamation Bureau matured as an agency, it had grown into a caricature of a wasteful bureaucracy serving and subsidizing a few special interests, principally corporate farmers. Conservation evolved into exploitation. The Bureau took the lead in developing Glen Canyon Dam and many other projects that became world models for wasteful destruction of natural beauty and renewable resources.

During the 1950s the Bureau of Reclamation joined forces with the old Corps of Engineers to ram through Congress, over the protests of Indians involved, the Pick-Sloan Plan authorizing 100 dams in the Missouri River drainage. Dams converted the longest river in North America to a staircase of reservoirs, largely to serve barge companies on lower reaches of the river. In the process of flooding 750 miles of prime agricultural land, the two federal agencies also flooded several Indian reservations. These lands, now under the flat water of the "Great Lakes of the Missouri," contained forests and historic forts and dozens of old villages as well as some of the richest archeological areas in the northern Great Plains—traditional burial grounds, religious shrines, and ancient homeland of Indians. Their ancestors had been living on these lands since the retreat of the ice age and had welcomed and sheltered the first Americans they saw, the Lewis and Clark expedition, in 1804.

But water projects such as those on the Missouri River failed to attract promised industry, to stop the migration of people from the area, or to enhance the local economy. Indians, their lands flooded for the benefit of a few barge companies on the lower river, were relocated on harsh and unproductive uplands. Thirty years later they still suffer from poverty, disease, and ill health as a result. Water development by the Bureau of Reclamation and Corps of Engineers converted them from a self-sufficient agrarian people to a welfare economy. The barge companies' welfare plan was more profitable.

Throughout the West, a legacy of misguided water reforms from the turn of the century lost public resources, destroyed renewable resources, and enhanced the fortunes of a select few. Roosevelt's land and water reforms had intended the opposite effect, but in California federal water is often delivered to company farms at less than $2.50 per acre-foot of water. Water from the same federal project often costs $100, $200 or more per acre-foot delivered to urban residents, who pay taxes for federal projects and pay the full cost of their own water as well as agriculture's. The subsidized federal water is nothing less than liquid welfare.

Such abuses evolved in part because the conservation movement was weakened and torn internally by differences in philosophy and personality. After Roosevelt stepped down as president, Taft named Richard Ballinger as his Secretary of Interior. Before long Ballinger and Pinchot were involved in a complicated, personal squabble over conservation tactics. The merits of the two individuals are not entirely clear. Gifford Pinchot, an aristocratic egoist, eventually offended President Taft and was fired. In any case, the controversy split the power and influence of the conservation movement at the end of Roosevelt's era as president.

The second split was more fundamental. John Muir was the inheritor of Thoreau's ideals and of the transcendental philosophy. Not only was Muir a charismatic leader, effective writer, and masterful publicist on behalf of wild America, but he brought a religious fervor to conservation. He founded the Sierra Club, the model for active citizen protection of the environment. At first he and Pinchot were friends, but the friendship could not last. Pinchot brought not only a strong ego, but also an equal dedication to the "wise use" and commercial management of resources. He was politically shrewd and had institutionalized his program in the U.S. Forest Service. Muir's personal fervor and loose affiliation of hikers in the Sierra Club could not match the day-to-day efficiency of the bureaucracy.

Muir's views were hindered in a practical sense by the lack of a tangible commodity. The mix of plants, grasses and forbs, shrubs and young sprouts, mature and even dead and dying trees made up Muir's magical world. The respect he and his followers brought to wild America was passionate and could be articulated eloquently and vigorously, but it was always interpreted personally.

One person's love was another's commodity. Pinchot and his followers offered the tangible products of resource development, and their view of forestry and conservation was regarded as scientific. Essentially it rested on a belief that nature's bounty of forest was renewable and could not only be reproduced but improved upon. It was as scientific as an engineer's perspective on the uses of a tree. It could be measured and put to work. It did not consider, or even have the ability to measure, subtle interactions of birds, insects, and habitat. It could not relate to or cope with Muir's holistic vision.

Multiple use and sustained yield became the foresters' clichés. Land could be used for several purposes—economic in nature—

most important of which was timber production. Properly managed, all these uses could continue to increase and to be sustained indefinitely. Wilderness, parks, and any Muir-like programs were opposed for "practical" reasons, largely because foresters feared they would have nothing to do. Unable to grasp the enormous complexities of protecting and maintaining a natural environment, foresters thought of preservation as a symbolic dark force. The fervor with which Pinchot's supporters opposed Muir's followers cannot be explained by the rational scientific principles they claimed to adhere to. They were as committed to a theology as Muir, and they also had the institutions and economic products of public land to deliver in the political arena. For this reason they were more successful than Muir.

The elasticity of the definition of conservation was soon evident. Before long everyone was a conservationist. President Wilson reflected a typical view of conservation, often describing what it was not. "A policy of reservation is not the policy of conservation." The most dedicated predators of public resources were claiming to be the finest of conservationists. That was usually only a preface, however; their views were qualified with "but. . . ."

The first national conflict over the split in conservation philosophy came in California. Muir, of course, was in the lead. Yosemite had been protected first as a state park since 1864 and as a national park after 1890. Yosemite was John Muir country, and he had worked for years to assure its protection. To his dismay, Hetch Hetchy Valley was proposed as the site of a dam and storage reservoir for San Francisco water. In the exaggeration and distortion typical of developers, Hetch Hetchy's supporters conjured up vivid images of children dying of thirst because of Muir's selfishness.

Pinchot saw the issue in terms of his own values. He and other foresters saw the national parks as a threat to their own bureaucratic turf; many of the early, large parks were carved out of national forests and then transferred to the Department of Interior. Pinchot had tried diligently to get the national parks transferred to the Department of Agriculture and the Forest Service. He was opposed by the likes of Muir, who was afraid the parks would become the object of multiple uses and would be considered just another crop. The Forest Service's antagonism to national parks began early, with roots deep in the agency's psyche.

In part because of his own principles and in part because he opposed parks, Pinchot supported Hetch Hetchy Dam. As the nation's leading conservationist, he had a critical influence on many organizations and politicians. Congress authorized the dam in 1913. President Wilson signed the bill into law. Pinchot, whom Muir had named an honorary vice president of the Sierra Club, helped degrade one of the finest parks in the world. A year later Muir died, leaving a legacy of a strong citizens' conservation organization. Pinchot left a bureaucracy.

Conservation policies were also compromised in many other areas. Western states have periodically opposed the very concept of federal ownership of western lands. Every protest was led by people with an economic interest in the federal lands. The first strong outcry came after Roosevelt established forest reserves, and more protests followed the first grazing controls on public lands. Illegal fences ranchers built on public lands had been a problem to settlers, wildlife, and other public-land users for decades. Roosevelt tried to restrict this practice; stock raisers continued to break the law.

Pinchot added to the controversy by imposing the first grazing permits and fees for using public grasslands in 1905. Opposition was vehement. One result was a cry from states'-rights advocates and sheep herders to transfer forest reserves to the states.

This was when Pinchot split the sheep and cattle ranchers; he favored cattle ranchers and forced sheep ranchers and small migratory stock raisers off public forest reserves and onto the lower, drier, less productive public-domain lands. Railroads and certain lumbermen, with large landholdings of their own, could see the advantage of working in concert with a sympathetic government agency.

Old aristocrats of the western rangelands were given preference rights without competitive bidding. Public-land leases essentially became property rights, bought and sold by ranchers as part of a ranch. No Forest Service administrator would dare substantially reduce or transfer a grazing lease from a large and influential cattle rancher, no matter how abused the public's land might be. The native wildlife that belonged to everyone were forced off the range.

The Forest Service ranges were high and well watered compared to lower public-domain lands. Deep snows usually closed them every fall, reducing the season of use. As a result, Forest Service lands recovered relatively quickly from overgrazing, in contrast to the lower public-domain lands, which, under the General Land Office, had virtually no protection or supervision.

The Taylor Grazing Act of 1934 institutionalized the arrangements. It brought most of the remaining public domain, eventually more than 150 million acres, under a leasing system. It established a system of grazing preferences that favored large and established ranchers—the old western range aristocracy. It established reduced fees and eventually heavily-subsidized public-land grazing. Most fees that were paid were returned to rural counties and ranchers in the form of range developments. Federal agencies assisted cattle ranchers in building fences, drilling wells, and constructing stock-watering tanks and other facilities vital to the ranchers' aspirations. As time went on, agencies plowed, burned, and sprayed rangelands with exotic chemicals and in turn planted them with foreign grass species intended to benefit one form of animal life—the domestic cow. Wildlife suffered. So did the peoples' land.

The largest profits were to be made not in ranching however, but in mineral development on public lands. Essentially, public lands were open to free development of minerals with no limitations. The 1872 Mining Law forsook the age-old tradition of paying a royalty or severance tax for the privilege of developing public minerals. Simply by "staking" a claim, the first person who found minerals had a partial property right in what were previously public lands. On unpatented mining claims, the miner enjoyed the best of all worlds; he could live on the property and exclude the public from its own land. He could develop and mine public resources without any interference or any requirement to share the wealth. He did not pay property taxes, because the land technically belonged to the federal government.

Early in the twentieth century, a major energy-mining boom was taking place. Coal, oil, gas, and other energy resources lands were being claimed on the public lands by land speculators. To protect the public interests, Teddy Roosevelt had withdrawn millions of acres of public lands from mineral entry, but under the terms of the 1920 Mineral Leasing Act, the government could lease energy resources such as oil, coal, gas, oil shale, and certain other resources. After development, land would revert to full public ownership. The so-called "hard rock" minerals, or resources found in granite-type rocks, were still managed under the 1872 Mining Law. Before long, the leasing system was abused. It remains a monumental subsidy of mining and energy to this day.

Albert Fall was the first prominent abuser. He had a buffalo hunter's perspective on public lands. Resources were to be used, not protected. They were best developed by private corporations, which in turn would pass the benefits on to the working class, a type of "trickle down" theory of developing public lands.

Although Fall went to jail, the basic mechanism for selling public oil, gas, and other energy resources was not modified. However, because of the outcry over the Teapot Dome scandal, subsequent secretaries of the interior were prudent in leasing public energy resources. Private and state lands were the major focus of energy development until the mid-1970s. Federal lands had been held in reserve. They were hoarded for the public good, in the national interest, for later generations.

The 1973 Arab oil boycott renewed interest in domestic energy production. Conservation was emphasized on one front, development on another. One fact became obvious: most energy resources left were on public lands. Their development remained essentially at the discretion of the secretary of the interior.

Forestry and forest conservation, on the other hand, remained largely the province of the Forest Service in the Department of Agriculture. After 1920 most big western forest reserves were completed. Some forest lands, however, had gone into national parks; others had been claimed by states or private individuals under various land laws. Private ranches and mining developments fragmented Forest Service lands. National park administrators, in contrast, protected their lands from development and periodically attempted to eliminate private lands and conflicting activities within park boundaries.

During this period, forestry became the first and foremost natural-resource profession. Pinchot had formed a professional cadre of foresters that was a model for all other resource disciplines. Such an approach worked well as long as the simple land-management goal of foresters was met—production of timber from public lands. But during the twentieth century, the process of managing natural resources and forest land grew increasingly complicated, both politically and technically. Foresters, long regarded as leading land managers, became watchdogs of tradition. They adapted poorly to social and political change.

An essential element of the Forest Service's success was a cozy working relationship with the forest-products industry. Unfortunately, most productive forest lands had passed into private ownership by various land laws and widespread fraud. Mining and homestead acts permitted loggers, farmers, and miners to claim millions of acres of prime timber land. The public was left with the poorest quality timber land. Until the 1950s private lands satisfied most of the national demand for timber. Public-land timber sales tended to compete with the private sector, except in certain locations.

The Forest Service held in reserve large virgin tracts of wilderness not open them to timber cutting and competition with private companies. These lands, when finally opened, were sold under terms that subsidized timber companies. In many cases timber was sold at a net loss to the public. Local Forest Service offices protected and enhanced the forest-products industry through timber sales, fire control, and other land-management practices. They also spent some time providing recreation to the public at large and protecting wildlife, although these were seldom large or important projects. The timber industry could always be counted on to oppose any political movement that would diminish its convenient relationship with the Forest Service and to oppose every national park and wilderness area created at the expense of the national forests.

During the housing boom of the 1950s, timber cutting on the public lands began to accelerate. As with oil and other resources, the largest timber reserves were protected on public lands. Private land was overcut and could not satisfy the demand. The post-World War II housing boom was accompanied by unprecedented demands for recreation, parklands, and wilderness. The historic approach of forestry and Forest Service land management was also running full speed into a major reform in the United States—the environmental movement. The stage was set for major conflicts.

Most forces of economic development had successfully converted public-land resources to private wealth through favorable leases, subsidized grazing, and logging permits. Other groups periodically called for transfer of federal lands to states or to people or corporations already enjoying their use and profits. The pattern became a regular one. Stockmen and miners would vociferously claim their "rights" to public lands of the West. Large development corporations, such as livestock and logging companies, which often benefited from the discussion, seldom publicly called for the transfer of lands. Instead, they quietly supported anti-conservation activity behind the scenes through political channels.

Opponents to national public ownership argued for states' rights using a particularly dishonest verb—"return" federal lands. The pattern of complaint became routine and produced predictable results. The attempt to transfer ownership would fail, but day-to-day administration would always shift from conservation to exploitation to pacify the complainers. Political pressure, not scientific management, had the most dramatic impact on the land.

The first widespread attempt to transfer ownership came from the livestock industry after Roosevelt created large forest reserves. Stock raisers wanted the lands "returned" to states, arguing—with little ingenuity—that states could better manage the forest reserves. Not one western state had a program of land management that went beyond short-term exploitation.

The second attempt came during the 1920s. The frontier was exhausted, settlement had virtually ended, and ranchers wanted the lands they used, but they did not want to pay for them. President Hoover appealed to western audiences with his belief the states could best manage public lands. Given the poor state record in land management, such a view was especially disingenuous. The important committees of Congress largely shared Hoover's view, however. Fortunately, debate broke down over the mechanism of transfer. Stockmen did not want to pay even a suggested minimum of $1.00 an acre for the arid western lands.

Congress passed the Taylor Grazing Act, named for Congressman Taylor of Colorado, himself a stockman. Federal rangelands stayed in federal ownership. Permits were assured, fees were a fraction of what it would cost to use comparable private lands, costs of improvements and administration were passed to the taxpayers. Competition for the privilege of grazing was not tolerated, nor any property taxes required. The western stock raisers retained their aristocratic position over western lands.

Nevertheless, some stock raisers wanted the public lands to be made an outright gift to western states and ranchers. Disturbed with efforts the Grazing Service, an agency established by the Taylor Grazing Act, was making to end overgrazing and soil erosion, a group of western congressmen attempted another land grab in the 1940s and 1950s. It was the same old group with the same tired arguments. This time the forces of conservation were growing and were armed with the acerbic pen of western writer and historian Bernard De Voto. Using his platform on *Harper's* magazine, De Voto exposed the hypocrisy and public-land welfare system better than anyone before or since. As embarrassed as chicken thieves caught red-handed, the land-grabbers quieted down during the 1950s. But the movement was not gone.

The last anti-conservation movement in the late 1970s was born out of a resurgence of political, not environmental, conservatism and a disillusionment with the federal government. More important, vast energy and mineral resources long hoarded for future generations had become vastly inflated in value because of the Arab oil boycott and because privately-held resources were exhausted. Suddenly public-land energy reserves were worth not just millions, but several trillions of dollars.

Greed disguised as political philosophy launched the fourth public-land grab of the century, this time quaintly labeled a "sagebrush rebellion"—a cover name for the same land pirates aided by the largest energy corporations. Starting with Nevada in 1979, state after western state passed resolutions and laws claiming "their" land. Secretary of the Interior James Watt, following the established pattern, defused the "sagebrush rebellion" by transferring the public wealth of those lands to private ownership. The fourth land grab ended largely like the others, with ranchers and other private interests making large and substantial gains of the public land and resources at a cost few understood.

The evolution of today's public-land system was more than setbacks and exhaustion of resources; patterns of conservation and responsible land management had also been established. With the decline in the golden age of conservation and the end of Roosevelt's term, however, exploiters gradually gained ground. Altruistic conservationists never had the political persistence of people motivated by greed and self-interest.

During the Harding and Coolidge administrations, special-interest groups largely had the run of public lands. Conservation made small gains in national parks and wildlife refuges, but most federal activity favored exploiting public resources. The notoriety of Teapot Dome altered but did not end that pattern.

The next great wave of conservation came with the administration of Franklin D. Roosevelt. The Great Depression had helped exhaust both land and people. Tens of thousands of farms failed as winds blew soil in black blizzards across the plains. An array of public works and conservation programs emerged. The Civilian Conservation Corps (CCC) put hundreds of thousands of men to work doing the back-breaking work of conservation; planting trees, controlling erosion, and building new facilities, campgrounds, trails, and roads in the national parks, forests, and wildlife refuges.

Franklin Roosevelt was instrumental in the creation of new national monuments, national wildlife refuges, and innovative forestry programs. Under his hand, large areas of cut-out and burned-over private forestland were purchased and converted to state and federal ownership.

Roosevelt was not content with existing agency structures. He created an innovative soil-erosion control program, the Soil Conservation Service. In one of the most original resource programs in the world, he encouraged and implemented the Tennessee Valley Authority, the first comprehensive land and water development organization anywhere. Soil and resource conservation became not just make-work programs, but an obvious part of restoring the strength and productivity of the American earth.

Roosevelt's program also stressed professional management and administration of federal lands. From forestry to water resources, rangelands, parklands, and wildlife management, the role of resource professionals was growing as it became clear how complex problems of resource management were and as demands increased to assure a productive land. The fervor of the second wave of conservation did not end until Pearl Harbor was bombed.

At the close of World War II another revolution began. The American nation grew rapidly, and people moved south and west in large numbers. Housing and other construction boomed, placing new demands on the resource base. Automobiles and other developments strained and finally overwhelmed national petroleum supplies.

In concert with population growth and resource development, people made unprecedented demands on wildlands for outdoor recreation. The public visited national parks in ever-increasing numbers on the interstate highway system, but they also demanded new and larger recreation areas close to cities. Their interests broadened and diversified. Mechanized vehicles that went over snow and sand and into back-country revolutionized outdoor recreation. Large campers and mobile homes designed for self-sufficient comfort grew affordable and popular. More and more people put packs on their backs and traveled into back-country, not only for exercise, but also to recreate a frontier experience. Every type of outdoor recreation grew and eclipsed earlier forms during the 1950s, 1960s, and 1970s. The American public was discovering the power of the public lands.

Many social and environmental problems came with the changes. Post-World War II development paved over many miles of open fields. Air and water became polluted on a scale the world had never seen. As people spent more time outdoors, they found a natural world that was being spoiled at a frightening rate. Western public lands were the focus of recreationists on a scale thought impossible a few years before. Urban visitors camped and saw obvious signs of overgrazing; hunters pursued deer and elk but found mostly domestic livestock; campers were locked out by mining developments; and all the visitors saw resources plundered without care for the future. Another major land reform was in the making.

The environmental movement had a thousand origins, dozens of leaders, and many organizations; no one person emerged as the parent. Its solutions rested on a bedrock of science. Its scope was broader than any other conservation movement and included the health of people and the earth itself.

Managing and protecting federal lands were obviously part of the movement, but not a dominant part. The environmental movement brought rapid change and many improvements, but the finest gains were made in restoring the health of air and water, not public lands. Like the conservation movement before it, the environmental movement failed to stop the plunder of public-land resources; it could not divert the forces of greed from their mission.

Pine Forest

6

The Nation's Largest
Welfare Program

My first summer on the public lands, I was in Yellowstone Park on a fire lookout fifteen miles from the nearest road. Nearly every afternoon fluffy clouds sailed into the park from Idaho to grow ominously into towering thunderstorms. The fall was shattered by the shrill bugle of elk and the return to the flatland. I never recovered from the mountain wind and wild music.

As a smokejumper I made nearly one hundred parachute jumps into remote regions of the western lands to fight forest fires. I learned the land in an intimate way, in part to survive. New Mexico's mountains are high and rocky, the air hot and thin. A parachute drops its cargo quickly, and rocks rush to break ankles if one is careless. Colorado's fires are few, but high in the thin air chainsaws, water pumps, and lungs gasp for oxygen.

Idaho's Salmon River country is steep and rugged. Branches of tall ponderosa pines reach out to pluck the chute from the air and drop a person like a stone to the grassy slopes below. But the land is rich in big game. Once on the rocks of the Seven Devils, I stared back at a mountain goat wondering about my crew and me and the smoke below. Wading a Montana stream in August brings numbing cold, even on the hottest day.

Alaska is in a class by itself. The tundra is soft and easy to land on, a place for old, prudent jumpers. Every plane flight offers the sight of moose in lakes, white Dall sheep in the mountains, and entire hillsides moving, alive with caribou. Every fire camp recklessly polluted with garbage could attract bears, including the awesome grizzly. Under all the personal experience was the land, public land.

Dozens of hiking, camping, and climbing trips onto the public lands opened another dimension to me. The land was alive not only with wildlife and beauty, but also with history. Every desert spring showed the signs of Indian hunters; every pass was marked by a pioneer trail.

When I began to study and teach about public lands, another dimension opened. There were visits to mine-polluted streams, overgrazed meadows, sterile clearcuts. Beyond the beauty and the wildlife, after the lessons of history and pioneers, came the understanding of greed and its persistent control over the public lands even through the environmental decade of the 1970s. The present course of events offers little hope unless there are major changes in the management and protection of the public treasure of land.

Some changes have been made. In reaction to the waste of the era of exploitation, large tracts of public land once given or sold to private developers and plundered of their resources have been repurchased for the public good. The Forest Service has purchased and rehabilitated cut-over eastern forest lands exhausted and sometimes abandoned as worthless during the 1920s and 1930s. Today, 27 million acres of purchased eastern forests lie within a day's drive of 80 percent of the American people, providing clean air, open space, healthy watersheds, and green islands of recreation. Entire national parks, such as Great Smoky Mountains, Shenandoah, Acadia, and others were acquired by conservation groups and donated to the public. Although most public lands are a long way from most people, Redwoods National Park and national seashores such as Point Reyes, Cape Cod, and Padre Island have obvious benefits and are close to large populations.

Nevertheless, despite the size of the public domain and impressive gains made for conservation during the 1970s, public land remains under age-old threats. Whenever public resources increase in value, economic and political forces work overtime to acquire them. For example, settling native claims and establishing new national parks and wildlife refuges in Alaska made the federal domain available for enormous state land claims and private mineral development. With new timber sales, the Forest Service is allowing the last pockets of virgin timber in the

United States to be cut in what is largely a subsidy for a few timber companies. Overgrazing western rangelands still desertifies large tracts of western lands. The Bureau of Land Management, western universities, and stock raisers assist poor land-management practices.

Mining-claim staking continues to accelerate. There are now more than 1.5 million claims, each nearly twenty acres. The old hard-rock mining law remains the foundation of welfare systems on public lands, exceeded in scope only by the Reagan-Watt administration's monumental transfer of the public energy resources to private hands. All historic land grants and waste pale by comparison, including the giant railroad land grants.

Finally, two serious reactionary political movements threatened the very concept of public ownership of the land. The first one was the "sagebrush rebellion," supported by ranchers and farmers, which advocated turning over the federal lands to the states. While that movement was going strong, free-market economists hired by corporate foundations started saying the land should be turned over to private individuals instead. Many "rebels," thinking that idea was even better, supported "privatization." Both "rebels" and the free-market theorists have strongly influenced policy in recent years.

In 1964 Congress called for a review of the public lands. A Public Land Law Review Commission issued its final report in 1970, Congress's fourth comprehensive review of the public lands since 1883.

At no other time in the history of the public lands has a policy report been so swamped by social and political forces. The 1970s started as the National Environmental Policy Act passed, and a few months later, Earth Day focused the attention of the nation and the communications industry on environmental problems. In this atmosphere the final public-land report, *One Third of the Nation's Land*, was launched.

The report largely reflected the views of western development organizations and ignored the powerful environmental movement. The reason was obvious; the commission chair and godfather was Congressman Wayne Aspinall, chair of the House Committee on Interior and Insular Affairs. For years Aspinall had been the bitter enemy of conservationists. He ignored popular programs for national parks and wilderness areas while successfully pushing subsidies to cattle ranchers, water developers, and miners in his western Colorado district.

Aspinall controlled the agenda of the House Interior Committee. Any bills he did not care for simply did not come up for a vote. A classic example of democracy foiled was the Wilderness Act. The Senate studied and passed the bill on three occasions over an eight-year period. Widespread public support for the concept of permanent wilderness was obvious. Thousands of letters, articles, and editorials supported the bill, but it never even came up for a vote in Aspinall's committee. Finally conservationists surrendered; the bill was severely limited in scope, and livestock grazing, water developments, and even mining were allowed in wilderness areas. All future wilderness areas were to be forced over a complex series of difficult hurdles before being protected. The process remains a dramatic contrast to the ease with which developers can exploit public lands. Once out of Aspinall's committee, the bill passed with only token opposition.

It was little surprise that the fourth public-land commission report, headed by Aspinall and staffed by his people, recommended disposing of large portions of the Bureau of Land Management lands in the West. The report ignored the fact that the lands had grown more valuable for recreation and other public purposes; it was oriented toward commodity users. It recommended subsidies for timber production and advocated grazing fees below a fair market value. The old beneficiaries of the public resources demanded more and more.

But events stalled their plans. The environmental decade had been born. Not only had public awareness of environmental problems crystalized, but legislators passed many laws attempting to solve a broad array of environmental problems. The Public Land Law Review Commission died a quiet death. Two years later Wayne Aspinall, his district reapportioned to include some suburban areas, faced reelection with a well-earned ranking as the number one "dirty dozen" Congressman on Environmental Action's list. He was defeated. Years later, still a relic of the past, he became a hired gun for the "sagebrush rebellion."

The environmental movement first developed in urban and suburban areas and focused on a broad array of fundamental problems. Most obvious were water pollution and air pollution. Major air-pollution controls were enacted in 1970 and water pollution controls in 1972. In both areas laws were broadened and strengthened in 1977. But the environmental movement, riding a crest of popularity, also scored major successes in pesticide control in 1972 and 1978. Endangered-species legislation was enacted in 1973 and 1978. Within a few years the environmental impact statements required by the National Environmental Policy Act (NEPA) radically changed the process of developing natural resources. Although the process itself could not stop developments, it forced public decision-making onto a reluctant federal land bureaucracy that had wanted to maintain as much autonomy as possible.

As a consequence, the 1970s brought major changes to the areas of land use and air- and water-pollution control. Other programs affected federal lands indirectly and directly as well. An executive reorganization established the Environmental Protection Agency in 1970. The new agency was delegated responsibility for maintaining water and air quality; for managing pesticides, radiological materials, and solid waste; and for other areas of environmental protection. The Coastal Zone Management Act provided states with planning funds and the discretion to protect coastal regions. Still later in the decade, legislation tackled problems of solid waste, noise, surface mining, and soil conservation.

While federal lands were not the primary focus of the environmental movement, several significant pieces of legislation markedly improved the policy direction for the public resources. The trend began with the Wilderness Act of 1964. Of more than 3000 public-land laws passed by Congress, the Wilderness Act was the first to mandate public hearings on federal plans for the land.

Despite improvements in some managerial areas, however, the federal acreage continued to shrink. The largest recent shift in the federal land system was launched in 1958 with the Alaska statehood act, in which the state received 104 million acres, 28 percent of the total state. The state was also given the option of selecting the choicest lands. Alaska not only chose those lands with high value, but also those with highest mineral and development potential. One result was the oil boom that began in 1967 with the Prudhoe Bay discovery. As a result of its extraordinary federal land grant, Alaska was nearly awash with royalties and revenues by the 1980s. But still the state wanted more.

In its zeal to select the most valuable lands, the state was thrusting aside its oldest residents. Alaska natives, both Eskimo and Indian, had never been allocated reservations; their livelihood, heritage, and traditional homelands were usurped. The people were legally regarded as squatters. To give justice a chance, in 1966 Secretary of the Interior Stewart Udall initiated a freeze on claims. Congress was expected to settle the issue.

The great Prudhoe Bay oil discovery created pressure to lift Udall's freeze, so Congress passed the Alaska Native Claims Settlement Act in 1971. The act provided Alaska natives with nearly a billion dollars in grants and 40 million acres of Alaska land, but it also contained an important public-interest provision. Its principal author, Morris Udall, is not only the brother of the former interior secretary, he is the finest environmental congressman of his generation. Few men carve such a mark on history. Udall's great gift to the nation's future was Section d(2) of the Alaska Native Claims Act. This section was based on a simple assumption: since both Alaska and its natives were selecting federal land, the public should have a share of Alaska's great land for parks, wildlife refuges, and wilderness areas. Section d(2) mandated that 80 million acres be withdrawn from state and native claims while it was studied for inclusion in national parks, wildlife refuges, and forests. The stage was set for a decade-long battle over the fate of Alaska's public lands.

In the contiguous forty-eight states the 1970s brought other major public-land legislation, too. Wild horses had been hunted to virtual extinction by the 1960s. Once numbering nearly a million head, they overgrazed and competed not only with domestic livestock, but also with wildlife. They were not a native species, but seeing a band of wild horses galloping across the sagebrush hills of Nevada, led by a powerful and aggressive stallion, was a thrill. It was part of the old West, part of the region's heritage.

Persuaded by Velma "Wild Horse Annie" Johnson, during the 1970s Congress protected wild horses and burros. Annie, herself a westerner, was an example of the influence of strong-willed westerners on federal land policy. Ranchers raged against the act and blamed easterners, but the bill was a product of the West.

Throughout the 1970s Congress added major parks and recreation areas to the national park system. In addition, long and bitter battles were fought over every addition to the national wilderness system. Sports enthusiasts and wildlife interests fought for and paid to establish new and important wildlife refuges. Every park, every wilderness area, and every refuge was opposed by an alliance of business interests led by chambers of commerce, miners, and ranchers. Developers, long-standing opponents of public benefit from federal lands, were always professionally represented in Congress. In contrast the public interest was protected by nonprofit organizations, many of which had small but energetic staffs and little financial support.

Every park, every wildlife refuge, and every wilderness area worked its way through a political minefield. Hearings, studies, testimony, letter-writing, and often political campaigns were led by volunteers cooperating with a few dedicated and hyperactive staff from conservation and environmental organizations. Protection for the areas was always won by people with nothing to gain except a future in which their children could share the American lands.

Long-standing problems over management of the lands produced two major bills in 1976. One was the National Forest Management Act (NFMA), which formalized a complex system of land planning and management on U.S. Forest Service lands. A major struggle over the Forest Service's failure to respond to the environmental movement and associated political and social changes during the 1960s and 1970s climaxed with the passage of the forest management act. The Forest Service won part of what it asked for, discretion to manage its land with professional resource managers.

The National Forest Management Act, like most public-land policies, was a compromise. Congress spelled out in some detail its concerns over clearcutting and species diversity on public forests, obviously different standards than for private forestry. The act also established new standards for marginal lands in the national forests, mandated more sensible economic development of public lands, and required a continued supply of timber from the public lands instead of permitting short-term profiteering.

Perhaps the most important feature of the act, and the one that reflected the success of the agency's reform, was the planning requirement. The national forests were to be planned by an interdisciplinary team that would consider a wide variety of concerns and resources. Before long, however, the planning process began showing signs of the usual agency bias toward saw timber. The final land-use plans for the Forest Service are not truly balanced for multiple uses. They continue the orientation toward producing timber for private corporations from the people's forests.

The second major act of 1976 helped trigger the "sagebrush rebellion" within a few years. The Federal Land Policy and Management Act (FLPMA) began with a simple premise. Most thought the era of disposing of public lands was over, so FLPMA established the policy of the United States to retain the public domain in public ownership. The act also mandated the Bureau of Land Management land to serve not just the usual multiple uses, but a variety of other public purposes including historical, cultural, and environmental protection.

Clearly 1976 was one of the most important years in the history of public lands. After two hundred years, not only national parks, wildlife refuges, and forests, but also remaining rangelands of the West and Alaska were to be managed for many public purposes. That was the law.

However, the law was not enforced. The many reasons for failure were as old as the nation. Comprehensive reform failed because of old tensions between opposing philosophies and between commercial organizations profiting from the lands. The congressional committees that oversee the lands remained controlled by developers. The budgetary process directing various management agencies remained easily manipulated. The secretary of the interior retained wide discretion to sell public resources. Finally, the nature of federal land-management agencies worked against public-land reform.

For over a century most legislation that directs the management and policies of the public lands has passed through some form of congressional committee or subcommittee on public land, the interior, or natural resources; recently the scope has expanded to include national problems of energy.

For over a century the congressional committees have enjoyed concentrated political power over public lands, and the members and chairpeople have represented rural regions of the West. Even as the West has become more urbanized, with rapid population growth in California and the Southwest, political power over public lands has remained with rural and arid regions. Urban congressmen represent urban concerns, such as welfare, education, and transportation, so public lands have been a congressional priority only for representatives from rural regions. After reapportionment of Congress, the power remained concentrated.

Occasionally conservation-minded members of Congress served on the various interior and public-lands committees. In recent decades such esteemed conservationists as Pennsylvania Congressman John Saylor and Ohio's John Seiberling have served with distinction. They have had a personal commitment to conservation and to the future of the land. But such far-sighted congressmen have been the exception. The committee chairpeople, chosen largely by seniority, have been, with few exceptions, westerners.

After the frontier closed and the nation became more involved in world affairs, the public lands became almost a quaint and unimportant congressional assignment. Yet to a congressman from Idaho, Alaska, Nevada, Utah, or Oregon, which all have more than 50 percent of the lands within their boundaries in federal ownership, an interior committee assignment was a prize. The leaders of land-management agencies understood the concentration of power in committees supervising their budgets and policies. Political power, delivered to rural districts of the West, was a mundane but vital influence that could translate into a large dam project, but more often brought funds for wells, fences, and "range improvements." These investments benefited a few stock ranchers, who often were political leaders in their local communities. The power of an interior-committee assignment might protect a cattle rancher from reductions in a grazing permit, or assure that money would be available for fire control or for roads in a national forest, opening areas for logging and mineral development. Assignments on public-land committees were the simple nuts and bolts of practical politics —regional politics.

A committee concentrates political power like a spotlight. The bills that pass out of the relevant committees are often passed without opposition or discussion by the full House or Senate. Especially in the House of Representatives, representatives defer to the specialized experience of long-standing members of the Interior Committee. Therefore, western representatives have extraordinary influence over public lands; no public-land law has passed in the twentieth century over their united opposition. Westerners are the gatekeepers of all public-land law, arbiters of the public allotment.

The power of a key committee assignment is more than just an influence over formation of public-land policy; it reaches directly to agencies that manage the lands. A personal relationship develops between important committee members and top-level administrators. The directors of the National Park Service, Bureau of Land Management, and Fish and Wildlife Service must work closely with key members of Congress or find themselves hamstrung and useless. A Park Service director may receive a dozen phone calls from congressmen from all over the nation but will personally respond first to those who sit on the National Parks Subcommittee, regardless of the urgency of the calls or the political affiliation of the member calling. William Whalen, a former Park Service director, was once asked how he responded to a House Interior Committee chairperson. "If my chairman only lifted an eyebrow, I jumped," Whalen responded, only half-jokingly.

Adding energy policy to the Interior Committee's concerns in the 1970s began to erode western influence over public lands. Nevertheless, the national interest has never been fully represented in Congress.

The second major institution at the core of public-land problems today is the budgetary process, which often works contrary to principles of democracy. Members of the Appropriations Committee become specialists in certain programs. Like public-land committee members, those who concentrate on the federal-land budgets are usually from western states. They scrutinize items of personal interest and assure that programs beneficial to loggers, miners, and stock raisers are well funded. Funds for roads, capital improvements, timber sales, and mineral leasings are virtually always fully funded. Educational, aesthetic, wilderness, and non-economic programs are never adequately financed.

The budgetary process frustrates public concerns in another way: special amendments, or riders, are sometimes attached to appropriations bills, radically changing the direction of public-land policy. When western congressmen were offended that Teddy Roosevelt was protecting large blocks of lands as national forests, they wanted to pass legislation removing his power to reserve such lands. Roosevelt would obviously veto such legislation, so they attached it as a rider to the appropriations bill. Roosevelt was forced to sign the legislation or have the government agencies run out of funds. Further establishment of national forests from the public domain has been blocked since that time.

In another case, for many years conservationists attempted to enlarge the Grand Teton National Park in Wyoming to include the scenic valley known as Jackson Hole. The Wyoming congressional delegation refused to permit such legislation to pass, despite national support for it. John D. Rockefeller had quietly purchased 33,000 acres in Jackson Hole to be part of the new park. After years of waiting for Congress to act, all the while paying taxes on property he had no intention of developing or exploiting, Rockefeller threatened to sell his holdings. Franklin D. Roosevelt declared the valley a national monument under the authority of the Antiquities Act. The Rockefeller land was accepted as a gift to the American people and incorporated into the national monument. Local resentment against the monument and park was high. Congress passed legislation abolishing the monument, but it was vetoed by Roosevelt. Then in 1944 a rider was attached to the Interior Department budget; funds could not be used to manage or protect Jackson Hole National Monument.

A young local county commissioner, shrewd and ambitious, joined two other cattle ranchers and moved their livestock onto the monument's lands. Legally they were trespassing, but the Park Service was powerless to enforce its laws. The cattle grew fat at public expense. For seven years the rider was placed on the annual Interior Department budget. The commissioner testified before one congressional committee that people could camp or do anything they wanted in Jackson Hole National Monument without interference from the Park Service.

In 1950 a compromise bill passed Congress permitting Jackson Hole National Monument to become part of the Grand Teton National Park. The bill permitted "valid existing grazing" to continue and established a precedent to allow hunting in a national park. The county commissioner, Clifford Hansen, went on to become governor and then senator from Wyoming. Senator Hansen sat on the Interior Committee, and eventually the Park Service adopted the most unusual practice of any national park: Park Service employees used public land to raise the cattle of a U.S. senator. The cattle remain each summer in the park on irrigated public land, the shameful legacy of a budget committee member's control over public lands.

The practice of directing policy with a budgetary rider is also a major problem for the Bureau of Land Management. Congress undoubtedly wanted public lands to be well managed and protected when it passed the Federal Land Policy and Management Act in 1976. The BLM set out to control overgrazing and provide forage on the public lands not only for domestic livestock, but also for wildlife and wild horses. This policy required drastic cuts in the numbers of livestock in some areas to protect vegetation and soil from overgrazing and to stop desertification. But this policy raised a bawl of protest from cattle ranchers. Obviously legislation permitting overgrazing on the public lands would not pass Congress, so Idaho's Senator James McClure attached an appropriations rider to the Interior budget. It severely restricted the BLM's ability to control overgrazing on public lands; no more than a 10 percent reduction could be made in the grazing levels each year. Some areas needed a 50 to 80 percent, even a 90 percent, reduction in grazing to prevent soil erosion and protect forage for native wildlife. Cattle raisers protected their interests at the public lands' expense, because McClure was chair of the Senate Energy and Natural Resources Committee.

The third institution that remains a major problem in forming a rational and balanced public-land management policy is the office of the secretary of the interior. As a presidential appointment, the cabinet position is normally not considered prestigious and a high presidential priority. Only perfunctory public concern is expressed in the position, and that is largely from the West. When Interior Secretary James Watt was appointed in 1980, many industrial interests in the West expressed relief that a westerner was named. Yet the previous interior secretary, Cecil Andrus, was a former governor of Idaho and lifelong westerner. Most interior secretaries are from the West, and many, such as Andrus and Stewart Udall, have records as conservationists.

The problems with the office of the secretary are several. Congress has given the Interior Department cabinet post wide jurisdiction over public lands. The interior secretary has broad authority to set regulations and policies on most of the public lands, even handling mineral leasing on the national forests and other federal lands. The interior secretary makes development decisions involving hundreds of billions of dollars' worth of public resources with little oversight by Congress or any other public body. The secretary has virtually unlimited power to sell energy resources on the public land. It is a system that encourages scandal.

The classic case of abuse by an interior secretary was the Teapot Dome oil lease on 9000 acres in Wyoming. Secretary of the Interior Albert Fall, a former U.S. senator from New Mexico, was convicted of granting this lease for a $200,000 bribe given by Harry Sinclair of Sinclair Oil Company. The scandal haunted conservation for years and shamed the Harding administration.

But the most infamous example of a secretary of interior violating the sacred public trust of his office was James Watt. He earned the dubious distinction of being the most corporate-minded individual who ever held such an important office. With his zeal and extreme right-wing views, Watt quickly became a household word and an embarrassment to the Reagan administration. While he was widely condemned and ridiculed in cartoons and the press, he proceeded to carry out his plans. He cleared out Interior staff members devoted to conservation. He intimidated and threatened career professionals. But more important, he began massive regulatory reforms that served special interests and sacrificed the public interest in federal lands.

Watt had earned his living for years as an agent for western corporate interest. As the top executive in the Mountain States Legal Foundation, which represents big business's interests although it is euphemistically termed a "public interest" organization, Watt led the attack on many of the environmental gains of the 1970s.

Once in office, Watt set out to sell at bargain prices to the oil and mining industry virtually all the remaining public-land energy resources. Conservation had protected public lands and continental-shelf lands containing not only wilderness and parks, but the last reserves of energy resources—oil shale, coal, tar sands, geothermal sites, oil, and gas. Watt set out to transfer this vast public wealth worth more than a trillion dollars to private and corporate ownership.

For his work, Watt earned the applause of developers, oil company executives, and the politicians they supported. He also richly earned the epithet of the poorest secretary of the interior in history from the public's perspective. He sold a nation's resource heritage for pennies on the dollar and cheated future generations. It is a dark and scandalous legacy. No secretary of the interior should ever be permitted to carry out such an awesome transfer of public wealth again.

The fourth problem in federal lands are the federal land-management agencies, which curbed the environmental gains of the 1970s and helped bar public-land reform. Each land agency is distinctive, with its own history, its own policy emphasis, and its own manner and style. Federal public-land policy has never had the benefit of united, cohesive management oriented toward the public interest. While land-management agencies in some cases have been heroic leaders in conservation and have often enjoyed excellent public relations, reform of public-land management must include reform of the land-management agencies themselves.

One of the oldest land-management agencies, and one at the center of public-land problems today, is the U.S. Forest Service, a study in contradictions. Its staff is the most highly trained and professional of the federal agencies. Not only has the Forest Service been one of the most independent agencies, but it has also resisted new values and policies of the 1970s. It is a master of public relations, policy manipulation, and behind-the-scenes maneuvers. Its large size, competence, and skill make it one of the most exasperating bureaucracies.

The 191 million acres of the national forest system today is guided by an overall policy of multiple use and sustained yield. Essentially this policy means the resources in national forests must be used for a variety of purposes in perpetuity. Yet in reality the Forest Service is dominated by foresters whose education, training, and philosophy is primarily oriented toward the forest-products industry. The agency does have professionals concerned with resources, but the route to the top levels has clearly been through the ranks of timber management. The bias is everywhere.

In both its professionalism and conservatism, the Forest Service provides a contrast with the National Park Service. The Park Service was created by a 1916 Act of Congress. Its first director was a wealthy Chicago businessman and active Sierra Club member, Steven Mather. Typical of many early resource leaders, Mather was a dynamic, impressive man. He is still venerated within the agency. Those Park Service members who knew Mather or had contact with him indoctrinated new staff members in his idealism.

Mather was a practical businessman who valued the Chamber of Commerce and other business organizations. He was a master at garnering support from the tourist industry for new parks, often carved from the domain of the U.S. Forest Service.

The basic, long-standing competition between the two organizations goes beyond their separate departments and is deeper than a mere turf battle. The Forest Service claims Park Service employees are only preservationists, not professional land managers. Their complaints are, for the most part, true. In terms of education and training, the National Park Service staff is far less professional. Its employees are seldom affiliated with any scientific organizations, and their education is usually not in land management.

Historically, the Park Service's mission has been simply and directly to preserve a park in its natural state. Preservation meant protection from forces such as fire, insects, and, most important, people. The problem of maintaining a park in a natural state therefore requires complex solutions involving historical, ecological, and human forces. Many historic sites and recreation areas also require restoration of land and resources.

The lack of professionalism is due to subtle and complex forces, such as a recent shift to law enforcement. More important, the agency became increasingly political, compromising its basic mission. Since World War II most newly designated park areas have involved complex political arrangements allowing areas to be mined, grazed, and developed. In some cases hunting and off-road vehicles, normally considered incompatible with parks, were permitted. Rangers and staff with urban and recreation-area experience were transferred to the old established parks and brought with them a tolerance for mechanized activities and multiple uses. They lacked the professional background in resource areas needed to be thoroughly competent. With political compromises and multiple-use management, the morale and *esprit de corps* of Mather's Park Service declined severely.

If the Park Service lacks professionalism, at least it enjoys the support and loyalty of the conservation community. The same cannot be said for the Bureau of Land Management. The BLM was born in 1946 from an unlikely marriage between the thoroughly fossilized General Land Office, dating from 1812 and designed to dispose of the public lands, and the Grazing Service, created by the Taylor Grazing Act of 1934 and designed to serve western stock raisers, especially cattle ranchers. With such unpromising parentage, the Bureau of Land Management took years to develop professional standing even comparable to the National Park Service. It was constantly hampered by the lack of any central legislation providing a coherent management direction. Nevertheless, it made progress.

The Bureau of Land Management managed, ambivalently, most of the western rangelands and, until recently, most of the lands in Alaska. By the 1970s the agency was expanding and hiring many idealistic and thoroughly competent resource specialists. It was changing rapidly for the first time and was grappling with complex environmental problems facing its lands. In 1976 the Federal Land Policy and Management Act spelled out a concise management direction and authorized many new programs, including a major wilderness review. During the 1970s, under the leadership of Frank Gregg, the Bureau of Land Management advanced professionally more than any other land management agency.

All progress halted in 1981 when a conservative rancher and politician, Robert Burford from Colorado, was appointed its director. Best known for his marriage to the discredited EPA Director Anne Gorsuch, Burford was a proven leader in the "sagebrush rebellion" in his home state. Like many other ranchers, he had a record of violating federal grazing laws. He was placed in charge of the agency he had previously favored disbanding. He and other members of Interior Secretary Watt's staff set out to pull the teeth from land-management and grazing-management regulations. Professionalism declined. People who favored exploiting public land and giving preferred treatment to miners and stock raisers rose to the top. Managers concerned with land and the integrity of its management were fired, retired, or moved into meaningless jobs. Others just became disgusted or quit. The Bureau of Land Management went back to being the lapdog of industries that damaged the land.

None of the preceding three federal agencies identified strongly with the environmental movement or its organizations. The Fish and Wildlife Service is the one exception. It is a highly professional and competent wildlife management agency. Its purpose and programs are complex and in some areas contradictory, but throughout, the agency is completely professional, with nearly all of its administrative staff both trained in wildlife and committed to the discipline as a profession. Unlike other agencies, Fish and Wildlife Service employees also identified with and belonged to conservation organizations, especially those concerned with wildlife protection and management.

The Fish and Wildlife Service administers the national wildlife refuge system. The refuge system recently doubled in size and is likely the world's finest. Yet the Fish and Wildlife Service has remained severely underfunded and hopelessly understaffed. During the 1970s, when other agency staffs were expanding rapidly, the Fish and Wildlife Service stagnated even though its responsibilities expanded. It gained new authority to protect endangered species, to protect wetlands, to guard against illegal imports of endangered species, and to comment on federal development projects. The staff also struggled to maintain a viable wildlife refuge system.

While other agencies expanded their political bases through programs involving commerce, the Fish and Wildlife Service has upheld its commitment to one resource—wildlife—better and more honestly than any other agency. It also has been the least successful in the political arena.

Politically, the U.S. Army Corps of Engineers is the largest and most omnipotent of the resource agencies. Although it is little appreciated by the conservation community, the Army Corps of Engineers is one of the oldest agencies in American government and is highly professional and competent. During wartime its exploits have been nothing less than heroic. It also has been incredibly insensitive to environmental concerns.

The Corps has international responsibilities as part of the American military force scattered around the world, but the agency's oldest civilian concern is to maintain navigation on streams, in rivers, and in harbors. In recent years it has expanded into flood control and multiple-use projects concerned with recreation. In fact, Corps of Engineers' reservoirs attract more people than do all the national forests or national parks.

But most important, the Corps is big, professional, national, and politically nearly invincible.

In contrast the Bureau of Reclamation is a newer, smaller, less professional regional federal agency. Restricted by law to the western states, the Bureau originated during Teddy Roosevelt's administration to develop water resources and to irrigate farmland in the arid West. It was intended to be self-supporting. It soon proved not to be, but the political power that launched the agency in 1902 grew with the amount of water delivered to western farmland. With political power came new and innovative methods of subsidizing federal water in the West, and the Bureau's mission has broadened to allow multiple-use management.

The Corps, with its large budget, has resources for staff and research that dwarf the Bureau of Reclamation. The Corps is a Cadillac agency, the Bureau a beat-up Ford pickup.

Another federal agency, smaller but with a comprehensive role in land and water management, is the Tennessee Valley Authority. The TVA is confined to the Tennessee River country of Kentucky, Tennessee, and Alabama but is noted throughout the world for its Depression-era innovations in land and water conservation. More recently, like many agencies, it has aged, has failed to adapt to new social and political forces, and has become a caricature of a bureaucracy out of control.

The federal land and water agencies are at the core of any land program. Progress has been made. In the past twenty years, starting with the Wilderness Act of 1964, there has been a consistent if uneven trend toward a more public decision-making process for public lands. Anyone can now walk into a federal land-management office, request documents and environmental impact statements, and receive them with a minimum of protest and complaint. That was not the case a decade or so ago. Problems still exist, and decisions are still made in back rooms to serve a few special interests, but the persistent citizen can discover and explore the paper trail of most decisions.

But the management of federal lands today is in great need of reform despite the progress made during the 1970s. The ease with which environmental progress was undone and professional management subverted for the profit of a few during James Watt's tenure is vivid testimony of the need for reform.

The old problems and tensions remain. The solution lies with a concerned and involved public.

Aristocratic and economic royalists, the miners, ranchers, and their corporate counterparts, remain largely in control of day-to-day decisions affecting public-land resources. Public information has helped broaden and democratize management of the public lands, yet the public does not receive profits and benefits from the lands and resources that are rightfully theirs. The fiefdom of public land is controlled by ranchers, miners, and energy corporations that take what they want and leave only damaged land, depleted resources, and a broken public trust.

The struggle between Hamilton and Jefferson over the use of public domain remains. Are the lands to be used for the good of the common person or the corporation? The answer today clearly is the corporation. Corporations take the profit, and the public gains little revenue from resources worth trillions of dollars. In many cases developing public resources drains the treasury. The most tangible way to assure that the benefits go to the common people is to maximize profits from public lands and return them to the treasury and to a trust fund for renewable resources, where they can benefit future generations. The other objective should be to provide for tangible benefits most Americans can enjoy—recreation and non-consumptive activities that have been at the bottom of public-land management priorities. The structure of public-land policymaking and management should shift to include national, urban, and suburban perspectives. National and conservation values should be considered.

Finally, the most recent tension over the management of the public lands is clearly not resolved. Since the days of Teddy Roosevelt there has been an outraged cry to conserve resources for the future. Instead the historic pattern has been to exhaust the resources and protect only what was uneconomical to exploit. When the remaining resources became valuable, they were then exploited and exhausted. It is time for a firm national commitment to protect the public-land resources for all Americans and especially future generations. The politics of resource exhaustion and massive transfer of public wealth practiced in recent years must never again be part of the national public trust.

Hydraulic Mining

7

Mining:
A Firesale of Gold
and Gas

M ore than 200 miners and pros-
pectors packed the Nevada public-land meeting. To the western
miners, any hint of government control is a battle cry. Every
threat to their activity rallies their troops from around the state.
On this occasion the Bureau of Land Management had proposed
weak regulations to reduce the environmental impacts of prospecting and mining. The BLM hearing on the regulations was
just one more skirmish in a hundred-year western war. The
miners had a list of victories reaching from the presidency of
Jimmy Carter back to Ulysses Grant. Like veteran Marines,
they were feisty and warming up for a fight.

Each speaker fueled the miners' anger and excesses. Strong
and symbolic words were thrown into verbal war—words such
as "freedom," "independence," and "constitutional rights."
From their perspective they were the last honest Americans and
were being oppressed by a ruthless government. When I rose to
talk about a public-land trust, environmental protection, and
conservation for the future, I was greeted first with silence, then
with hostility. When I pointed out the welfare aspects of free
mining on public lands, the crowd shouted, jeered, and called
me a "communist." Many people rose to their feet, shaking their
fists and bellowing threats. There are few miners, but they
vociferously defend their unique subsidy. They speak of freedom but ignore the public rights in federal lands. Theirs is a
freedom to exploit the public lands for private use.

The miners brought to the hearing all the logic and judgment
of a lynch mob, but they carried the day and the skirmish. A few

weeks later, BLM officials meekly withdrew the proposed controls. A few years later, miners helped lead the ludicrous "sagebrush rebellion," one more battle in their century-old war against the public trust. Once again they had beaten conservationists and professional resource managers. In the Reagan-Watt administration they had sympathetic friends. The BLM was intimidated and submissive; the agency even ignored illegal mining forays into areas that were being studied for possible designation as wilderness in California, Utah, Nevada, and elsewhere in the West. Once again miners proved that the shrillness of greed is audible above the muted obligation to the next generation.

The most dramatic public-land issues focus on minerals; geology has sharply polarized the debate. The conflict between renewable and nonrenewable resource development always requires a compromise because mineral extraction is the most absolute and irreversible way to use land. The immediate economic value of the minerals almost always exceeds the values of resources such as trees, soil, recreation, or mere scenery. Yet once minerals are mined, without conservative practices they may be lost to future generations. After they are taken from the earth, only recycling will sustain their productivity. But recycling and conservation have not been priorities in the mining industry.

Much of the cost of scattering irreplaceable resources to the winds is measured in public lands scarred, ripped up, and left worthless. The pick and shovel were replaced by dynamite, then by more potent explosives and mining equipment. Today giant electric shovels several stories tall devour the earth, wolfing great hunks of ore and rock to feed modern industry and technology, and excreting sterile rock and toxic chemicals. They leave the earth shattered. The public pays the price; the miners profit.

Ironically, the issue of freedom often emerges in discussions of minerals policy. Every prospector with a beat-up jeep and every sophisticated mining company regards the freedom to find, locate, and develop minerals as a sacred, inalienable right. Forgotten in the arguments is the concept that minerals are a part of public wealth, a public trust. Freedom to claim public-land minerals without payment to the public is nothing less than freedom to steal, and the miner steals not just from this generation, but from every generation yet to be born.

Human perspective defines the problem. Hikers and mountaineers are inspired by rock and mountains. The red rock canyon country of the Colorado Plateau moves the human spirit in the deepest religious sense. The native rocks seem eternal; humans are humbled, inspired, and awed. Conversely, professionals associated with the minerals industry are usually trained in engineering and earth science. Many of them regard the thin top layer of the earth—plants, trees, soil, and biological life—as part of the "overburden." The highland ranges are a resource, not an inspiration. The U.S. Geological Service in the Department of Interior, staffed with earth scientists, rushes in to develop and move soil and rock. Other agencies, the Fish and Wildlife Service, the Park Service, and even the Forest Service have much more respect for the thin veil of life on this earth. Education, environment, and perspective define the values of people and organizations.

Near the Utah border in eastern Nevada is the magnificent Snake Range. Its highest mountain is Wheeler Peak, rising over 13,000 feet above sea level. Ancient bristlecone pines, some believed to be the oldest living things on earth, are found high on its ridges. A person can hike to the top and wade through summer snow to find the century-old graffiti of early surveyors etched in tidy hands on burnished rocks. The range is surrounded by wide valleys and ancient dry lakes. Streams run out of the range past green meadows and shady aspen groves, into the hot, dry lowland. Because of its central location and diverse elevations, it holds the most representative Great Basin vegetation. The area has been repeatedly proposed over many decades as a Great Basin National Park.

But Nevada is a materialistic state not sympathetic to parks, conservation, and environmental issues. Politically it has been dominated by gamblers, who leave the politics of isolated public land largely to the miners and ranchers. They in turn have usually seen that any Great Basin park proposal is quietly sidetracked in one of the House or Senate subcommittees by an obliging member of the state's congressional delegation.

Senator Alan Bible was a member of the Nevada delegation to Congress for many years and chaired the Senate Subcommittee on National Parks. He helped plan, authorize, and develop many national parks and recreation areas. He favored a Great Basin National Park. His reasons were practical and obvious—

a park would benefit the tourist industry in nearby Ely and in communities dependent only on mining and livestock. Twice Bible's park proposal was ushered out of his subcommittee onto the floor of the Senate, where it promptly passed with little opposition. However, Nevada's lone Congressman was Walter Baring, who strongly supported the mining industry and chaired the House Subcommittee on Public Lands. Despite public support, the park proposal never budged from Baring's subcommittee. No votes were taken.

At one point Senator Bible was chairing hearings on the Great Basin National Park when the dean of the University of Nevada's School of Mines testified. The dean spoke long and eloquently about the obvious: "minerals are where you find them." When they were found, the welfare of the nation and world depended on their development. The dean vividly sketched a bleak image of how our nation would be starving and backward without wide-open exploitation of minerals on public lands. At one point Bible pressed the point that no mines were operating in the region of the Great Basin Park. Never mind. One never knew when the next mining strike would come, replied the dean condescendingly.

Somewhat in exasperation Senator Bible pressed the dean about his philosophy of mineral development. Were there not some areas in which scenery or wildlife values would outweigh minerals? The dean could not think of any example. What about Yosemite or other national parks? The dean replied, his silver hair bristling with patient indignation, that science could not tell what was below Yosemite and never would if it remained a national park. Finally, the Senator said, certainly there are some places, such as Yellowstone and Old Faithful, which should be spared the damage of the miner's profession. The dean could not agree; even Yellowstone should be free and open to miners and their machinery.

The self-serving philosophy of miners can survive intact and exclude public values today because of the successful long-term defense of the 1872 Mining Law. It permits free exploration and development of most public lands for "hard rock" minerals, those non-energy resources found in granite and other age-old rocks. Gold, silver, copper, zinc and a host of other minerals are classified as hard-rock minerals. They are contrasted with the phosphates, oil, gas, coal, and other energy resources found largely in softer sedimentary formations and leased without claims.

The operation of the 1872 Mining Law is simple. Most public lands (except most areas administered by the National Park Service) are open to claiming. The prospector must first locate the mineral; the amount is immaterial for a valid public-land claim—any trace amount is sufficient. The miner then "stakes" a claim by marking the corners with rocks or posts and files a written notice in one corner. The claim is usually about twenty acres, equal to three or four city blocks. Each claim must then be recorded at the nearest courthouse and, in recent years, with the Bureau of Land Management. There is no limit on the acreage or number of claims a person may commandeer. Each summer day thousands of mining claims are staked on the public lands of the West.

By staking a claim and filing a notice, the prospector owns an unpatented mining claim and shares part of the title to the land with the American people without paying a fee or royalty. Mining claims are free. After staking a claim, the prospector may sell the land for cash or trade it. It has real property value. The prospector may even post it as "private" property and keep the public out. It is little wonder miners have defended this give-away program so vigorously. Every natural resource taken from public lands for private use is subsidized in some fashion, but none is such a blatant giveaway as mineral claims.

Acquiring a patented claim, which becomes private property with fee-simple title, is more difficult. The person who gains such a claim must pay for it at 1872 prices: $2.50 to $5.00 per acre. To patent the claim, the prospector must establish that it is profitable to operate a mine there. Instead, most prospectors prefer to retain only unpatented claims because they are essentially speculators who want to tie up the resources and prevent anyone else from developing the land. Meanwhile its value often escalates, and the property may be saleable to a developer.

Each year the prospector must spend a minimum of $100 in "improvements" on the claim to continue its validity. Despite intervening inflation, the cost was fixed in 1872. Often "improvements" involve merely pushing soil into piles with a bull-dozer or building a road, usually a meaningless but damaging exercise to prevent the claim from being "jumped" by another prospector. A plane flight over public lands reveals the widespread and useless scarring. Mineralized areas are marked by piles of eroding rock and wasted roads. Building them should be a crime; instead, it is required by the 1872 Mining Law.

The prospector may build a cabin on the site, and often the claim is used for a summer home or hunting camp. When the claim is staked, the public becomes a trespasser. Most active claims bristle with bright and sometimes threatening "No Trespassing" signs. It is common for the prospector to cut trees on the mining claim to build a cabin or to provide raw materials for a mine. Both are permissible under the 1872 Mining Law. Because timber is free, some claims are staked for their trees. In essence the miner is almost unrestricted and often ignores the public values in federal land. Abandoned mining claims are usually tainted with patches of oil, littered with equipment, and scarred with gaping holes and unsightly tailings. Frequently water flowing through mines or their tailings pollutes streams because it leaches acids from rock exposed by prospectors. Environmental damage from mining and prospecting is shocking, lasts for centuries, and robs the public of renewable resources such as timber, wildlife, and pure water.

Throughout the miner's development program, land-management agencies have little control over the operation. Neither the public nor the U.S. Treasury receives a royalty for the sale of a mining claim or development of public-land minerals.

The system is unusual by historical or world standards. For most of America's history mining was a privilege, not a right. Throughout the world, minerals are regarded as a gift of nature. The miner does not create the land's wealth; it rightfully belongs to the entire nation and future generations. Exploiting it requires returning a portion to the public in the form of a royalty. In most states and nations, such revenues are invested in a trust fund for education, for reclamation of mineral land, and for development of renewable resources.

The concept of returning revenue to the national treasury is almost as old as civilization. In ancient Rome and Greece, miners paid a royalty. The tradition lasted throughout the Middle Ages and was part of the precedent in English, French, and Spanish law. When Sir Walter Raleigh received a colonial land grant from England on March 25, 1584, it provided royalties for the mother country. All Spanish land grants incorporated into American land law in California and the Southwest originally included royalty provisions. Such a policy was regarded as fair and logical because minerals bring wealth to the miner, yet losing them makes the nation poorer.

The first American land law, written by the Continental Congress in 1785, provided that miners pay a one-third royalty for gold, silver, and copper taken from public lands. Like much of public-land history, the mining system we have today was a result of frontier disorder. During the California gold rush civil authorities in the territory were overrun. It was useless to attempt collecting royalties from miners. There were too many of them, and their lawlessness threatened all authority. The 1872 Mining Law was a practical compromise in the face of illegal frontier conditions; it essentially legalized the theft of minerals and rewarded outlaws. Today supporters of the 1872 law claim it is a patriotic policy serving the national interest.

Supporters of the act also insist the federal government should not hinder their operation with environmental regulations. Instead they often insist the government should be run like a business; they fail to realize that no rational corporation would give away wealth found on its property, but would sell the minerals to the highest bidder. So should the people of the United States. The market should operate equally for public and private minerals.

One example of the complete impact of abuse is the Leviathan Mine east of the Sierra and south of Carson Valley. The area is rugged with sweeping views of the Sierra and the clear sky. The Leviathan Mine extracted millions of dollars' worth of copper. Today, a gaping hole covering several hundred acres remains. Crumbling buildings and still more land covered with tailings and waste have outlasted corporate responsibility. Hundreds of pinyon pines and Douglas firs have been stripped from the land, but more seriously the entire mountainside is moving downhill. The stream has been pushed out of its channel and eats vigorously at the pile of terrain forced in front of it. The stream is heavily laden with silt and exotic chemicals leaching from the mine tailings above. A forested area of several hundred acres, relatively undisturbed during the days of mining, is now restless. Great gaping fissures have opened as the entire mountainside, undercut and destabilized, has moved. The cracks in some cases have split ancient Douglas fir several feet thick.

Despite environmental damage, the Leviathan Mine sits neglected and isolated, like hundreds of others on public lands in the West. The Anaconda Mining Company took the soil, trees, and minerals, took the profit, and returned to the public a broken land. Leviathan Mine is but one example of the price of free mining on the public lands, a frontier practice in a modern society.

In some cases western mining corporations such as Anaconda dominate the politics and economy of entire states. In Montana, Anaconda Company was—until it closed its Butte operation—not only a mining giant, but also for many decades a logging giant. The bedrock of its wealth was public land. Politically Anaconda ran Montana like a Central American banana republic. The company took more than 17 billion pounds of copper from the earth in mines and open pits around Butte, but it returned not one cent of royalty to the American people for the use of their lands. For years the Anaconda smelter belched arsenic and heavy metals into the atmosphere, killing horses and cattle as far as forty miles downwind. For decades the smelter's pollution wiped out the fishery in the Clark's Fork River for a hundred miles downstream. But The Company dominated the state's legislature, news media, and political life. The miners carefully nurtured their welfare system.

The scope of problems from mining on public lands grows every year. There are now more than a million claims on public lands, an area the size of Maine. The number grows every day. Not only is the public locked out of its own domain, but lands long thought to be protected are now open to mining. The secretary of the interior retains wide discretion to open the lands to mining, and even areas administered by the Park Service such as Death Valley and Organ Pipe Cactus National Monuments and Denali National Park contain many valid mining claims. In 1981 Secretary of the Interior Watt opened national recreation areas, including Whiskytown, Lake Mead, and Glen Canyon, with no public hearings. His purpose was simple —to give more public-trust land to a few prospectors and miners.

Even the nation's 70 million acres of wilderness areas were available for prospecting until 1984. Tens of thousands of old mining claims that checkerboard dozens of wilderness areas and proposed wilderness areas are like time bombs. They remain valid long after 1984 if the mineral-assessment work is continued. When the price of copper, gold, zinc, silver, or any other of dozens of minerals rises, these wilderness areas will be opened to miners. Neither the public nor land-management agencies can prevent access. Economics, not laws, protect most wilderness areas.

There are periodic rushes to develop public-lands minerals. Mining is historically a cyclic process—a boom-and-bust economy that has scattered ghost towns around the West. Those protected as historic sites are pearls of the past; but recent towns from the 1950s or '60s lack the character and quality of earlier days. There is little romance in an abandoned town with rows of tract homes or broken-down mobile homes. Mutilated land and abandoned towns are the ultimate result of mining.

Mineral development proceeds, however, and its success is partly due to its having been warped by misguided patriotic fervor. Often leaders of the mining profession talk pretentiously about loss of independence and threats to national security unless all public lands are available for exploitation. It is an appealing argument for its simplicity, but it is without historic merit. Wasting and exhausting resources have threatened national security; conserving them has not. It is not the only time the flag has been wrapped around a cause that is more profitable than patriotic.

In a well-orchestrated campaign during the reign of Interior Secretary James Watt, the mining industry and government raised the specter of "resource wars," in which this country would fight to retain access to other countries' resources. The solution proposed was easy access to our own public lands to assure "independence." It was another industry rush to exploit, to grab public resources for private benefit. Yet as President Theodore Roosevelt understood so well, a nation's strength lies first in its resources, not in its weapons. A rush to exploit brings waste and weakens the country's foundations. Wasting and failing to recycle resources threatens the nation's wealth and security. Conservation is a fundamental application of patriotism.

The arguments used by Watt and others for wide-open mineral development are specious at best. The United States enjoys abundant mineral resources, including reserves of critical minerals that could be traded on the world market for others we need. Nations such as Japan, which have complex and modern economies with few natural resources, have sustained their production in peace and war by trading, recycling, substituting, and stockpiling key minerals. The entire issue of national security may even be a bit of old-fashioned thinking, because the next war would probably not provide time to experience the effects of embargoes on critical minerals; the world could be reduced to rubble in a matter of hours.

There are historic examples of substituting resources during shortages. The British Navy could not guard its mast trees, so it developed new techniques of lashing and laminating ship masts. When supplies of natural rubber were cut off during World War II, alternatives were developed, and widespread conservation eased the problem in the interim. Recycling and reusing minerals have been largely ignored in our disposable economy, although they remain workable alternatives to uncontrolled development of the public lands.

The strategic-minerals argument ignores the complex economic forces acting on all minerals. When a shortage exists, whether from an embargo or a decline in resources, the price promptly rises. When prices rise, other ore bodies, some far away or deep in the earth, become economically attractive to develop. Marginal bodies of ore become profitable. More important, the technologies of manufacturing change. For example, copper has been affected. Once copper prices rose to high levels, substitutes entered the market. Industries adapted alloys and processes to use less copper, and consumption declined. Recycling became worthwhile; scavengers prowled dumps and storage areas.

Opening national parks or wilderness areas to mining only delays the necessary complex economic response to mineral shortages. The market cannot respond quickly when public-land minerals policies subsidize miners and hinder recyclers and conservation.

In a true crisis, the current policies reveal their deficiencies even more clearly. The ownership of mining claims is scattered among tens of thousands of prospectors, who are speculators. During a crisis, they are motivated not by patriotism, but by self-interest. During World War II, when trade was disrupted, some minerals were in short supply. Military demands for them had top priority. Yet because of the haphazard system of claims under the 1872 Mining Law, the claims on public land were legally off limits to the federal government. In a hopeless hodge-podge of overlapping and confusing claims, any given body of ore might have dozens of claimants with an array of conflicting records. Conflicting claims could only be resolved in lengthy court battles. In many areas, resources went undeveloped. Patriotism and military security were not served then, nor are they with today's methods of developing public minerals.

The law has not encouraged discovery, either. One study from the University of Nevada School of Mines revealed that not one single new body of minerals had been discovered by small miners in recent decades on the state's 60 million acres of public land. Instead the new minerals came either from reopening old lodes or from areas discovered by major companies using sophisticated exploration techniques. However, the basic elements of the 1872 mining law are directed toward the small miner. In particular the requirement for a $100 worth of annual "improvements" on each claim is absurd; the figure was established eleven decades ago, when the average wage for mining labor was 20 cents per hour. Today the requirement is met with one day's labor or one hour of bulldozing.

No other public-land policy is so undemocratic. The mining law makes a mockery of multiple-use policies and a rational public process. Virtually every other form of development on the public lands requires public hearings; not the 1872 mining law. Its cure is more public influence and power over the allocation of public lands.

People have been trying to reform the 1872 law for more than fifty years, but they have always been crushed by the miners' political clout. Soon after the 1920 Mineral Leasing Act passed, affecting energy resources on public lands, President Warren Harding called on Congress to reform the hard-rock mining law. It did not happen. During the Truman administration in 1949, the prestigious Hoover Commission recommended reforming the mining law as well as restructuring the natural-resources administration. Again in 1952 the Paley Commission advocated reforming mining laws. In 1970 even the pro-development Public Land Law Review Commission, chaired by Congressman Wayne Aspinall, called for changes in hard-rock mining. A complete reformation of mining is essential for democratic use of the public lands.

On a small portion of the federal lands, hard-rock mining has been reformed. Federal lands purchased from private owner-ship are excluded from the provisions of the 1872 Mining Law. They account for about 8 percent of the total public lands and include most of the federal lands east of the Mississippi River. On the eastern lands, a prospecting permit is required, road-building and other environmental damage is controlled, and the public receives a royalty. As a minerals policy, it is far from perfect. But it is far superior to the 1872 Mining Law.

Energy resources are regulated still differently. Public-land energy resources are awesome in size and are worth trillions of dollars. Their value dwarfs that of the other federal resources. Although they are not claimed under the 1872 Mining Law, they have never been effectively managed or protected.

Since the days of Teddy Roosevelt there have been many attempts to reform the development process. The earliest poli-cies provided that coal lands be sold to the highest bidder for a minimum payment of $20 per acre. These lands were subject to fraud and abuse under various land laws. Conservation was not a priority. Quickly the Roosevelt administration began to pro-tect forests, parks, wildlife refuges, and other resources. Roose-velt felt strongly that it was in the national interest to withdraw portions of public lands containing coal, oil, and potash from sale to protect them for future generations. Conservation was a moral imperative. Roosevelt also feared the trend of a few corpo-rations monopolizing public-land energy reserves.

Roosevelt was not reluctant to take on big business. Between July and November 1906, he had his secretary of the interior withdraw approximately 66 million acres of coal lands from development. It was a spectacular, dramatic, and imaginative way to force Congress to consider public-land energy problems for the first time. Congress joined railroad and mining corpora-tions in bitterly complaining about Roosevelt's conservation ethics. After the withdrawals were complete in February 1907, Roosevelt asked for legislation to lease coal but retain surface rights to the land. Coal was to be leased and a royalty paid to the public. Roosevelt lamented that more than 30 million acres of rich lands had already been pirated from public ownership. It did not seem fair or sensible to him to allow the remaining coal to slip away.

As a compromise to legitimate homesteaders, Roosevelt

agreed to allow them to settle western coal lands for agriculture. The energy minerals were severed from surface rights. About 50 million acres of rangeland and farmland in the West passed to private ownership while the minerals below stayed in public ownership. Recently Secretary Watt began to sell the public coal under millions of acres of private surface land. Using today's strip mining techniques, the coal is exposed by giant electric shovels that dwarf even homes and barns. They devour the earth. Millions of acres of western ranches and farms are endangered in this ironic result of Roosevelt's desire to protect both coal resources and homesteaders.

Like coal lands, oil lands were withdrawn from entry under the homesteading laws during and after the Roosevelt administration. Nevertheless, millions of acres of oil and gas lands passed to private ownership under the homestead laws. By 1909 the director of the U.S. Geological Survey pointed out that the United States was forced to purchase the same oil it had given away. The director recommended a series of petroleum reserves for the government, including naval reserves like the old Royal Navy reserves for Great Britain. The oil reserves protected by executive order totaled three million acres in California and Wyoming.

Congress squabbled over executive mineral withdrawals for years. Yet key committees responsible for interior legislation were controlled by western congressmen who took care of corporations first instead of the public at large. No energy legislation for public lands was enacted for ten years. At the same time private lands in Oklahoma and Texas produced oil and gas, reducing the need to open the public lands for more energy resources.

Finally Utah's Senator Reed Smoot, chair of the Committee on Public Lands, offered a compromise. The basic system was to be leasing, and title to the land would rest with the American people. It was a major improvement over the hard-rock mining law, but generally the 1920 Mineral Leasing Act favored energy corporations. Lands with proven oil reserves were leased gradually over twenty years by competitive bidding. The leases were continued as long as the wells were profitable. Royalties were to be paid at 12.5 percent of a well's gross revenue. Even that low rate was reduced by fraud, and the distribution of the payments was hardly favorable to the public; 90 percent went to the states or into the reclamation fund, which served water-development interests. Only 2 percent was returned to the U.S. Treasury. Unlike other nations, the U.S. allocated no funds for conservation or for a trust fund to provide benefits for future generations.

In 1920 the act passed. Soon the Department of the Interior had received thousands of lease applications, but it processed only a few. The following year Warren Harding became president, and as is the custom he named a western politician, New Mexico's Senator Albert Fall, as his secretary of the interior. By then several important naval oil reserves had been protected for national security reasons. Fall had them quietly and secretly transferred from the Department of the Navy to his own agency. One reserve was the Elk Hills in Southern California; the other was Teapot Dome in Wyoming. Fall secretly leased Teapot Dome to Harry Sinclair and the Sinclair Oil Company.

As was often the case, there were other conflicting claims for the Teapot Dome under other land laws. While Harry Sinclair was boasting he would make $100 million on his new leases, Fall arranged for U.S. Marines to evict people squatting on Sinclair's lease. Fall also began to make a number of expensive improvements on his New Mexico ranch, improving the bloodline of his stock and expanding his ranching operations. A lengthy Senate investigation followed, led by Senator Thomas Walsh from Montana. By October 1923 Walsh had revealed that Albert Fall had accepted over $200,000 in cash bribes from Harry Sinclair for the Teapot Dome leases. Teapot Dome became synonymous with public-land scandals, and Walsh became a national hero, like Senator Sam Irvin during the Watergate era. Later Franklin Roosevelt chose him to be attorney general, but he died of a heart attack two days before the administration began.

After the scandal the naval reserves were transferred back to the Navy Department, and other similar reserves remained under the jurisdiction of the U.S. Department of Defense until 1980. In 1981 the lands were transferred back to Interior. Secretary of the Interior James Watt then quietly speeded up the production of Elk Hills oil to help reduce the Reagan budget deficit. Watt also leased to private oil companies the first lands in Petroleum Reserve #1 in Alaska, which had been protected by the U.S. Navy since the 1920s. He offered the largest oil leases in history on the old naval reserves. "The nation must become energy independent," he claimed. His objective was to transfer resources, even the military reserves, to private corporations. Then, according to his belief, the free market would serve the nation. Under the terms of Watt's leases the big oil companies received subsidies of public oil worth hundreds of billions of dollars.

Unlike Albert Fall, Watt did not stop with the naval reserves. He also leased unproven lands with presumed energy resources under a noncompetitive lottery system. The leases were given for a small entry fee and an even smaller annual rental fee. On those where oil or gas was discovered, the "owner" earned millions in windfall profits. The practice is comparable to a man selling a handful of one-dollar lottery tickets, then giving away his home as the prize. It makes little sense. Yet during James Watt's administration, tens of millions of acres were leased in this manner, essentially giving away public oil on a scale that would embarrass the most hardened robber baron.

Secretary Watt gave away coal, too. Sixty percent of the coal in the West lies under federal lands, largely in Wyoming, Montana, and Utah. It was common for Watt to claim that "extreme environmentalists" locked up lands so the energy could not be developed, but such statements were more than distortions; they were dishonest. As has been the case in other resource industries, coal companies turned to federal lands when their privately-held resources were dwindling. Between 1950 and 1980, leased coal lands rose from a total of 50,000 to nearly 800,000 acres, and another 30 million acres had been transferred to private ownership years earlier. By the end of the 1960s, the federal government had already leased a surplus of coal, and energy companies were reluctant to open more land to production. President Nixon then ordered a freeze on leasing in the early 1970s. Even with the freeze, production of coal from the public lands rose from only 1 percent of the industry's total in 1970 to 10 percent in 1980. Since the leasing program began, some 17 billion tons of coal have been leased.

In recent years there have been two major changes in the system. First, many leases are being acquired and traded by speculators, not by people or companies that want to develop the resources. Second, major corporate ownership of the leases has risen rapidly. Between 1950 and 1980 individual ownership of federal leases declined from 27 percent to only 5 percent. During the same time corporate ownership of public-land coal leases rose from 26 percent of the total to 78 percent.

The corporate share of public-land energy grew even more during Watt's administration from 1981 to 1983. Until the mid-1960s, no large energy company was involved in coal leasing. By 1980, 20 percent of all leases, and most of the new ones, were held by energy companies. Giants took over fast. One company, Peabody Coal, owns more than 8 percent of all leases, more than are held by all private individuals. In April 1982 Watt sold the largest coal lease on record—1.5 billion tons, the Powder River tract. Shell Oil received the largest share and paid three cents a ton for the coal. Some portions sold for less than a penny a ton. At the same time energy companies were marketing coal for $20 to $25 a ton.

Major steel companies such as U.S. Steel, Republic, and Kaiser also hold large tracts of public-land coal. Virtually all the major corporations in the energy field hold leases, partly because Watt's leasing strategy favored large companies. The corporations with the poorest environmental records, such as Exxon and Mobil Oil, gained major leases. Western energy companies with long, distasteful records in the environmental area, such as Montana Power and Utah Power and Light, have been significant lease-holders in recent years. The same holds true for mining companies with dismal environmental records, such as Asarco, Amax, Phelps Dodge, and St. Joe Minerals. Their influence over public lands has grown, not lessened, in recent years. Only the public trust has been reduced.

The most important mineral-leasing area is the outer continental shelf (OCS). Vast amounts of public lands and resources extend far out to sea. The continental shelf is larger than all federal lands on shore, and would cover about one-third of the United States. New technology has made more and more of the OCS area available for oil and gas production. In the future, mining the ocean floor for phosphorite, manganese nodules, tin, platinum, and gold may be possible on a large scale. Minerals on the OCS are subject to the enormous powers of the secretary of the interior.

Most of the country's remaining energy reserves are under

federal lands; two-thirds are under the outer continental shelf. The OCS lands are subject to leasing. Their importance to the public and oil companies can hardly be exaggerated. According to some studies, they may hold 710 billion barrels of recoverable crude oil and some 1640 trillion cubic feet of natural gas. They will be worth trillions of dollars when they are eventually developed.

The outer continental shelf lands were the focus of a long, bitter battle between the coastal states and the federal government. Both claimed ownership. Harold Ickes, Franklin Roosevelt's acerbic Republican secretary of the interior, believed the wealth of OCS lands belonged to all the people, not just to coastal states with oil resources, such as Louisiana, Texas, and California. In 1937 Ickes laid claim to the so-called tidelands in the name of the entire United States. The battle lasted until 1950, when the Supreme Court ruled that the federal government did indeed hold title.

But the war was not over. The Congress has a clear constitutional authority to dispose of the public lands as it sees fit. In 1953 Congress passed the Submerged Lands Act, which gave the coastal states the tidelands area from their coastline to three miles out. Although some states claimed a wider zone, the act largely resolved the issue. At the same time, Congress passed the Outer Continental Shelf Act, which established the lands beyond three miles as part of the unreserved public domain and subject to leasing. The leasing provisions were similar to the 1920 act except the royalty rate was raised to 16.66 percent. The revenues from selling leases were not given to the respective states, nor was a resource trust fund established to sustain renewable resources, as other nations have done. All OCS revenues went into the U.S. Treasury. Unfortunately, federal leasing terms remained below the state rates in many areas and competed with them. OCS leases provided extremely generous terms for the oil industry.

The importance of the OCS lands was not realized until 1981, when Secretary of the Interior James Watt announced that he intended to lease all the OCS lands with oil and gas potential within five years. A billion acres of public resources would be sold. Public debate focused largely on small but controversial leases off California and New England. They were blocked for environmental reasons, but the remaining leases went for the most part unchallenged.

During the previous thirty years, the Department of the Interior had leased a total of 40 million acres. Watt set out to grant five times that acreage each year for five years. The estimated known offshore oil and gas reserves, a fraction of the potential resources, was worth $1.4 trillion dollars at current prices. With the OCS lease plan, James Watt launched the largest transfer of public wealth to corporate hands the nation had ever seen. Watt's leases would last for twenty-five or thirty years, even longer in some cases. Depending on the rate of development, some leases would last well into the twenty-first century. Based on inflation and future price increases, Watt's leases would be worth several trillion dollars by the turn of the century.

The news media were attracted to Watt's colorful antics while he attempted to open wilderness areas to development, authorized toxic poisons to control wildlife, and took controversial positions on snowmobiling and the Beach Boys rock and roll band. The scope of the energy leasing was not seen in its entirety. Watt, in his first year in office, had launched not only a billion-acre OCS program, but a 100-million-acre onshore leasing program in Alaska, including the sale of the largest and oldest naval reserves. He opened millions of acres of public lands in the West to noncompetitive energy leases sold for a dollar an acre. In addition, he accelerated production of oil at California's Elk Hills Naval Reserve and launched major leasing programs for public-land coal, tar sands, oil shale, and geothermal resources. He sold the largest coal lease in history and ordered the sale of all geothermal resources in a single year. In one short term, the secretary of the interior had proposed selling, through mineral leasing, all the economically recoverable reserves of energy the federal lands held. Once again the public lands faced the exhaustion of their resources. Once again the public lost its wealth.

Leasing minerals is superior to actually transferring public lands to private ownership. As practiced by Watt, however, there were several serious problems. First, the leases in fact transferred the wealth without a fair return. Obviously the lessee must be able to make a profit from development, but the fixed royalty schedule and noncompetitive leases serve only the oil-company profits. Additionally, rapid leasing as practiced by Albert Fall and James Watt is competitive with private and state minerals production. Watt's unprecedented program drove down the price on other mineral lands. Everyone lost—states with minerals, private individuals, and the American public. Everyone lost, of course, but the corporations that received the leases.

Second, rapid development of resources sacrificed environmental quality. The top priority of the Reagan administration was to transfer public energy to corporations. Mineral development became the dominant objective for public lands. The array of multiple-use values—wildlife, recreation, forestry, and watershed integrity—were not considered in the process. More seriously, the rapid leasing was not the practice of conservation; it was the politics of exhausting natural resources. Watt held what the General Accounting Office called a "fire sale"—with public resources. He ignored the future.

The strength of a nation lies in its resources, and conservation is an act of patriotism. Yet under a pseudo-patriotic banner the Reagan administration attempted to lease all energy resources in a few years' time. It scrapped conservation programs, abandoned alternative energy development, and sold and scheduled for use only by this generation our vital fossil energy reserves. It was as if Reagan and Watt called for national strength through the consumption of the public resources.

The final problem with the federal leasing program is that it serves not the national interest, but the growth and power of a few corporations. The federal coal-leasing strategy during the Watt years served the monopoly interests of major energy corporations and utilities. It served speculators. It concentrated production of energy in a handful of vertically-integrated corporations. It turned the public's control of policy over to energy companies.

The leasing program was the opposite of what was needed. Reform of the entire federal mineral policy has been overdue for more than a century, since the policy creates many insoluble problems under the present system of management. Reagan's secretary of the interior transferred awesome resources to private corporations for only pennies on the dollar. Yet the leases are contracts and cannot be cancelled without due process and just compensation to the corporations. The terms offer none of the most basic and fundamental protections for the environment. Such resources are developed with no democratic process concerning the use of the most tangible sources of public wealth. The public lacks any mechanism to influence mineral development. A fair and just return for the use of public resources is impossible under existing law, and interior secretaries periodically forget their duty to provide for future generations. In no other area is the public-land wealth so squandered. No other resource area is as hopelessly outdated as the mineral development on public lands.

The solution to the problem of public-land minerals is relatively simple. First and most urgent, the power of the secretary of the interior to dispose of the public wealth must be curtailed. An office charged with conserving resources must be stripped of its power to waste them. Never again should any one person have the power to liquidate public resources as James Watt did. President Reagan's first secretary must be the last public-land robber baron.

Second, the outdated mining and mineral-leasing programs must be replaced with a democratic leasing process. Such a process would provide three important public elements: all mineral lands would stay in public ownership; all resources would be sold at fair market value; and leases would be let by competitive bidding, ending low royalty rates and the giveaway lottery system. The environment and renewable resources would be protected and sustained.

A thorough reform would return a fair market price to the public, and a share of this income would be invested in a perpetual trust fund to sustain public-land productivity. Such a fund could support soil conservation, land reclamation, reforestation, and development of new parks, recreation areas, and fishing resources. If the public received a fair return from selling its resources, the federal lands would not subsidize one organization or group of people and would not compete unfairly with private or state lands. Reform would require the free market to operate on behalf of the owners of public lands as well as the developers.

Public-land minerals are a storehouse of treasure that have been squandered and stolen. Their development has been guided only by awesome greed. Yet these resources do not belong to this generation; they belong to all Americans, including those yet to be born.

Yellowstone River

8

Water:
Dammed For The Few

The path of a trek on the western reaches of the California Trail was dictated by pearls of water along the route. For the first western explorers, following the thin line of the Humboldt River across Northern Nevada was a logical course. Not so logical were various routes unscrupulous guides sold like patent medicine to unsuspecting pioneers. The unfortunate Donner party took the Hastings Cutoff north of the Great Salt Lake. After suffering terribly from thirst in Utah, at a spring near Pilot Peak west of the Great Salt Lake the group rested, wasted time, and sowed problems reaped in the Sierra snow. A route across dry western land laid the foundation for the horror of starvation.

Other routes to California had little more promise. The route through Black Rock Desert and High Rock Canyon killed dozens of people. The stench of rotting livestock on the desert playas haunted people who rode that route. Thousands of people went to the south along the forty-mile desert, an alkali flat between the Humboldt and Carson River sinks. Today any of these desert routes, all on land still owned by the public, can be visited. But visiting is intensely personal. Scattered on the desert are rusting metal from long-rotted wagons, pieces of broken purple glass, and shattered pioneer dreams.

The West is arid and water is life, health, and wealth. The urban oases are deceptive products of technology and manipulation of limited water supplies. Without water the land is dry, with a sparse and simple ecology. Riparian areas, in contrast, are diverse and highly productive. The boundary between land and scarce water provides the key environment for hunting, birdwatching, recreation, and, in the past, survival. Epics have been written around the rivers, springs, and lakes of the West. Water brought settlement, crops, cattle, and sometimes cities. The story of the West is written with thin blue lines of water.

If you hike the deserts, you quickly discover the abundance of life and restful camping areas at the bases of rugged mountains or at the mouths of steep canyons—where water is found. Travel the Great Basin, and you see and feel that springs and wet meadows have been overgrazed and trampled by cows, horses, or sheep. Fly over canyons of the West, and you see concrete plugs holding back blue water and contrasting sharply with red rock and dark canyon walls. Trace the lines of water from reservoirs to towns, cities, green fields of alfalfa, and humming power plants, and you track political power in the West. Water and public lands are linked by geographic imperative and economics.

The water cycle is one of nature's many rhythms. The oceans hold 95 percent of the world's water. The power of the sun lifts moisture from the sea, distills the salt and other material out, and drives the clouds of moisture over land. There, winds and masses of air rise, and moisture is wrung out as rain, or in western states, more commonly as snow in the high country. More than three-fourths of the world's frsh water is solidly locked into ice caps and glaciers. Almost all the remainder, over 22 percent, is locked below the surface as groundwater. Large aquifers of groundwater under much of the western dry land were deposited during the last ice age, when mountains were full of ice and the land was soaked with rain and runoff.

The pure underground water now lifted from thousands of western wells fell on the backs not of buffalo, but of mammoths and saber-tooth tigers. The wells tap fossil water, that rises into a new world after thousands of years slumbering beneath a dehydrated land. Stand under a farm sprinkler on a hot summer day. Feel the cool water from a deep well. Look around you. The water was left there when ancient glaciers chilled the weather, retreated to high mountains, and then evaporated into the thin blue air. Feel pure water that was distilled by a sun unshadowed by pollution, and that fell on a wild, untainted land. It emerges into the modern western economy as a fossil resource.

Using old groundwater is like mining a nonrenewable resource. So is disrupting riparian areas along streams and springs. Their ecology is a stone-age relic, like old water. Depleting them is like exhausting minerals. The complex community of plants, animals, and aquatic life allied with a western stream is like a vein of gold; once it is dissipated, a glacial epoch is needed to replace it.

New water falls unevenly on western lands, usually as snow. The areas receiving the most moisture are the seaward-facing mountain ranges—the Cascade, Sierra, and Olympic ranges. The highest peaks rising from dry valleys capture additional water from winter storms, as do the highest peaks of the Rockies: Utah's Wasatch Range, Arizona's White Mountains and San Francisco Peaks, Wyoming's Wind River and Teton ranges, the high plateau of Yellowstone, and the Blue Wallowas in Oregon. Lesser mountains, and those such as the Great Basin ranges in the shadow of hulking seaward ranges, wring only residual moisture out of storm clouds. Western valleys are watered by light winter snows and isolated, irregular summer thunderstorms. Snow, stored in white cushions and pillows for much of the summer, is intimately tied to elevation. The higher the mountain, the deeper the snow. These highlands, unsuited for agriculture, homesteading, irrigation projects, or scattered mining, remain largely in the public domain. As a result, approximately 80 percent of western water falls on only 20 percent of the land, mostly federal land.

The geography of water produces one of the many ironies of America's public-land policy. Water from the world's vast ocean-commons sails inland with dark fleets of winter storms. Carried on clouds in massive banks of moisture, it is then clearly part of nature's public resources. In the western United States, this liquid gift falls on public land. It begins a long journey from the mountains. En route, it is transformed from public ownership to private not by nature or reason, but by tradition and law. Once it is captured and diverted from public streams, it becomes a valuable private property. In the West, it is often appropriated, stored, and transported by federal development projects. The public pays for it to become private property. At the same time, public claims to fish, wildlife, and aquatic and riparian resources, as well as the pleasure of recreation and the enjoyment of a free-flowing waterway are shunted aside and lost.

Water law came to the West with more than passion; it came with violence. Probably more blood has been shed over water than over all the livestock and gold mines. Diverting public water onto private property is now one of the most cherished and defended forms of property right in the West. In many western states, a public trust in stream flows is not even recognized as a legal right. Today, vested water "rights" are entrenched in the economy.

Starting in the 1820s the agency that managed and controlled water and land was the U.S. Army Corps of Engineers. The Corps began operations twenty-five years before the Department of Interior and nearly eighty years before the Forest Service. Managing and controlling the water was an early development mission of the federal government. When the frontier reached the invisible but critical line separating the arid West from the humid East, Congress responded with a water-development agency that attempted to overcome the geographical limitations of the land. The agency not only failed, but also became a caricature of a federal welfare agency.

Early in his administration President Jimmy Carter made a naive attempt to strip both the federal funding and the authorization for approximately thirty dams and water projects. A leading environmentalist, in a euphoric mood, stated: "The President is in the process of destroying the cozy relationship among powerful governmental bureaucracies, pork-barrel Congressional committees, and water development and user interests." Environmentalists' elation was short-lived. Within a year, most of the "hit list" was restored. Construction continued on projects authorized by Congress despite high economic and environmental costs. A backlog of more than 800 water projects with a $34 billion price tag remained authorized despite the administration's efforts to reexamine their rationale and to cancel inefficient ones. The federal water-development agencies and congressional public-works committees and subcommittees remain as cozy with their clients as ever. President Carter joined a long line of people who have tilted at the water-development windmill and failed. Presidents, environmentalists, and people concerned only with efficient government have all broken their lances against the triumvirate guarding water development. The historic saga is long, wasteful, and littered with casualties.

Water projects are the oldest form of federal development programs. Time has produced three federal agencies concerned with major engineering projects—the Army Corps of Engineers, the Bureau of Reclamation, and the Tennessee Valley Authority. A fourth, the Soil Conservation Service, is concerned with planning, assisting, and constructing small ponds and dams.

The scope of water development in the United States is impressive. Approximately 50,000 dams twenty-five feet or higher have been constructed. Although many large dams are privately owned, the very largest world-class dams and projects are federal. Federal technical assistance and funds have helped build many of the 2.5 million small dams less than twenty-five feet high. One flight across the nation will usually convince the most persistent skeptic that federal water policy is a major force shaping the land.

The contrast between dam construction and stream conservation is worth considering. In 1968, Congress established a policy of protecting some streams in their free-flowing condition, through the National Wild and Scenic Rivers Act. After fifteen years, some 7000 miles of free-flowing rivers have been covered under some form of federal protection, or four miles for each major dam constructed in the United States annually. That is, for every eight major dams in place, one mile of free-flowing river is protected by federal legislation. If all dams large and small are contrasted with protected streams, then for every dam there remains less than fifteen feet of wild, free-flowing stream.

The federal role in water development dates to a Supreme Court decision of 1824, which firmly tied the interstate-commerce clause of the Constitution to the regulation of rivers and harbors. The decision cleared the way for the federal government, specifically the Army Corps of Engineers, to develop canals and river-improvement projects for commerce and trade. Originally this mission consisted of removing snags, rocks, and sandbars that threatened barges and steamboats. Successive acts of Congress increased the Corps' authority to regulate bridges, wharves, piers, channels, harbors, diversions of water, and eventually garbage dumping.

Inside the huge Defense Department, the Army Corps of Engineers has been insulated from periodic budget cuts that affect other federal agencies during war or economic stress. The Corps remains well funded and supported.

The Corps is really far different from the way it is commonly perceived by environmentalists and people concerned with government efficiency. It is an elite organization, selecting the cream of West Point's graduates for its few hundred uniformed-officer positions. More than 98 percent of the employees are civilians. During war the agency has heroically and rapidly developed airfields, harbors, bridges, and other engineering marvels. During peacetime, despite its well-deserved reputation for environmental insensitivity, it has been professional and competent. Scandals and inferior physical projects are practically unknown in its long history.

The government moved into the irrigation or reclamation business in 1902 by passing the Reclamation Act. First proposed by John Wesley Powell, the concept had been strongly supported by President Theodore Roosevelt and had been debated for years. Since the Corps of Engineers was opposed to the idea, a new agency was created—the Bureau of Reclamation. The agency was limited to the arid western states and was directed by the western-oriented Department of the Interior.

Originally the Bureau of Reclamation was to be a self-supporting agency. It would lend money for large irrigation projects, and fees from selling water would repay the cost of construction with interest. There was one problem: the marginal western agricultural conditions could barely support farmers. As a result, farmers could not make payments when they were due. Reclamation interest rates were kept much lower than those of banks. Prices for federal water were minimal. The projects were obviously not self-supporting.

As a result the Bureau expanded its mission. Soon it was concerned with power production, flood control, recreation, and fisheries. Such activities were credited on the account ledger as public benefits, so large portions of projects' costs were written off as general public benefits. The result today is that only a small portion of the costs of the Bureau's dam projects are charged to irrigation. Water is welfare for those fortunate few people who hold federal reclamation contracts.

The Bureau of Reclamation was originally supposed to help the family farmer and to provide federal assistance to the struggling homesteader. The acreage limitation built into the law was a legal mechanism to assure program assistance to small farmers. The actual limit was seriously debated by Congress, which eventually reached a compromise: subsidized federal water was to irrigate no more than 160 acres owned by any one person. This 160-acre limitation was soon circumvented by large landowners and by the blatantly dishonest Bureau. By the 1960s thousands of acres on some corporate farms were flushed with cheap federal water. Attempts at reform made during the Carter administration were promptly abandoned by the Reagan administration, which instead worked successfully for legislation to end the limitation. It was an end to an old Jeffersonian model of public-land policy.

The demise of the 160-acre limitation demonstrates the perversion in federal land and water policy. Congress clearly intended to limit the delivery of water and to prevent a few large landholders from gaining more than their fair share. John Wesley Powell, the father of federal reclamation, had advocated limits decades before the 1902 Reclamation Act was signed by Theodore Roosevelt, who clearly considered the acreage limitation an anti-monopoly mechanism. Yet, as has been the case with land disposal, the development and disposal of federal water was subverted repeatedly and consistently by economic forces.

The most creative shift in federal water policy came when the Tennessee Valley Authority (TVA) was established in 1933. The TVA arose out of the Great Depression and was the world's first attempt at comprehensive regional land and water development. It was widely heralded early in its history for bringing power, prosperity, and development to the Tennessee Valley region. The agency was concerned with the health of the residents, soil conservation, reforestation, and dam construction. But in later years it focused single-mindedly on producing cheap electrical power while ignoring the environmental impacts of its programs. By the late 1970s the TVA had reached as far as Wyoming for coal to drive its turbines and pollute the air.

The early success of the TVA prompted President Franklin Roosevelt to advocate similar comprehensive development authorities for the Columbia, Red, Missouri, and other rivers. But the case of the Missouri River illustrates the difficulty in creating alternatives to existing programs.

Except for Fort Peck Dam, a Great Depression make-work project, the Missouri River was largely undeveloped. The river is the nation's longest and drains one-fifth of the country's land. In the spring of 1943 record floods caused $50 million in damages and covered 2.4 million acres of farmland. Congress requested a review of the Missouri's flood-control needs from the Corps of Engineers.

Fifteen years before, the Corps had developed a 1245-page wish-list of dams and flood-control proposals for the entire Missouri River. In the spring of 1944, it summarized a portion of the earlier work in a twelve-page "Pick Plan," named for the district engineer. The document was not a plan but a general proposal to build dams for navigation and flood control on the lower Missouri. The major projects were hundreds of miles of levees, five large main-stem dams, and six dams on tributaries. The proposal promised to stabilize Missouri Valley economic life, encourage industry and civic growth, and relieve distress caused by the Big Muddy.

Critics of the Pick Plan from the West howled in protest. The arid region in the Rockies and the West from which the Missouri flows needed dams for irrigation, not flood control. The western states supported the Bureau of Reclamation, the region's own water-development agency. Their proposal was soon called the "Sloan Plan," named for the regional director of the Bureau. In contrast to the Corps of Engineers' proposal, the Sloan Plan was five years in preparation and was more comprehensive and detailed. The plan stressed irrigation and power development, the Bureau's twin missions. It proposed ninety dams, facilities to irrigate 4.7 million acres of land, and many large power plants.

Congress was faced with two opposing and contrasting proposals for the same watershed. Both agencies sent emissaries around the region publicizing their own plan and criticizing the opponents'. Regional newspapers ran editorials extolling the virtues of one plan over the other. Congressmen advocated one as opposed to the other. The Bureau of Reclamation staff insisted the Corps' proposal for Garrison Dam in North Dakota was unsafe. They even quoted a detailed Corps of Engineers' report to substantiate the argument.

In the middle of this debate, on September 21, 1944, President Roosevelt asked Congress to create the Missouri Valley Authority, a new, independent multiple-use agency patterned after the TVA. Within a month, on October 16 and 17, representatives of the Corps of Engineers and the Bureau of Reclamation met in Omaha and reached an agreement. In two days they buried the hatchet and reconciled the Pick and Sloan plans into the "Pick-Sloan Plan." In two days the competing agencies settled the entire water-development scheme for the largest river in North America. The public was not involved; neither was the White House.

The agencies' response to the threat of a Missouri Valley

Authority was as simple and direct as it was self-serving. The Corps and the Bureau decided behind closed doors to build the projects proposed by both agencies, including two of the world's largest dams. Reconciliation meant each agency accepted the other's works, except one Corps project was eliminated. The proposed dam would have been submerged by a larger Bureau dam downstream; the larger one was to be built. Garrison Dam's safety problems were ignored. The "compromise" did not consider the serious question of how to allocate water to navigation, flood control, power generation, and other conflicting uses. Vital questions of land use and regional distribution of benefits, as well as social and economic impacts, were ignored. Essentially, navigation and flood-control interests won the lower basin, and irrigation and power prevailed in the upper basin. No one knew if enough Missouri River water was available for both.

The *St. Louis Post Dispatch,* long an advocate of a Missouri Valley Authority, provided the classic description of the Pick-Sloan Plan in an editorial:

> The resumption of this old and apparently irreconcilable feud between two vested government interests convinced many people that the time had come to cut the Gordian Knot by advancing the MVA (Missouri Valley Authority) idea. The idea would reserve the Missouri Valley from contending factions and place it under harmonious and scientific, but above all, under united and non-political management. As the MVA idea took instant hold upon the imagination of the country and won the ultimate endorsement of the President in a special message to Congress, a strong and wonderous thing occurred. The feudists, fearful of the MVA idea, lest it invade their bureaucratic precincts, began to murmur softly to each other and how marvelous they relate—a marriage has been arranged. A loveless, shameless, shotgun marriage of convenience, arranged between old and bitter enemies, not only to kill off MVA, but to save the interests jealously guarded by two powerful government agencies.

Within weeks Congress agreed to the Pick-Sloan Plan, and President Roosevelt signed it into law late in 1944. For more than thirty years Congress continued to authorize spending for the Pick-Sloan Plan, and more than 100 dams were built for more than $6 billion. During that time no one asked if the plan's objectives had been achieved. Only one thing is certain—the development agenda for the nation's longest river had been decided. Nowhere else in the history of water policy were so many dams approved in such a short time by so few people.

From the 1930s through the 1960s many massive federal water projects were planned and constructed. Large-scale technologies emerged to solve the problems of water distribution and use. Large earth-moving equipment and new techniques made it possible to build dams on a scale never before seen. Unfortunately, the increased size of water projects increased environmental impacts, social and economic problems, and unanswered questions concerning efficiency and equity.

Many people's perception was fixed on the Tennessee Valley model for water development. The region did prosper and emerge from the Depression with a far stronger economy and facilities to enter the mainstream of American life. However, the technology that made larger dams possible also helped transmit power over greater distances without losing efficiency. Instead of attracting industry and prosperity for the region, the TVA transmitted power to existing urban and industrial centers, in some cases even accelerating the migration of residents from rural areas. Construction brought a temporary boom but left in its wake a discouraged local population.

The history of water developments has been fairly simple. Private power companies and irrigation districts captured the best sites early, leaving the costly and inefficient ones for federal agencies. In turn, federal agencies developed their best sites during the first decades, then later turned to the less efficient sites and those with high environmental costs.

The first government agency to consider a spectacular public site for a dam was the city of San Francisco early in the century. The city proposed a dam and reservoir in the Hetch Hetchy Valley of Yosemite National Park. The small but principled Sierra Club, led by John Muir, fought the idea for years. The dam split the friendship between Gifford Pinchot and Muir; Pinchot opted for development. In 1913 Congress authorized the dam, which today produces electricity for San Francisco to sell. Domestic water sources are now available elsewhere, so the dam's major justification today is to serve as a cash register to defray part of the city's operating cost. New development proposals now being discussed would permit a downstream dam to be built on the Tuolumne River or would raise Hetch Hetchy and flood more of Yosemite Park. Water developers are only temporarily satiated as long as a river flows free.

Visiting Hetch Hetchy today involves driving on miles of

gravel road. Even in summer the site is little used, hardly an example of multiple use. Crossing the dam, one looks into cool, clear water and at steep canyon walls plunging into the reservoir. The dam bears the water with colorless efficiency, its face marked with a dimly visible crack painted by some adventuresome climber who rappelled over the face to mark a protest.

If one sits quietly, he or she can almost feel the raging of John Muir's angry soul at the sight of such a project in the heart of a national park. His words practically ring from the flooded canyon walls: "Dam Hetch Hetchy! As well dam for water tanks the people's cathedrals and churches, for no holier temple has ever been consecrated by the heart of man." Some future generation will break the offensive dam, scour the debris, and nurture the natural healing forces of the valley.

The flooded Hetch Hetchy became a tragic symbol for the flowering conservation movement. The nation continued to dam and build as if there were no end to wild and free-flowing rivers. In the early 1950s the Bureau of Reclamation proposed the Echo Park Dam in the remote and obscure Dinosaur National Monument on the Utah-Colorado border. Led by David Brower of the Sierra Club and members of The Wilderness Society, the publicity and organizing that became hallmarks of conservation organizations in the 1960s and 1970s brought Echo Park to the nation's attention. Conservationists were so successful that Congressmen received more mail on Echo Park than on any other issue of that era. After a long and bitter fight, Echo Park Dam was blocked.

But the victory was bittersweet. As part of the compromise over the Colorado River Storage Act, which passed without Echo Park, Congress authorized the Glen Canyon Dam. It was literally *The Place No One Knew,* as a later Sierra Club book was entitled. The quiet and beautiful canyon was a remarkable resource of rich and diverse archeological ruins, petroglyphs, and peaceful canyons. But the Colorado River was blocked by a 710-foot dam in the 1960s, and the water flooded dozens of side canyons and refuges of peace and beauty. It backed water to the very foot of Rainbow Bridge National Monument, the world's highest rock arch. It also changed the complex ecology and character of the Colorado River in Grand Canyon National Park. Of all the changes the Glen Canyon Dam brought, converting the warm, muddy Colorado into a clear, cold trout stream was most startling. Changes came like falling dominoes to the riverbank vegetation, animal life, even the geomorphology of the Grand Canyon.

If wild canyons were lost, conservationists still won a few small but symbolic, and perhaps temporary, victories. None was more important than defeating the Bridge Canyon and Marble Canyon dams, proposed for the Grand Canyon by the Bureau of Reclamation during the 1960s. Like the Hetch Hetchy Dam, the two proposed Grand Canyon dams would have served as cash registers to generate money for water projects in southern Arizona. After a long and bitter national campaign, again led by the Sierra Club, the proposals were defeated.

The 1960s and 1970s brought more awareness of the complexity of environmental problems. Water was interrelated with other resources, and developing it spurred many questions and problems.

One problem was the loss of agricultural land. The river bottoms along the Missouri River and other western streams were not only diverse and complex environments, but they held the best agricultural lands. Once the best dam sites in the rugged canyons had been used and federal projects moved into broader valleys, more agricultural land was threatened.

The irony of the issue in the West was the Bureau of Reclamation focus on irrigating farmland. The Pick-Sloan project was designed to irrigate more than 4 million acres of farmland. Building the large main-stem Missouri River dams such as Garrison, Oahe, and Fort Peck flooded hundreds of thousands of acres of prime agricultural land. Yet when the nation was facing a huge grain surplus, Congress could not see the logic in funding irrigation projects to subsidize even more crops, so it built the dams but not some irrigation facilities. Some lost prime Missouri River farmland was partially replaced by marginal irrigated farmland. One succinct and caustic farmer, commenting on Montana's Canyon Ferry project, a Pick-Sloan project on the Upper Missouri, summarized the federal reclamation problem: "I never could understand why they flooded 20,000 acres of rich bottomland so they could irrigate 12,000 acres of rocks."

In addition to losing farmland as a resource, rural western counties often lost value from their tax bases. The western water projects also increased transportation problems in some areas, because the reservoirs are inland seas. In the process, traditional patterns of communication and other activities were disrupted. The reservoirs brought a seasonal influx of tourists, boaters, and fishermen, who only proved to be an additional disruption.

For nearly fifty years federal water projects have been required to be cost-effective. That is, the benefits are supposed to exceed the costs. Several problems are inherent with the cost-benefit analysis. First, the process is not honest. Ridiculous interest rates sometimes as low as 3 percent are used in the comparison. Benefits are inflated in creative ways, while costs are studiously minimized. Subsidies to special interests are evident to anyone involved in the process, yet in classic bureaucratic fashion, the agencies never honestly discuss them.

Less obvious is the geographic distribution of costs and benefits. Benefits such as flood control, navigation, and power have tended to flow downstream and to urban areas. The costs are borne largely by local rural residents near the project. Family farms are flooded, roads blocked, and communities altered. The tax base is weakened, costs of police and social services rise, and a stable rural style of living is disrupted.

For American Indians on reservations, the Corps of Engineers has replaced the Seventh Cavalry as an object of fear and hate. Federal water projects have been located to protect urban centers from temporary floods while permanently flooding homes and lands of reservation Indians.

Missouri River Indians who had lived in harmony with the river since the last ice age welcomed the first Americans they saw, the Lewis and Clark expedition. But the Pick-Sloan project replaced their ancient subsistence economy with a welfare economy when the Missouri River main-stem dams flooded sparsely-populated reservations to protect the land and resources of cities downstream. The positive cost-benefit ratio was enhanced by flooding cheap reservation land on the cost side and protecting expensive urban land on the benefit side.

The impact on the Indians was devastating. The Missouri River bottomland provided three important elements in the Indians' subsistence economy. First, the excellent soil, moisture, and temperature provided high-quality cropland not found elsewhere on the upland plains. Second, the riverine area furnished habitat for game animals, as well as pasture and shelter for domestic stock. Finally, the bottomlands supplied timber for heat and shelter. Building the Garrison Dam required relocating 1700 people whose entire social, economic, and cultural lives had been disrupted. The Indians lost 90 percent of their timber and much of their most valuable wildlife habitat. Burial grounds and ancient religious sites were flooded. When the entire cost of taking the area was considered, the Army Corps of Engineers paid the Indians less than $100 per acre.

Cultural and social values are not limited to ethnic minorities. Rural residents or religious or political groups may be concentrated in the area taken by a federal water project. These peoples' values are seldom represented. Older people are hit especially heavily by forced relocation. Dreams, memories, and old loves do not fit into tidy economic formulas.

Many archaelogical sites have been flooded by federal water projects. The main-stem Missouri River projects wiped out historic frontier sites, including the village where the Lewis and Clark Expedition spent their first winter—in the Louisiana Territory. Fort Randall Dam on the Missouri flooded 120 historic sites and features. Garrison Dam buried not only Indian land, but 77 historic sites and hundreds of archaeological sites. In a futile attempt to salvage some of the best sites, the developers replaced the precise techniques of archeology with bulldozers.

By the mid-1960s, only one 175-mile stretch of the Missouri River, the Missouri River Breaks in Montana, was undeveloped. The Corps of Engineers proposed to flood the entire primitive, historic stretch. But local and state residents rallied against the threat. The late Senator Lee Metcalf led the way. After years of citizen involvement and struggle, in 1978 the Missouri was added to the Wild and Scenic Rivers System.

Today, anyone can float for a week on this stretch of the Missouri and find the magic wilderness Lewis and Clark found. On several occasions I have camped where these explorers camped and listened to the coyotes howl. The river still flows, dark and powerful, and elk live in the shade of the dense river-bottom foliage. I have found the ashes of old campfires and mouldering bones of buffalo in the banks of the river. Each year swallows nest along the river bottoms, and prairie dogs guard their towns. Soaring hawks send them diving for cover. They welcome coyotes with a shrill cry of warning.

If wild rivers take us back in time, then reservoirs and dams are a reminder of short-sightedness. Over time, several problems with engineered projects emerge after being ignored in the tidy cost-benefit analyses. Time is a forgotten variable in the equation for building dams.

First, some projects are outdated before their planned life span has passed. Errors in construction have ended some projects prematurely; rapid siltation has reduced the usefulness of others. In some cases, projects have had to be modified and rebuilt at an expense exceeding the cost of the original dam.

Associated with the problem of time is the problem of safety. The hazards associated with old dams are only now being appreciated. In the aftermath of the Teton Dam failure, new inspection programs have revealed dozens of federal projects with safety problems threatening thousands of people downstream. Dam safety will be the next great concern in water-development policy. As 50,000 dams over twenty-five feet high age and weaken, their safety decreases. The policy of building large dams has traded a predictable and relatively low level of risk from flooding for the possibility of rare but catastrophic dam failures. Environmental disruptions from dams create often-pathetic human problems, but dam failure can be a colossal disaster.

In many areas large dams have given people living below them a false sense of security. Housing and other buildings have been encouraged on flood plains where periodic annual floods have been controlled. However, a recent inventory of dam safety has shown that in many cases, dams are unsafe. The future will bring only new problems and expensive mandatory repairs.

Some types of construction are now considered so unstable they are no longer used to build large dams. One is the hydraulic fill method, a form of construction used early in this century in which mud-laden water was pumped between dikes. The water drained, leaving sediments and material that slowly accumulated and formed the axis of a dam. Such dams were subject to wholesale slippage and, in some cases, a phenomenon called liquefaction, in which the solid material would suddenly flow like a fluid. Once engineers understood the problems of this type of construction, the technique was abandoned. In California, a state with a model dam-safety program, all such dams have been reconstructed to prevent failure.

The largest dam ever built by the hydraulic fill method was the Army Corps of Engineers' Fort Peck Dam on the main stem of the Missouri in eastern Montana. The dam's axis is nearly four miles long. The dam is a linear hill more than 300 feet high and 20,000 feet long that holds back a reservoir with more than 1500 miles of shoreline. During the initial filling of Fort Peck Reservoir, the dam suddenly slipped and a chunk 4000 feet long flowed into the new reservoir. For many hours it appeared the entire reservoir would fail, but the slippage was halted and then repaired. In more than forty years of operation the reservoir has never been completely filled.

During the early 1950s the Garrison Dam was built downstream from Fort Peck. A Corps of Engineers' report called the geology unsafe, yet economists considered the location desirable because the reservoir flooded a large Indian reservation. The dam was built. If Fort Peck Dam liquefied and suddenly collapsed, it would send a wall of water down the 180-mile-long Lake Sacajawea to Garrison Dam, which rests on a geological foundation long regarded as weak and unstable. If Garrison should fail, then almost certainly Oahe, Fort Randall, Big Bend, and Gavins Point dams downstream would fall like dominoes. Nearly 700 miles of flat water, two and a half years of the Missouri River's average annual flow, would head downstream for Omaha, Kansas City, St. Louis, Memphis, and New Orleans. A multiple dam failure on the longest river in North America, involving three of the world's biggest dams, would be the largest human-produced disaster in history.

One of the fallacies of dam policy is ignoring the risk of failure. The cost of possible flood damage or its insurance premium should be a cost of development. One of the best examples is the Teton Dam failure in Idaho. The Teton Dam, constructed by the Bureau of Reclamation, was a 310-foot-high earthen dam built largely for irrigation. Eventually, according to the plans' optimistic promise, it would return $20 million in benefits to the area. However, through a dismaying set of blunders, the dam was built over volcanic rock laced with caverns and pockets. The Bureau ordered grouting, or pumping liquid cement into the dam foundation, to seal the maze of holes that resembled underground Swiss cheese. The rock absorbed tons of cement, and still the pumps did not register the rise in pressure that would indicate the holes and cracks were filled. Although the reasons were never clear, grouting was stopped, construction resumed, and the underground curtain to prevent leakage was left tattered.

The dam was built and filled rapidly to catch the spring runoff in 1976. The filling was rushed despite the risk, in an attempt to satisfy the irrigators. On the day the reservoir reached capacity, leakage increased rapidly and was far higher than anticipated. The project manager sent a memorandum to his supervisor in Denver—by mail. Engineers attempted to blast open the partially-completed flood gates. The effort failed. Finally, the next day early in the morning of June 5, 1976, the synthetic springs flowing at the base of the dam turned brown with sediment. It was a stark, deadly sign: the bowels of the dam were being flushed away. Warnings were issued to residents of Sugar City and Rexburg, Idaho, that the dam was failing. Even with the warnings, a few hours later the flood killed eleven people and caused an estimated $1.17 billion in damage. Teton Dam held less than one-half of one percent of the water stored in the Missouri River dams.

The Bureau of Reclamation later asked itself, in its press release, "Could the Teton Dam disaster have been avoided?" The agency piously answered, "No, the collapse was an 'Act of God.'"

There are many other water problems in the West not directly related to federal lands. Irrigation practices have leached soluble salts onto agricultural lands. Both soil and groundwater have been contaminated. Aquifers have been mined for irrigation and other uses. Depleting the groundwater has brought land subsidence, which damages structures and developments as well as disrupting natural drainage patterns.

However, as the West continues to expand its use of water, the greatest problems remain in the variability of supply. Stream flows are both declining and becoming more variable. Overgrazing and overcutting the land is partially responsible. Stability is a primary lesson of nature, yet federal land and water policy has encouraged instability.

The problem of federal water policy is complex, but one thing is obvious: the question of development on the grand scale practiced by federal agencies is not simply a matter of thirsty urban residents opposed by people concerned with protecting the environment. The predominant question is not protecting remaining wild rivers but achieving economic efficiency and rational use of resources.

Federal water in the West goes largely to irrigate low-value crops such as alfalfa, which are seldom used to feed people, but instead to feed cattle. Beef price-supports, subsidized irrigation, and low grazing fees on federal lands all help to keep the western cattle ranchers solvent but not as self-reliant as they like to view themselves.

Public-land water, first diverted to private ownership by

western agriculture, is now being converted into energy and taken for urban uses. Rights to the water flowing from public lands have property value. Originally free, they now are bought and sold in a specialized market. The value of water transferred from agriculture to urban or industrial use explodes like a family farm subdivided for condos.

The business side of western water development is simple and direct; the motive is profit. The political side is less obvious. Again, as with public-land policy, the linchpins of power are in the key congressional committees, in this case the Water Resources, and the Water and Power Resources committees in the Senate and House, respectively.

The geography of water projects is closely related to the lines of key congressmen's districts. Even after the death or demise of a key congressman, the district will be awash with water projects. Western Colorado and Northern California were for a long time the political turf of Wayne Aspinall and Bizz Johnson. Long after they retired, their districts still have many federal water projects they crafted.

Both the politicians and the business people are assisted by the top personnel in the federal water-development agencies. To the public, the agency personnel present an image of dull professionalism, responding only to the demands of the people. However, behind their professional façade, top agency people hide political skills to rival the finest Irish ward heeler. Data are manipulated, public opinion formed and molded, key people in Congress and the business community quietly courted. Water projects do not spring from the nebulous demands of the public at large; they are carefully nurtured and promoted by a few key people and organizations, who often invest years of effort in one project. When they emerge for public review, key supporters have already agreed on the basic agenda.

At the core of the federal water-development problem are people who profit from federal pork. First are the construction companies, irrigation districts, and individuals who stand to benefit from the pork-barrel projects. Their influence is facilitated by election laws that permit political action committees (PACs) to mask campaign contributions. People who stand to benefit make campaign contributions to politicians sympathetic to their views and who are in a position to usher their favorite project through Congress.

Solving the many problems of federal water development

demands major reforms in how we view public water and land. Water must be seen as a vital public resource not to be severed from public lands and rivers without a substantial benefit to society. Politicians and the public must firmly accept the concept of public title to water. Once they accept a trust obligation to the future, the solutions become reasonable and obvious.

There are several solutions. First, the concept of water conservation must be studiously applied everywhere water is used, from urban showers and toilets to massive irrigation projects. Most of the western United States uses water far less efficiently than other regions of the world where water is in short supply. The waste is a product of federal subsidy; federal aid, which makes it cheap to use water, is a disincentive to conservation. Conservation such as Israel practices could open more land to agriculture without demanding more from a limited water supply. Such a policy is only prudent. Rainfall and snowfall during the twentieth century have been well above long-term averages, according to tree-ring analysis. We can reasonably expect long and devastating droughts in the future, which will have severe impacts without strict conservation.

Obviously, a major way to induce conservation is to require users to pay the full cost of the water. Full-cost payments would produce better management of water projects. In many areas the management of water, for political reasons, has benefited only a handful of users, although all the taxpayers bear the cost. The irrigator or power company has first claim on the water, and the public and other users usually suffer. A rational policy would consider an array of users, from recreationists to irrigators, fishermen, and waterskiers, and would balance the management of water for everyone's benefit.

A major part of a good water strategy would be to protect minimum flows on all important streams in the West. Today, power plants and irrigators literally dry up many streams. This would not be economical if developers were not subsidized. The public benefits of fisheries, recreation, and aesthetics are lost, although in many cases they far outweigh private benefits. The priority of uses must include instream flow protection for the sake of environmental stability.

A successful program that needs to be rapidly expanded is the national wild and scenic rivers system. The act that created it, passed in 1968, states that it is a worthwhile national policy to keep rivers in a free-flowing condition. The act permits either states or Congress to designate free-flowing rivers. Depending on the stream-side condition and development, the rivers are classified wild, scenic, or recreational. All classes forbid building dams above the level of banks, or other forms of development. Since the act passed, many rivers have been protected, but developers have prevented protecting other qualified rivers.

All water developers should have to meet new democratic standards, including a complete and thorough accounting of the social, historical, cultural, and environmental values that would be lost. The accounting must consider dam failure, the costs of repairs required for the project's safety, the true environmental damage, methods to mitigate the problems, and whether the benefits over time outweigh the costs.

The array of biological and physical changes large projects produce are seldom anticipated or studied prior to construction. We are only beginning to understand the drastic impacts that dams and reservoirs have on fish and wildlife. Some projects have endangered both plants and animals. In the physical dimension, large reservoirs have triggered earthquakes and landslides. Such processes must be part of the development equation.

Both geographical and temporal benefits and costs must be presented. The useful lives of projects are limited, and the life span must be clearly understood, as should future problems and costs to the next generation. Benefits and costs are unequally distributed geographically, too; all social and economic groups should clearly understand that process. Benefits and problems for local populations or minorities have been ignored in the past. That is a dishonorable practice for this nation.

Cost-benefit analyses and assessments of physical and environmental impacts must be performed completely independently from the agency that would do the construction. Today water projects are proposed, built, and managed by the same agency, which has an incentive to find a positive cost-benefit ratio to justify its new project, larger staff, and budget. The system invites dishonesty.

A more difficult reform will require severing campaign contributions from development organizations to members of Congress. Congressmen and women should, first and foremost, be concerned with the public trust, not the campaign chest. Obviously this is not the case. A major reform of land and water policy would require public campaign financing and prohibit people who stand to benefit from federal pork-barrel projects from contributing to political campaigns. It should be illegal to purchase political support. Today members of the key water committees in Congress are awash in contributions.

The final element of reform is both logical and long overdue. An independent institution is needed to undevelop large federal water projects. We need a federal agency to tear down dams and reclaim the flooded land. Many projects are built poorly, and others are approaching the end of their usefulness because of siltation, age, and other problems. For still others, the environmental and social costs far outweigh the benefits. Many large projects did not optimize benefits, but only foreclosed other land-use options.

A Department of Dam Termination would break down projects that no longer serve the public interest, are wasteful, or need redevelopment. The water level of these archaic projects would have to be lowered slowly to stabilize soils and vegetation. Historic monuments such as Hetch Hetchy Dam, Glen Canyon Dam, and Fort Peck Dam would be phased out, and the dams themselves could become national monuments to past wastefulness and greed. Redeveloping a river system would be complex and challenging and would require years of study by ecologists, soil scientists, wildlife experts, and other specialists. Reintroducing agriculture, wildlife, and plant species to balance the habitat would be a major question. Cleaning up and recycling the detritis of a civilization marked by beer cans and plastic would be, in itself, a considerable effort. Soil deposited in reservoirs could be recycled into productive use. Crews of youth, similar to the Civilian Conservation Corps or the California Conservation Corps, could clean up debris, plant trees, and revegetate. It would be an exciting challenge, easily more complicated and rewarding than building a large dam and casually flooding a complex riparian system.

In the end, the rivers would begin to heal themselves. New trees would sprout, and the winds would sow pioneer plants and animals. The rivers would carve out the silt and cleanse themselves. Fish would return, and so would people. Long-buried rapids would sing again to strong young boaters. Lost rivers and canyons would be brought back to life. In place of Glen Canyon, Hetch Hetchy, and Fort Peck dams would be a more complex and balanced system resting on conservation, intelligent management, and a sacred public trust in the waters of this nation.

Big Trees—Mariposa Grove

9

Forests and Foresters

In 1864, George Perkins Marsh published *Man and Nature: Or the Earth as Modified by Human Action*. Marsh, a remarkable linguist, world traveler and scholar, had served the United States in many capacities, including Ambassador to Arabia for Abraham Lincoln. Marsh's prophetic book focused on human effects on the land. The man and his book began a revolution. They also helped launch the environmental movement more than a century later.

Marsh studied how browsing goats and sheep had deforested Greek and Roman lands. Trees had many special properties, according to Marsh and his prescientific judgments. They brought thunderstorms and rain and protected people against malaria by preventing the passage of air fouled with miasma; trees reduced pollution. More accurately, Marsh noted that forests absorbed flood waters and protected mountain villages from avalanches. His warning on deforestation attracted the attention of many early conservationists and helped advance the forestry profession. He introduced an original concept, "But the vengeance of nature for the violation of her harmonies though slow, is sure. . . ."

Marsh wrote of how deforestation affected history; Julius Caesar burned the Gaul forest in the Roman war of conquest. Emperor Constantine built aqueducts and cisterns that supplied Constantinople with water, then passed strict laws to protect the watersheds, the Belgrade forest and springs that fed the aqueducts. Marsh's ability to translate historic records, observe changes in the land, and understand the cause and effect between humanity's impact on forest land and environmental problems was unique. Marsh, the restless intellectual, was a pioneer in both forestry and the environmental movement. In his thinking the two disciplines were in harmony with each other; a hundred years later they are essentially opposed.

American forestry's roots are in Teutonic and aristocratic efficiency, but the promise of public-land forestry is progressive and democratic. The struggle to conserve forests led the way for later battles to protect parks, wildlife refuges, and watersheds, resource values often downgraded by today's foresters. Forestry was once part of a progressive political movement, yet in recent decades has been noted for its conservative, even reactionary, response to changing social values, including environmentalism.

Forestry was once based on a firm gospel of efficiency and science, but the profession has in recent years ignored basic tenets of ecology and the scientific method. The national forests were the first large reservations created for the public good out of the public domain, but the Forest Service continues to resist letting the public become involved in the most fundamental decisions taking place on the forests. The discipline rests today on technical and aristocratic values instead of democratic principles. Foresters have practically worshipped a patrician and politically shrewd forester, Gifford Pinchot. But before Pinchot a quiet Prussian forester and intellectual laid the groundwork for American forestry.

In 1851 Bernhard Eduard Fernow was born into Prussia's land-owning elite. Fernow was interested in forestry and forest management from a young age, so he worked for the Prussian forest service, attended the famous forestry academy at Munden, and studied under the leading foresters in the world. He was an officer in the Franco-Prussian War and was by temperament an austere, realistic, patriotic German. His later pictures reveal a stern man with a bristling, handlebar mustache. His writings express a discerning mind with the instincts of a scientist, combined with Teutonic practicality and efficiency.

In 1872 a traveling American girl, Olivia Reynolds, met Bernhard Fernow. They fell in love and planned to marry, but when Bernhard took his girl to meet his aristocratic family, they were appalled at his common choice. He had a promising future managing the impressive family estate, but he chose to follow Olivia to the United States even though it meant the collapse of a promising career and the end to both his own and his family's ambitions for him. Forestry was unheard of as a profession in the United States.

After three decades of marriage, Olivia Reynolds Fernow wrote: "If anyone should ask me who was the originator of the forestry movement in this country, I should modestly reply, 'It was I.' If a certain young girl had not gone to Germany in the year 1872 and fallen in love with a certain young forestry student, who knows but that the movement might have been delayed for a decade or more? Said young girl imported the young forest candidate soon to become the first forester of the United States at a time when the very words forester and forestry were unknown in this country. . . ."

Fernow launched the first forestry research programs and played a major role in the passage of the Forest Reserve Act of 1891, which led to the first national forest reserves. He began the Division of Forestry in the Department of the Interior, then started the first professional forestry training program at Cornell University in 1898, and two years later helped found the first professional forestry organization. More than any other person, this studious Prussian introduced forest conservation to the United States.

The public was in a receptive frame of mind. The disposal of public timber lands, widespread fraud, and reckless destruction of virgin forests by fires and loggers helped prompt the establishment of forest reserves. Many people thought the American forests were going the way of the bison. The early reserves were considered essential protection against timber famines. Decades before, Marsh had warned of the ancient lesson of deforestation.

Teddy Roosevelt said in 1908 that the nation could live in an iron-less age, but not in a tree-less one. Public-land forest reserves were regarded as trees in the land bank. Under Roosevelt's leadership, nearly 150 million acres of forests were protected, the first sizeable reservations of public domain for the public good. Their establishment was a turning point in the history of public lands.

Gifford Pinchot was a close advisor of President Roosevelt's. On Pinchot's advice, Roosevelt moved the Bureau of Forestry from the Department of the Interior to the Department of Agriculture. Pinchot worked for years to bring about this transfer. Locating the Forest Service in the Department of Agriculture was a recognition that trees were a crop; they differed from corn or oats only by the length of time it took to grow them. After the transfer the Forest Service grew quickly, becoming independent from the political pressure Pinchot regarded as the corrupting influence in Interior.

At the time Pinchot was maneuvering the transfer, he was laying the service's political foundation. Along with other foresters, including Fernow, he helped organize the Society of American Foresters (SAF). The SAF was to encourage research and professional forestry in the United States, to aid in the political arena, and to support the policies and practices of the forestry profession. A major underlying purpose was to assure the Forest Service's independence. The society was highly successful initially. In recent decades, however, with its leadership drawn from the Forest Service, the timber industry, and academia, it is neither truly respected scientifically nor effective politically. Its policy recommendations have been cautious, struggling to meld the canons of forestry with the economic objectives of the timber industry and the politics of the Forest Service. To many trained biologists, foresters are as scientific as witch doctors.

Long ago the forestry profession gave up leadership and began defending the status quo. There are at least three elements in the Forest Service's built-in conservatism: education, recruitment, and promotion. The first is education. The number of forestry schools in the United States is very limited. In the West most states have one forestry program, commonly in the land-grant colleges, often in colleges of agriculture. Faculty traditionally are educated in only a handful of major universities that have doctoral programs. An incestuous pattern exists. Many academics started their careers with the Forest Service or the forest products industry and work in the public or private organizations during the summers. Often their research is funded by the Forest Service and is concerned with applied problems common to the profession. Most faculty are products of this program.

For their part, the faculty serve both government agency and the profession of forestry. They immerse the freshmen students in the tenets of the faith. The heart of these beliefs is that forests are for "multiple use." The centerpiece of the uses is commercial wood production. But people who profess this doctrine usually lose its complex subtleties, and when pressed, they will admit such a multitude of activities cannot reasonably be practiced on a single plot of ground. It is obvious to unbiased land managers that, as currently practiced, "multiple use" is for public relations, not for real forestry.

The second major belief has its roots in democratic populism: forests are to be managed for the greatest good for the most people. A right-sounding proposal, this tenet is usually altered in reality to provide the greatest good to a few local economic interests, such as lumber companies, an obvious compromise for a federal agency that is supposed to serve the national public.

A third tenet is that goods should be produced from forests for the longest time; in this way a "sustained yield" will result. This belief rests on the reasonable assumption that trees are a renewable resource and, correctly managed, can provide perpetual benefits. But the concept falls apart when the subtleties of a complex forest ecology are considered. Modern forest management is not very concerned with mature climax forests or the plants and animals that depend on them.

Another belief is the profession of forestry can improve on nature. Mother Nature's timber production is viewed as inefficient and wasteful. An acre of forest, properly managed with rapidly growing hybrid species that are harvested before they grow old, can be a veritable factory producing wood and fiber. The forestry profession is literally guilty of failing to see the forest for the trees. The complex values of ecology, wildlife, watershed, and spiritual sustenance of a mature forest are not part of an efficient forest. Increased tree growth is a forester's fundamental objective, but such growth is achieved at the expense of other biological communities.

A corollary of the improvement-on-nature theme is the tenet that to be managed well, forests are not to be "locked up." Foresters speak of "losing" land to wilderness when Congress has protected such areas. To a forester what is lost is the opportunity to meddle with nature, to improve on the basic scheme of things. This anti-wilderness perspective has haunted the profession and has left foresters perplexed by environmentalism's success. After decades of leadership in conservation and wise use, the forestry profession, and the Forest Service in particular, became the bitter priests of an outdated theology of managing public land for commerce.

Another aspect limiting the forestry profession and the Forest Service is how new employees are recruited. Standards for professional positions are rigid; specific course work is required. Entry-level Civil Service positions are offered only to people conditioned with the forester's view of resource management. Cooperating forces are forestry faculty and a summer work program that evaluates and selects only people with acceptable attitudes and values. The route to permanent employment in forestry is a major obstacle course for a young person. As a result, people trained in biology or ecology are not qualified for key jobs in the Forest Service.

A survey of Forest Service leadership revealed the results of selective recruitment. The agency was the most homogeneous of the federal land-management agencies. Nearly everyone in a leadership position was a trained forester. Only a few had backgrounds in other resource disciplines. Most came from a handful of universities, such as the University of Montana, Utah State University, Colorado State, and Oregon State. Despite years of equal-employment opportunities, all Forest Service managers were males with a middle-class background. Most were members of the Society of American Foresters, but only a small fraction belonged even to traditional conservation organizations. Fewer belonged to an environmental organization.

The basic field-management position is the ranger. He is the boss of a district staff and makes decisions regarding approximately a quarter of a million acres. Rangers are white males who think and look so much alike, a meeting of them makes one consider the possibilities of cloning.

Yet the Forest Service is professional, smooth, and sophisticated in handling diverse constituents. While the Park Service, Fish and Wildlife Service, and especially the Bureau of Land Management were ravaged by development-oriented political influence during the Reagan administration, the Forest Service resisted the winds of political change and kept much of its integrity.

It is this very aloofness and immunity to public pressure that frustrates the concerned citizen trying to change Forest Service policy. One has the sense of fighting a giant marshmallow. The agency's answers are always reasonable and cautious, the tone professional, the attitude compromising.

Even with compromise and conciliation, the Forest Service

staff have historically faced deep-seated resentment in some regions of the West. Not only did the ranchers hate the Forest Service, but Pinchot alienated Department of the Interior leaders by fighting with Interior Secretary Richard Ballinger. Eventually Pinchot's strident rhetoric offended even President Taft. Pinchot was fired, and his demise helped end the golden age of forestry. At the close of this era, the national forests totaled over 190 million acres. Pinchot went on to be Governor of Pennsylvania for two terms and lived until 1946. He defended the independence and professionalism of the Forest Service until his death, but his aristocratic manner and uncooperative habits had offended many people.

Even so, the Forest Service was conciliatory on early problems. When hostile western interests wanted all potential homestead land within national forests opened to development, the Forest Service compromised and accepted new policies directing them to open lands suitable for agriculture. This action fragmented forest lands and remains a problem even today. Some 1.8 million acres within early national forests were settled by homesteaders. Another 12 million acres were eliminated from the system by boundary adjustments.

Although the Forest Service was losing some land in the West to political forces, it was gaining in the East. The Weeks Act of 1911 authorized the government to purchase forest lands to protect watersheds, eventually resulting in more than 24 million acres added to fifty eastern national forests. Most of the lands were acquired during the 1920s and 1930s, after they had been cut over and were essentially useless for timber. They were originally reforested to preserve their timber and watersheds, but after World War II they became some of the most valuable recreation lands in the United States.

In 1916 the National Park Service was established. Pinchot had tried but failed to transfer all parks and monuments into the national forest system. When the Park Service was established, its first director, Steven Mather, a successful businessman and active member of the Sierra Club, was becoming uncommonly successful in selling the public on the benefits of national parks. He worked closely with western railroads and chambers of commerce to demonstrate the practical economic benefits of tourism. He also worked to establish new parks from national forests.

There are few threats more serious to any land-management agency than the loss of turf. The territorial imperative is a fundamental competitive force. Pinchot's followers searched for an alternative to national parks. They made providing outdoor recreation a function of the Forest Service to seize the territorial initiative. One program inaugurated in the 1920s was designating some areas as wilderness, not because the Forest Service agreed with the Park Service's philosophy of preservation, but to wrap the agency's most scenic and wildest lands in the mantle of protection to prevent a Park Service takeover. To this day, few things upset a forester more than losing land to the Park Service. Even designating some lands as wilderness is preferable.

Between the world wars, the Forest Service developed effective fire-control and cooperative-extension programs. Recreation projects expanded, but they were not a priority. Instead, the agency focused on and publicized the issues regarding forest devastation, including fire and insect problems. The timber reserves were largely withheld from production, in part because of the belief timber shortages were imminent, and in part because selling the logs would compete with private-forest owners. At the same time, the agency improved forest lands and recreation areas using the Civilian Conservation Corps (CCC).

Politically, the Forest Service continued its battles with the National Park Service, frequently over wilderness areas. Relations deteriorated to a new low when acerbic Secretary of the Interior Harold Ickes made a long, concerted effort to transfer the Forest Service back to Interior. The Forest Service's land management was clearly superior to Interior's, because Interior's public-domain lands, administered by the General Land Office, received little care or management whatsoever. Only after 1934, when the Taylor Grazing Act passed, was even limited management brought to the remaining public domain.

After World War II, the modern conflicts and problems began to emerge. The boom in outdoor recreation brought record numbers of people to the forest lands. Rapid population growth, better highways, more leisure time, changing social values, increasing disposable income, and longer vacations all combined to make record demands on the public lands. The bulk of the recreation hordes pressed on the national parks, but they also used the national forests heavily. At the same time, private forests were being cut for the post-war housing boom. Conflict was inevitable.

Once timber lands were in demand, the foresters were quite willing to open previously protected wilderness areas to roads and developments. Conservationists became alarmed. In some cases they advocated that wild, scenic areas become national parks. They began a long process of establishing wilderness areas through congressional action. The Forest Service consistently opposed both ideas.

The Forest Service pressed Congress to formalize with legislative action what the agency had used as its management guidelines for many years. The result was the 1960 Multiple Use and Sustained Yield Act, which defined multiple use and instituted into law the forestry profession's tenets of faith. Politically it promised something for everyone forever. In practice, the agency favored timber first and foremost.

Then, after nearly a decade of debate, Congress passed the Wilderness Act of 1964 and for the first time seized the discretion in establishing wilderness areas. The bill also provided the first mandated public hearings in the public-land policy process. Both points became major problems for the Forest Service. The period of great autonomy in managing public lands was coming to an end. It was the start of a difficult time for the agency.

While the Forest Service often boasted of establishing the first administrative wilderness areas, it opposed the Wilderness Act. It continued to resist and oppose every new wilderness area, or it supported only the minimal areas that satisfied even the most gluttonous developer. In the 1970s the agency administered two major wilderness reviews, the Roadless Area Review and Evaluation (RARE) programs, which were so biased and discredited that federal courts held both to be essentially useless for their purpose. A new generation of environmentalists learned to distrust and dislike the agency, which constantly and consistently distorted reports, information, and its own management processes.

The agency found itself embroiled in a national controversy over a subject it long had regarded as its own special area of expertise—managing timberlands. The issue centered around a management technique, clearcutting, which had found favor among foresters. Clearcutting is cutting all the trees at once from large areas, sometimes hundreds of acres. Clearcutting did not balance multiple uses. On the contrary, it was often detrimental to wildlife, watershed integrity, recreation, and other uses. Nevertheless, clearcutting was the cheapest and most efficient method of removing timber products.

In the late 1960s, first in the Monongahela National Forest in West Virginia and then in the Bitterroot National Forest in Montana, the agency was put on the defensive. The West Virginia State Legislature chastised the Forest Service twice for clearcutting ancient oak forest lands. Sportspeople and others were outraged at losing hunting grounds. But the forestry faith was stronger than public opinion. Finally, the Sierra Club and Natural Resources Defense Council filed a lawsuit, with other groups, to challenge clearcutting. The case was won, clearcutting was banned, and the Forest Service was left clucking with industry friends over the ignorance of environmentalists.

Foresters continued to insist they were the professionals and therefore the only ones qualified to make judgments on forest lands. In the rich and beautiful Bitterroot Valley, Forest Service clearcutting aroused not only sportspeople, but farmers and ranchers who found sediment from upland forest soils filling their irrigation ditches. A constant burr in the agency's side was a retired Forest Service Supervisor, G. M. Brandborg, who regaled the agency at every opportunity for what amounted to heresy—poor forest management. The agency grew defensive and launched a meaningless internal review that did not mollify its critics.

Finally Montana's independent and conservation-minded Senator Lee Metcalf asked the University of Montana School of Forestry to investigate clearcutting on the Bitterroot National Forest. Forestry schools, including the University of Montana, had worked closely with the Forest Service for years and had never been critical of the agency. The report, titled *A University View of the Forest Service,* was reprinted as a Senate document and was widely discussed. The impossible had happened. The report accused the agency of timber mining—harvesting the timber at such a loss of soil and other resources that the site would never again regenerate a viable stand of commercial timber. The Forest Service was blasted for spending more public funds for the harvest than it realized in revenue. In other words, the Forest Service was subsidizing timber cutting with public funds.

The agency's relationship with the University of Montana suddenly grew cold. Forest Service grants were not renewed, and privately the agency condemned what it regarded as traitorous behavior. The agency failed to distinguish the public's and the university's real concerns. First, subsidized forestry was unacceptable on public lands. Second, environmental impacts and public preferences made indiscriminate clearcutting unacceptable. Still the agency persisted. Politicians from Wyoming and Idaho became involved. Controversial hearings were held, and Congress set out to rewrite the laws for managing national forest lands.

At the time of the clearcutting controversy in the 1970s, environmental movement was sweeping the nation. It was the third wave of conservation in the twentieth century and was the most comprehensive, because it included the total view of the land, air, and water together as interacting forces. The fundamental principles of ecology, not the narrow precepts of forestry, guided environmentalists. Previous conservation movements focused individually on forest lands, water development, soil, or parklands. The environmental movement was different. Its net encompassed the earth and all life.

The Forest Service not only ignored environmentalists, but aloofly held them in contempt. Environmentalists were upstarts with no real understanding of the practical side of land management. Their concern with the aesthetics of land and life was a quaint reminder of past battles with the likes of John Muir and other effete snobs.

The Forest Service did not appreciate the depth of national concern for the environment, nor the impact the environmental movement would have on public-land management through the National Environmental Policy Act. Environmental impact statements changed many of its activities, but the agency resisted the trend toward more open and democratic decision-making. Foresters could not be experts when every concerned citizen could walk in off the trail and make his or her wishes felt regarding the management of his or her own land.

Finally, the agency did not perceive the balances changing among the conservation organizations. First, traditional organizations such as the American Forestry Association and the Izaak Walton League were no longer potent political forces. Militant environmental groups such as the Sierra Club, the Wilderness Society, and the National Parks and Conservation Association were gaining not only new members, but large, professional staffs. Finally, new groups formed that were impatient with the conservatism and old-boy network of older organizations. New organizations like the Natural Resources Defense Council and the Environmental Defense Fund dealt with the law, not cozy personal discussions and negotiations. Collectively, all these changes shocked and distressed the Forest Service.

Although most of the environmental decade's gains were made in air and water quality, public lands were affected. The Endangered Species Act required federal agencies to actively protect species threatened by development. The Coastal Zone Management Act reached far inland to change Forest Service cutting practices on the west coast. The 1972 Federal Environmental Pesticide Control Act removed some Forest Service discretion in spraying toxic chemicals on insects and shrubs. During this same period, the Forest Service lost land to the Park Service in the North Cascades and other areas.

The agency was embroiled in controversy. There were dozens of new wilderness proposals. The Roadless Area Review and Evaluation (RARE) I and II programs vividly demonstrated the Forest Service bias toward timber. Its policy of converting complex forest and range lands into monocultures for timber or livestock interests created even more conflict and illustrated its single-use orientation. The Forest Service could still maintain it was a more professional agency than the Park Service, and its staff was better educated and its decisions were based on more data than other agencies'. Yet the Forest Service was threatened by more groups than ever before. This time the agency was no longer considered to be on the side of the public interests, but in the pockets of industry.

Three years after the West Virginia District Court shut down clearcutting on the Monongahela Forest, Congress passed the National Forest Management Act. Foresters wanted the act to maintain professional decision-making and were supported by many pleas from their university and industry friends. However, neither the public nor Congress trusted its management, so they forced the agency to consider new social and economic criteria. Congress and the public essentially concluded that professional forestry could not manage public lands as it did private lands. A different standard was required.

Overall, the National Forest Management Act increased the public's control and regulation of national forests. The Forest Service still retained a large measure of management discretion, but it was clearly warned that its freedom had been restricted. Clearcutting was to be controlled, and a diversity of plant and animal species was required. Marginal lands were not to be developed where timber resources could not be economically justified. More important, the act's language assured perpetual timber supplies and restricted the Forest Service's ability to cut old-growth timber. Finally, the act required a lengthy, interdisciplinary planning process that would lay out the specifics of future forest land uses. A wide range of values were to be incorporated into the plans, including not only environmental concerns, but social, economic, cultural, and other resources.

Today management of the national forests remains far from ideal. The agency manipulates the complex planning process. The Reagan administration quickly reversed environmental reform efforts, and the timber industry, followed by stockranchers and miners, remain essentially dominant. The first priority for the public forests is private enterprise. The public bears the cost; the private sector enjoys the profits.

Inherent in the Forest Service is a basic orientation toward harvesting timber. Unlike other public agencies, the bias in the Forest Service lies largely within the personnel instead of archaic policies and laws. The basic management directives from Congress have been adequate for a true multiple-use agency, but the Forest Service's staff and budgets reflect the timber-industry orientation. Recreation, wildlife, water, and minerals management receive small portions of the total appropriations.

Part of the fundamental problem of the Forest Service is its innate conservatism and distrust of public involvement. Its staff are the classic technocrats who confuse and complicate planning and management to assure that they will make the final decisions. The agency needs not only foresters, but wildlife managers, recreation specialists, watershed experts, and people trained in the broader fields of ecology and environmental management. Having foresters manage public land alone is like having a dentist practice medicine.

Another major problem is that the Forest Service has been captivated by the industry it is supposed to regulate. During the Reagan administration, the appointment of John Crowell, Jr., to the key position in the Department of Agriculture overseeing the Forest Service did not excite much interest in the press. Crowell had spent much of his career working for the Georgia Pacific Corporation, the largest purchaser of public-land timber. He declared that when public opinion conflicted with Forest Service plans, then urban citizens and environmentalists should be disregarded. He argued that city residents, therefore most Americans, had no ability to decide what was appropriate policy for public lands. Therefore they should be ignored.

Crowell soon pushed for more timber sales from the public lands, which in effect drove down the price to industrial foresters. He offered longer contracts and more generous terms to the private sector and advocated that past timber contracts sold at high prices should be cancelled. Such political control of forest lands by special-interest groups and their representatives should be illegal; it clearly is unethical.

The politicization of the public lands is not new. What is new is the complexity of the issues, which masks the public interest. The forest lands do not have an ethic nor a political constituency that requires a clear and honorable standard for their management. Public lands should not be confused with private forest lands, whose purpose is obviously to make a profit. Yet today public forest lands largely serve as welfare tree farms for timber corporations.

The ideal national forest system would unquestionably be managed for multiple use, not primarily for timber harvesting. An authentic multiple-use program would give priority to future uses of the land. Exactly the opposite is the goal today; old-growth timber is considered "decadent" and undesirable. Industry advocates like Crowell often use terms such as "inefficient factory" to describe an old-growth forest, although these forests are now rare and should be treasured for their variety of resources. The wealth of the virgin forest is not just its timber, but also rotten log that hold insects, and the variety of plants, animals, and birds a young forest does not have.

The greatest wealth of virgin forests lies in its ties to our history and primal land and in the inspiration it offers, which is far more rare than sawlogs. Private forest lands can be made efficient, along with selected public land; all remaining pockets and tracts of virgin forest in public ownership should be left in their wild state, protected for the future. The same should hold true for unique forest resources, those that cannot be found elsewhere. Rare environments are as priceless as classic paintings or old coins. Their development degrades a civilization.

An excellent example is the spotted owl, a furtive bird that survives only in mature forests of California and Oregon. Birders can approach it because of its propensity to answer even an amateur's imitation of its call. Unfortunately, great horned owls prey on spotted owls that leave the dense and dark protection of a mature forest. In the clearcuts of a managed forest, the owl is an easy victim of the night. Yet John Crowell changed the Forest Service regulations that used to protect the spotted owl. He objected to the "loss" of timber, the same old trees needed to protect the gentle species. Crowell compared sawlogs with spotted owls, a commodity with an heirloom.

Another example of a unique resource being threatened occurred on Grider Creek, a heavily timbered roadless area on the Klamath National Forest in Northern California. The area adjoins the Marble Mountain Wilderness Area, is bisected by the Pacific Coast Trail, and protects a prime salmon stream. It also is the home of the endangered peregrine falcon, whose awesome dive for prey has inspired humans for thousands of years. The Forest Service planned to log the area, but the California Secretary of Resources, Huey Johnson, brought a wilderness lawsuit. Despite the lawsuit and federal court injunctions, the Forest Service repeatedly attempted to "harvest" the timber. It wrote a shoddy Environmental Impact Statement (EIS) with sixteen pages on the problems of dead or rotting trees and one sentence on the fastest bird on earth. Despite the protest of the U.S. Fish and Wildlife Service, the Forest Service failed to mention that foresters planned to clearcut the area surrounding an active nest of falcons. Only the protests of environmentalists and the California Secretary for Resources stopped the loggers.

True multiple use of public forests would give priority to fisheries and watershed integrity. The Forest Service harvests timber at the expense of salmon and high-quality fishing. Rather, at any point when the fisheries would be threatened by timber harvesting on public lands, logging should cease. Protecting soils, ground cover, and fishing is more important than the value gained by sawlogs. On the South Fork of Idaho's Salmon River, the Forest Service insisted on harvesting timber from an area previously subject to landslides, which wrecked extremely valuable fisheries. True multiple-use would protect endangered species and diversity of life as the highest priority, particularly since a non-economic orientation to the future is seldom found on the private lands.

A few years ago, a group of college students visited the Los Padres National Forest in Southern California. During a discussion of the problems the forest faced, one forester brought up the "problem" of the last California condors on earth. He pointed out management restrictions and difficulties in fighting forest fires. He then insisted that protecting condors costs over a hundred dollars per pound of bird per year. What the nation needed, he said, was lumber for homes. The students, appalled at his insensitivity to the rare birds, learned a vivid lesson in national forest priorities.

In 1981, Forest Service staff members on the Los Padres proposed extensive oil and gas leases on the forest, including wilderness areas, proposed wilderness areas, and lands within the boundaries of the Sespe Condor Sanctuary.

Ideally, the national forests should be managed in the interests of the national public. However, the opposite is true. Forest lands serve the local sawmill, chamber of commerce, and concerns of the local congressmen first. The national perspective, concerned more with the future, wildlife, wilderness, and true multiple use, commonly comes last. The Forest Service's public hearings and methods for evaluating public desires respond first to local concerns, except in those rare cases when a controversy gains national attention.

In timber management, the agency has had an affinity for clearcutting and other timber-management practices best confined to private forest lands. Complex environments are reduced to simple tree farms. Public forests should have a very different standard for all management of commodities. A harvest or management practice that conflicts with a non-economic public concern should be avoided. Instead, the Forest Service subsidizes private corporations and individuals at the public expense, rationalizing with the trickle-down theory of economics. According to this theory, granting public-land privileges to private individuals will eventually provide jobs and benefits that will trickle down to others. This idea provides well for the top layer, but in the meantime, the public values in those resources are sacrificed. Public forest lands should not always be managed for maximum economic development.

When resources are sold from the public lands, however, the public deserves no less than maximum market value for those resources. Free and open competitive bidding without hidden subsidies for industry would bring a fair return to the public.

Currently, subsidies are large. Range in forests, as on other public lands, is grazed by private livestock for a fee that is a fraction of what range resources are sold for on private lands. In the case of timber, the timber is sold under a bidding system to assure maximum returns. In practice, it costs the Forest Service more to administer the sale, build the roads, and protect the land from fires than industry pays for the trees. The result cheats the American public and is unfair competition for private landowners trying to grow trees commercially.

Part of the timber subsidy has considerable impact on the environment and on people. In much of the West, the Forest Service sprays the compound 2,4-D on the forest lands to poison brush and create a more desirable environment for certain species of softwood trees. While the evidence on all impacts is not entirely clear, the chemicals definitely hurt fisheries and many plant and animal species. The chemical may also cause birth defects and other problems for human health. Spraying benefits helicopter contractors and chemical sales but not local employment. Many timber workers feel it is at least as cheap to remove the brush with hand labor, especially if it is done promptly after cutting, without the secondary impacts of the chemical. Despite strong opposition to chemicals and employment benefits from safer methods, the Forest Service continues to spray large amounts of exotic chemicals on public forest lands. The result is special-interest forestry.

In Northern California, public forest lands are often used illegally to grow marijuana. The practice in some areas is the largest local industry and is ignored by local law enforcement agencies. Nevertheless, the Forest Service has used SWAT teams to protect its spraying of the region with 2,4-D and has considered applying the herbicide paraquat on the illegal herbs. Paraquat's environmental impact is unknown. Even its chemical manufacturer abhors the practice.

The public-land priorities are askew in many aspects of recreation management, too. The national forests are often used in the western states, through leases, for ski areas. At the base of these public lands, the ski corporation typically develops and sells real estate. Public lands help inflate the value of private lands, and the ski area pays a small fee for leasing the public lands but does not begin to share the economic windfall that goes to the developer.

Other problems are more direct. Early in the Forest Service's history, the agency leased forest land for summer homes and cabins. These leases, providing long terms and low rents, have persisted long after the high alpine lakes and scenic regions they are in have become overcrowded. The result is severe competition for public recreation sites, with cabin owners receiving some of the best areas. The Forest Service is reluctant to cancel the leases because of political opposition. Therefore the cabin owners treat the land as private property, and the general public is faced with no-trespassing signs and locked out of its best recreational lands.

For example, southern Arizona's spectacular and popular Arivipa Canyon is widely known by birdwatchers as the northern habitat of many exotic birds and is the site of an annual migration of ardent birdwatchers. The surrounding canyons and mountains are laced with scenic trails and hiking areas, but the canyon bottom, which is severely limited in size, is mostly taken up by summer cabins on national forest lands. The few public camping facilities are perched on the upper reaches of the canyon.

The ideal role for the national forest lands is not to serve primarily the commercial interests of timber corporations. The federal government has far too many resources to compete fairly with private land owners. While trees should be harvested from public lands, they should be cut only when it can be demonstrated the land and other resources will not suffer. The traditional forester is not suitable for managing public forest lands. Forestry must be replaced with a genuine multiple-use policy and administered not only by professional foresters, but also by scientists and land-management professionals from many disciplines. The public interest should be served first, with protecting the future a basic tenet of faith.

Sheep Raid in Colorado

10

Grazing
the Range

To the early pioneers, the Great Plains were like an ocean. In diaries, books, and journals, pioneers described Great Plains grass and hills as a sea with gentle waters. From the edge of the midwestern forests and the dark Mississippi River bottom land to the Front Range of the Rockies spread a sea of grass. From the Gulf of Mexico, an ocean of grass reached north to the spruce forests of Canada.

Spring rains bring water to the Great Plains. The big sky lowers until it meets the wide land, and the two seem to fuse during spring, when the land is bathed in rain for days or weeks on end. The rain makes small lakes and pockets of mud, filling depressions between hills and sometimes even on hill tops and ridgelines. The climbing sun brings the incredible greenness, followed by flowers and clouds of insects. The muddy ponds brewed a myriopod stew. For thousands of springs hordes of insects rose from simmering ponds and drove millions of bison to seek the balm of mud.

Tormented bison wallowed in mud and became agents of geomorphic change. Great Plains mud, gumbo-slick, coated their velvet hides and dried in the ever-present Plains wind. Millions of bison each year for thousands of years carried mud a few pounds at a time and scattered it into the summer wind across the Great Plains.

Later the wind and sun dried all but the deepest, most persistent mudholes. Lusty wind drove before summer thunderstorms, lifting billowy clouds of dust like prairie smoke from dried mudholes. Common wind and shaggy bison moved tons of

Great Plains soil. Buffalo wallows pockmarked the plains like moon craters.

Today the buffalo wallows are grassed over. The wind remains but lifts little dust from them. Still, the few depressions retain their unique plant ecology, a reminder of past herds.

But buffalo wallows were a subtle symptom on the land. The plains changed when the plow traced black lines on the blue-green sea. Prairie grass was replaced with exotic alien plants, flowers with crops, buffalo with cattle, all bound together with barbed wire. Only the sky and clouds remain of the pristine scene pioneers witnessed. Even the bisons' bones have baked and dried to dust or were collected long ago for fertilizer. Dull herefords, often packed in rank and colorless feedlots, have replaced the courageous bison, and the velvet hides of buffalo carry no more prairie mud into the summer wind.

Range management affects more land than any other single activity on the public domain. Rangeland problems are widespread throughout the West, but the impacts are subtle, almost imperceptible. The harsh appearance of the land belies a fragile environment. In the eleven western states, rangeland conditions are, as they have been since the buffalo fell, deteriorating.

The practice of grazing livestock on the western lands, 60 percent of which are publicly owned, is the least understood activity. Although grazing is widespread, on the public range it produces less than three percent of the nation's beef. The public is misled by the Bureau of Land Management, which touts the land's importance for "red meat production." Confusion is aided by the Marlboro Man image of the western stockrancher. The stockraiser who sincerely believes he is a conservationist raids and degrades the rangeland. Rangeland management is the most provincial natural-resource profession. More than any other group rangemanagers are tethered by their chauvinistic devotion to ranching.

Herding domestic livestock dates back 4000 years or more. It remains the most widespread agricultural activity in the world and, in its tenuous manner, one of the most environmentally destructive. The first domesticated ungulates came into the American Southwest in 1540 with the gold quest of Francisco Vasquez de Coronado. The thirty-year old Coronado was drawn north by fabulous tales of riches. With 300 soldiers, 1000 Indians, and uncounted sheep, horses, and other stock, Coronado reached the legendary Seven Cities of Cibola in July, hoping to find gold in the sun-baked Zuni pueblos in what is now New Mexico. He and his lieutenants searched throughout the Southwest and found no cities of gold. They left, in their disillusioned wake, a tradition of grazing livestock on open rangeland. Grass was a poor substitute for gold, but at least it was free for the taking.

More than one hundred years ago, George Perkins Marsh in his classic book *Man and Nature* described "grazing quadrupeds" and said civilization constantly brought with it "inferior animals." The buffalo were perfectly adapted for the Great Plains but were replaced by stock that used grassland inefficiently and lowered the land's capacity to support life.

Wild ungulates migrate, and their sparse populations seldom suppress native plants. The bison, which roamed the Great Plains from the Pleistocene to the arrival of the white settlers, migrated hundreds of miles each season, spreading their impacts and protecting plant diversity. Domestic livestock are bound not by the limits of ecology, but by their owners' property and understanding. The result is a concentration of livestock and disappearance of certain plant species.

Livestock are selective and prefer some plants; ice cream plants, the range manager terms them. The result is that those species are first suppressed, then eliminated, simplifying the complex native-plant environment. With simplicity comes instability, since diversity is the strength of a living land.

Once the ice cream plants are removed, the foraging ungulates select less and less desirable species. If they graze when plants are flowering, storing nutrients, and expanding their roots, the plants' vitality and growth suffer. Especially in mountain areas of the West, livestock often graze during the weeks most critical to plant growth and development. The gradual simplification of the plant environment may take decades, even a lifetime, or more. We see a snapshot view of the land, one freeze-frame in the ecological movie of a declining community of life.

With the plant cover removed and the environment simplified, the land is exposed to wind, rain, and sun. Rangelands are almost by definition too arid or extreme for growing domestic crops. In the western United States a lack of moisture and a short growing season characterize public rangelands. The soil is thin and usually poorly developed. In some areas the soil, like the groundwater, is a product of the Pleistocene. It formed and developed in moist conditions with abundant organic matter. Consequently, soil in some areas is like a living fossil. When it is lost, it cannot be reconstructed again; vegetation is its protection.

Exposing such soil to overgrazing is hazardous ecologically. Rainfall, scant and irregular, averages ten inches or less in many rangeland areas. In some years, however, torrential thunderstorms or unusual tropical lows sweep into the desert regions. In such storms, and in the spring after a heavy snowfall, the land is awash with water. The aboriginal soil is easily lost. Once exposed, the soil bakes in the summer sun and shrivels pioneer plants attempting to grow. Without shade and the nursery protection of other plants, the only plants that can grow tend to be thorny and unsuitable to any herbivores, domestic or wild.

The land's ability to support life is reduced slowly and, at first, imperceptibly. Erosion may be gradual but is as effective as a bulldozer. Federal records show the impact of overgrazing. For a hundred years the number of livestock grazing on public lands has been declining.

Richard Henry Dana sailed aboard the *Pilgrim* from Boston around Cape Horn to California in 1813 and 1814. In *Two Years Before the Mast* he reported the vessel picking up 40,000 steer hides in San Diego, Monterey, and Santa Barbara. In the early 1800s the range livestock prospered. With the rush of California's gold seekers in 1849, the stockraisers thrived. They moved their cattle into the rangelands of California and onto the virgin grasslands of the Great Basin. The great trail drives moved out of Texas north to the railroads and to plains rangelands. Cattle began to replace buffalo throughout the region.

By the late 1870s European speculation in western livestock had reached its peak. Cattle by the hundreds of thousands moved into empty tracts of public domain. Trails were built to drive cattle into high mountain ranges in summer and to open springs and seeps to them during the winter on the low desert. Indians' tribal lands were overrun, and the invasion was often backed with rifles. Within a few years cows or sheep occupied almost every acre of grazing land in the West. Dry and desert rangelands seldom visited by native wildlife were teeming with cattle. Rangelands suited for only one cow per hundred acres had one cow for every ten acres.

Native grasses soon disappeared. Then in the winter of 1886 and 1887 record-breaking storms hit the northern Great Plains and Rockies. The cattle piled up before winter gales in gullies and arroyos. By spring many stockranchers were bankrupt, and cattle had died by the tens of thousands. The grass was exhausted and could no longer fatten cattle and the livestock industry. The limits of a dry land broke the stockraisers' appetite.

The next phase in the western livestock industry brought sheep west to isolated and brushy pockets of rangeland. The woolly animals could graze plants and rough country unsuited for cattle. Herds moved into new areas as the lower ranges became depleted, causing bitter range wars that cost many lives of both cattleranchers and sheepherders. In the Tonto Basin of Arizona, more than thirty men were killed over a three-year period. In the Blue Mountains of Oregon irate cattleranchers killed thousands of sheep. The tradition that emerged was clear: the first one to the range had tenure on the public lands. In the eyes of most stockraisers, public land became their own. Homesteaders, like sheepraisers, faced the monopolizing cattleranchers.

The stockraisers had little respect for outsiders or for public-land laws. Every Act of Congress passed to help homesteaders was bent to profit the livestock industry. In 1883 Congress's first report on the public domain detailed stockraisers' illegal use of fences and general lawlessness on the public lands, which had become the industry's tradition.

One of the first acts stockraisers distorted was Abraham Lincoln's Homestead Act. Clearly the law was intended for bona fide settlers. But as a condition of employment, many ranch-hands were expected to file homestead claims on public range-lands adjoining the ranch. The hired hand then signed them over to the reigning cattle baron. Thus many western ranches grew and expanded using the Homestead Act as a tool. The 1887 Desert Land Act was even more suited to ranch enlargement. It permitted settlers to purchase up to 640 acres for as little as 25 cents per acre. Once the land was irrigated, the settler acquired full title for an additional dollar per acre. Boundaries could follow stream bottoms and riparian areas, creating irregular but highly valuable parcels. Since whoever controlled the water controlled the surrounding dry land, 640 acres were often scattered for miles up and down a stream. The person who owned a few thousand acres of well-watered land would tie up hundreds of thousands of acres of dry public rangeland.

Another common practice was to pour a bucket of water over a parcel to be claimed under the Desert Land Act. Then, at the local government land office, the rancher could claim to have "irrigated" his parcel. The legacy of lawlessness is recorded on the geography of the West. Ranches fence streams and prime hunting land, often preventing access to hundreds of thousands of acres of public land and hunting areas. The regional landed aristocracy that emerged, with its attitude of aristocratic lawlessness, dominates public rangeland management to this day.

The first controls on public-land livestock grazing came not from the Department of the Interior, but from Agriculture in 1905. New grazing fees and a permit system launched one of the first "sagebrush rebellions" when the stockraisers demanded federal forest reserves be transferred to state ownership so the stock raisers could be assured control. The move was unsuccessful, in part because the Forest Service successfully split the cattleranchers and sheepherders by favoring cattle over sheep. The move to transfer the lands failed, but it established a predictable pattern of response from the ranchers when their control over the rangelands was threatened.

From 1910 to 1920 agricultural prices were high, so both farmers and stockranchers pushed into the last arid and remote regions of the West. More acres were homesteaded and plowed during that decade than any other period in American history. For several years rainfall was above average, so the residual moisture nurtured wheat and other grain crops. The World War in Europe raised grain prices to record levels. But in the end, grain prices fell, the cycle of drought returned, the land dried, and both crops and homesteaders failed. The population in hundreds of counties declined decade after decade.

During Herbert Hoover's administration the stockranchers precipitated a second "sagebrush rebellion." The stockranchers, wrapping themselves with the righteous flag of states' rights, pressed for the disposal of the 200 million acres of western rangeland to the states or to the ranchers themselves. President Hoover, with his business orientation, favored such a plan. Various proposals were submitted to Congress.

The proposed plans soon split stockraisers and other public-land developers. Stockpeople, insisting they were the rightful owners, claimed the first opportunity to purchase the public domain. Soon they were arguing with miners over mineral rights and with each other over boundaries. They also insisted that no minimum price be set, not even $2.50 per acre. Neither the states nor the federal government could agree on the transfer, and the idea quietly died amidst the economic morass of the Great Depression. The ranchers continued to have free rein on the range.

Failed homesteads often returned to the administration of the General Land Office in the Department of the Interior and were then added to the ranches' grazing allotment. The cattleranchers continued to turn out a surplus of cattle every year, and sheepherders drove their flocks from desert wintering ranges to summer grasslands in the western mountains. The grass and land, overused, continued to emaciate and erode. Finally even the most myopic rancher recognized the need for rangeland controls.

After a long debate rancher Edward Taylor, a representative from Colorado, pushed a grazing act through Congress in 1934. In a classic example of western control of federal land, the Taylor Grazing Act retained the elite stock raisers' dominance using a permit system, a small grazing fee, and a weak agency to manage the program. From the beginning the agency, now the Bureau of Land Management, was staffed by range people who came from western universities and had ranching backgrounds.

Fees from grazing, although small, were earmarked for range improvements and local governments. Local grazing boards, governed by the largest, most influential stockraisers, would allocate permits and establish grazing levels. The act gave preference to stockraisers with base lands or home ranchers. Because the migratory sheepherders seldom held base lands, the war between the sheepherders and cattleranchers, which had lasted for generations, was over in 1934. With the Taylor Grazing Act, the sheepraisers lost.

The war between homesteaders and stockraisers was over as well. Once areas were placed in new grazing districts, the public domain was withdrawn from homesteading. In the words of presidential advisor Rexford Tugwell, the Taylor Grazing Act "laid in its grave a land policy which had long since been dead and which walked abroad only as a troublesome ghost within the living world."

For the first few years the operation of the Grazing Service suited western stockranchers. Secure grazing permits were institutionalized and the old rancher aristocracy continued its control over the public lands. The Grazing Service, weak and regional, funneled money and labor onto the rangelands. Staff served the ranchers like indentured servants. Staff dug wells and developed water to distribute livestock better. They built fences, usually at public expense, to divide up the rangeland empire and control livestock. They supplied equipment and materials to reseed worn-out rangelands and to plow and replant others. They fought range fires and trapped and poisoned coyotes.

For these and other Interior Department services, a rancher paid a nickel for every month a cow grazed. The same person might rent pasture for several times that fee from another rancher, magnificently insisting he received no subsidy from the federal government. The rancher's self-image as the last hardworking, most independent member of American society grew with the popular western movies. Western stockranchers, as Bernard De Voto explained, believed in their own mythology. No finer welfare system was ever developed. It combined aristocratic arrogance toward a public agency with high social status and financial rewards.

The pattern of control grew more complex as the years went by. Grazing permits were theoretically a mere license subject to renewal every year, but in reality, the "right" to graze was seldom challenged. Permits took on a ghost market value and were incorporated into the sale price of every ranch holding a permit. It was a tangible byproduct of federal aid.

Whenever a rancher retired or sold his operation, the market price was a combination of the base land value and the value of the federal grazing permit. Grazing Service managers sometimes attempted to reduce grazing levels to protect the soil and rangelands; legally the grazing permits were privileges, not rights. The ranchers reacted with righteous fury not only at the loss of public grass, but because a reduction in allotment meant a loss in the ranch's capital value. They continued to demand secure tenure rights.

Soon after World War II, the Bureau of the Budget began looking into various federal subsidy programs. A small but obvious one was the public-land grazing permits. The difference in cost between grazing on private and public grass grew more embarrassing each year. Over objections of the Interior Department and the domesticated Grazing Service, the Bureau of the Budget proposed to raise the grazing fees from 5 cents per cow per month (Animal Unit Month or AUM) to 15 cents. The ranchers were predictably outraged. Once again, following their established habits, they demanded the federal lands be transferred to the states. Wrapped in patriotic verbiage and in all the righteousness they could muster, they beat back the threat of fee increases. They proposed studies and programs to evaluate the "problem" of grazing fees. More than twenty years of the next three decades involved some sort of federal "study" of rangeland fees, which were left low during the evaluations. The solution was obvious: the ranchers should pay a fair local-market value for public grass. But politics are stronger than logic.

Nevada's Senator Pat McCarren took up the battle against the Grazing Service. He hammered the agency mercilessly at meetings, in hearings, and in speeches. The agency's budget was slashed by two-thirds and its staff severely reduced. The lesson was pounded home to the demoralized staff: serve the ranchers well or find the agency crippled. The "McCarren Reduction" became a painful lesson to the agency and one not easily forgotten.

Grazing fees were eventually raised slightly, but the agency remained crippled and demoralized. In 1946 it was merged with the General Land Office to form the Bureau of Land Management, a relatively obscure organization that oversees more land than any other but is still a regional agency. As such it remains a servant not to the nation's people, but to a region and to economic interests, particularly the western stockraisers.

The Bureau of Land Management was not so fortunate as the National Park Service, the Fish and Wildlife Service, and the Forest Service, as well as agencies such as the Geological Survey and Soil Conservation Service, which were blessed with dynamic, charismatic leaders early in their history. For the first year and a half of the BLM, no director was named. Finally a respected scientist, Dr. Marion Clawson, was named its first director. A scholar and competent civil servant, Clawson failed to provide the type of dynamic leadership other land agencies had enjoyed in their early years. The agency drifted and earned the epithet of the BLM—Bureau of Livestock and Mining. The agency was decidedly inferior in staff quality and lacked the esprit de corps of the Forest and Park services.

In the early 1960s, Secretary of the Interior Stewart Udall named the dynamic and courageous Charles Stoddard to be director of the Bureau of Land Management. Stoddard reorganized the Bureau and moved it rapidly toward professional management and planning. He inspired young, idealistic staff members with his vision of a multiple-use agency that would serve all the public, not just special interests. But he was sabotaged by provincial career staff members with close ties to industry and tradition. Stoddard was fired, and the agency drifted again.

Slowly even the BLM felt the nation's environmental ethic and conservation values. The post-war recreation boom burst out of the mountains and parks of the West onto the open desert lands. Especially in Southern California and the southwestern deserts, the Bureau of Land Management's resources were used heavily. Recreationists were not just young motorcyclists and dune-buggy riders, but retired people who began to spend weeks traveling around the Southwest each winter in search of sun, leisure, and open space. They found gates locked by stockraisers, springs and wells polluted by livestock, mining claims closed to public entry—all on public lands.

The problems inherent with Bureau of Land Management slowly became more and more obvious. Clearly, grazing was the most dominant use of the public lands in the West and was having a severe impact on the land and its basic capacity to produce life.

The BLM's solutions to overgrazing were expensive programs designed to benefit livestock, not wildlife or the public. Large tracts of the western public lands were plowed, burned, sprayed, and otherwise denuded. These lands were then fenced and planted with crested wheatgrass and other exotic species cows favored. Domestic animals fattened. Wildlife such as antelope and sage grouse were eliminated or severely reduced in numbers. The simplification of the complex and vulnerable arid-land ecology brought more and more problems. Endangered plants and animals in unique ecological niches were falling like dominoes with BLM's assistance.

The debate over the use of rangelands was compounded by an interesting academic phenomenon. The influence of the western stockmen was part myth and part Hollywood hype, but it was definitely politically potent. Stockranchers also influenced the western land-grant universities. The conservative colleges hired and supported staff members in animal science departments, range management, and other natural-resource programs who were inherently sympathetic to stockraisers. Agricultural extension programs worked at the interface between the rancher and the universities. Job security for extension agents, agriculture faculty, and deans came from serving the rancher client.

In western legislatures, line-item budget appropriations provided land-grant colleges of agriculture and livestock with the means to conduct "studies," a popular academic industry during the 1960s and 1970s. Many of the studies were at best pseudo-scientific and were designed with obvious biases, often to establish a need for predator control, lower grazing fees, vegetation manipulation, or simply the importance of the livestock to the state's economy.

At one point, many responsible wildlife researchers expressed the fear that livestock on the public lands competed with big game for the available forage. Before long the western colleges of agriculture were grinding out research papers to show there was no competition. Most studies were superficial and ignored the complex interrelationships between large herbivores and other plant and animal life. Other studies were plain silly. Out of this phony research the argument emerged that cattle were a wildlife management "tool" that could benefit many wildlife species. Before long, both stock raisers and academicians portrayed the cow as the finest friend of the western rangelands. Such a conclusion was ridiculous, but the ranchers had "scientific" evidence to rationalize their livestock grazing.

The story about the horse's place on the range reads differently. A small primal horse once roamed the Great Plains in untold numbers. During the Pleistocene Ice Age, this early American species of horse became extinct, one of many animals that disappeared during this era, which coincides with primitive people arriving from Asia. The horse came back to the West with Francisco Vasquez de Coronado and his men. Before long the animal began to run wild on the American land again. Soon it became part of the culture and tradition of the West. A horse was a swift and mystical being to the American Indian and was responsible for the flowering of the Great Plains warrior culture. Wild horses captured the imagination of many people and began to be a staple element not only of stories for girls, but also for men in the macho novels of Zane Grey and other writers.

When homesteaders failed, mining ventures ended, and the frontier closed, many horses and burros were released on public lands. By the turn of the century a million or more wild horses roamed the West. They were strong foragers and without a doubt competed with both wildlife and domestic livestock, but they were for many people a romantic and important symbol. They also served a useful function: the U.S. Army purchased the best of them for the cavalry, and each war brought renewed interest in the animals. Capturing them supported many small ranchers during lean times.

World War II brought a mechanized cavalry and an end of the wild-horse roundups for the cavalry, but not for dog or fish food. Such roundups were often cruel and offensive to anyone civilized. But few people saw the process or the cruelty. The number of wild horses on public lands dropped to less than ten thousand, and still the slaughter continued.

However, one day in the 1950s a prim, delicate, and sensitive lady was driving to work in Reno, Nevada. She was raised on a ranch, had married a rancher, and had lived all her life in the West. Frail and scarred by polio, she was tenacious. She drove up to a stop sign behind a stock truck loaded with horses bound for slaughter. Out of the truck poured a fluid. She first assumed it was water, then feared it was gas. Finally she was horrified to find it was blood. The load of horses had broken legs; barbed wire had been forced through their noses; blood poured from their wounds.

The life of this gentle woman, Velma Johnson, changed in an instant. Soon she earned the epithet "Wild Horse Annie" from stockraisers. She wore it with pride. Ranchers vilified her and professors joked about her, but she devoted her life to the humane treatment of wild horses and became a legend. Annie was first a lady, but she was tougher than the strongest rancher.

First in 1959 and again in 1971 congressional acts passed with her leadership protected wild horses from cruel treatment. Velma Johnson insisted the animals remain part of the public-land heritage, important symbols.

A band of horses galloping across the Nevada desert is a

tangible link to a machineless age. The dust stirred by the horses, the power of the herds, and the stallion's strength offer a glimpse of some power older than us, a power the Great Plains warriors felt when they saw Coronado's soldiers astride the animals. To watch a wild stallion run on the dry land with head raised high, nostrils flared, and dust rolling up from his hooves is to understand the craving of any earthbound warrior to ride such a force, to fly with the wind chasing dreams embedded in the soul.

Wild Horse Annie's first congressional act passed in 1959 but proved difficult to enforce, and the cruelties continued. She worked, organized, and successfully led the fight for another act that passed in 1971. Despite the law, some ranchers continued their tradition. A band of wild horses was driven over a cliff in Idaho and brutally killed in defiance of federal law. Stockraisers began to howl about the growth in wild-horse herds and the threats to wildlife and their stock. Exaggerated stories told at livestock conferences were endorsed by agricultural extension agents and pseudo-scientists of the range livestock profession. According to stockraisers, extension agents, and professors, the wild horses were breeding like rabbits.

Everyone, including Wild Horse Annie herself, realized the wild horse population must be limited. But the leaders of the stock associations abandoned their perspective in their hysterical opposition to wild horses. During this period Annie died after a long battle with cancer. By 1978 amendments to the Wild Horse and Burro Act permitted the management and disposal of surplus animals. Still the ranchers complained. A BLM study of how the agency allocated forage illustrated the ranchers' unreasonableness: 7 percent of all the grass forage on the public lands went to native wildlife such as deer, bighorn sheep, and antelope; 13 percent to wild horses and burros; and the remainder, 80 percent, to domestic livestock.

Not only were domestic livestock granted most of the food, but they have also been given the right to eat it without worrying about being eaten themselves. Predator control programs, a subtle subsidy, are designed to aid only the livestock industry. Any ecologist knows predators such as mountain lions, bears, coyotes, and eagles serve a vital function on wild lands. They are natural population-control devices as well as sources of inspiration. For the public, seeing a golden eagle rising from the carcass of a jackrabbit, hearing a coyote on a moonlight night, and glimpsing a mountain lion are inspiring and priceless gifts. But the stockraiser views the eagle, coyote, and lion as threats to livelihood.

Some conservationists would agree a mountain lion on the back of a colt or a coyote feeding on a lamb gives the rancher a license to kill. But stockraisers have gone far beyond self-defense. The entire Animal Damage Control Program in the Fish and Wildlife Service serves the livestock industry. At the end of the first year of James Watt's administration, more money had been spent to control predators by killing them than was spent to protect all endangered species.

Government agents, as many as 75 or 100 in some western states, use highly toxic poisons as well as the more traditional trapping and shooting to kill predators. It is a rangeland subsidy. An indication of the ranchers' influence was the plan to use Compound 1080, supported by the administrations of James Watt in the Interior Department and Anne Gorsuch in the Environmental Protection Agency despite widespread opposition and after being banned for ten years. The poison is non-specific; it kills all members of the dog and cat family and does not target the offending predator. It often kills hunting dogs and family pets. Although it had been banned for a decade, it was available and used by some stockraisers throughout the period it was illegal. People in Elko, Nevada, and elsewhere could purchase the banned Compound 1080 at local outlets.

Despite the stockranchers' pressures, the Bureau of Land Management was changing throughout the 1970s, although it remained inferior to the Forest Service and other agencies in its professionalism. A study revealed BLM managers often belonged to the Society of Range Management, a semi-professional organization largely influenced by stockraisers and other people whose orientation to the public lands is based on livestock. Some 40 percent of the BLM employees did not belong to any professional organization whatsoever, indicating they lacked a commitment to the scientific management of resources.

Nearly 85 percent of BLM's line managers have academic degrees in range management, forestry, or agriculture. Virtually all were educated in western universities, especially land-grant colleges that cooperate closely with the livestock industry. Fewer than 2 percent hold degrees in wildlife management, recreation, or a broad natural-resources discipline. Inherent in

BLM employees' education and professional affiliations is a bias toward using resources to produce commodities and livestock. Membership in a conservation organization is an indication of support for environmental issues and a conservation viewpoint; fewer than 20 percent of the agency's managers belong to any conservation organization. Only the Forest Service came close to the BLM's non-involvement with conservation. The BLM managers did not originate in an urban or cosmopolitan setting, either. BLM employees have the most rural and western backgrounds of people in the major federal agencies. The result is an agency orientation toward the stock raisers and their values, ignoring or misunderstanding the national public. No wonder the BLM has long been known as the Bureau of Livestock and Mining.

Despite the basic sympathy and nature of the Bureau, it made progress internally during the 1970s because of new staff. The agency hired recreationists, wilderness specialists, even sociologists and archaeologists. Each new professional added yeast to the internal BLM ferment. The contrast in many field offices became striking. One group of employees, usually the range-management staff, could be seen, coffee cup in hand, emulating ranchers. The signs included rodeo belt buckles, western shirts complete with a can of Copenhagen in the pocket, well-worn cowboy boots, and twangy western accents. The caricature was startling, and the similarity to the rancher impressive. However, one difference was in attitude; in the presence of an influential rancher, the BLM cowboy was deferential. The rancher was aloof and superior.

New staff were often products of the Earth Day movement. Their hair was often longer until singer Willie Nelson led the cowboys into a longer hairstyle. Their dress was casual but not western. Often they grew beards. Most startling, the BLM began to hire both women and minorities, virtually certain to have been trained in one of the new disciplines. New BLM employees were more oriented toward urban areas, more concerned with an array of land uses, and sometimes even concerned with conserving wilderness. They were not in awe of the stockraisers but saw them as only one part of the public.

The new breed of BLM-er was encouraging for the public. The agency was changing, although the leadership continued to be dominated by old-time values and range managers. The overall result was positive, but the ranchers and the miners resented the BLM's newfound concerns for the environment and for urban citizens.

Then after thirty years of custodial management, the BLM received a clear, comprehensive managerial direction from Congress. Internal changes in the BLM were institutionalized into law in 1976 with the Federal Land Policy and Management Act. At the time it appeared to hold great promise for the agency; later it proved to be a threat. The BLM Organic Act, or FLPMA as it was soon nicknamed, took years to pass through Congress. Most important it clearly established a policy of federal ownership for the lands, with a multiple-use and sustained-yield directive. For the first time, on 175 million acres of land in the West and an equal amount in Alaska, ranching and mining were by definition only part of the management objective. FLPMA included a badly needed wilderness provision, to steer the agency toward protecting wild lands. The act was far from perfect; badly needed reforms in mining and grazing policy were not included. However, other important reforms were there—consistency with local and state planning, wildlife management, wild horse management, wilderness inventory and protection, and a clear policy to protect the heritage of old cultures and historic sites.

The BLM under Director Frank Gregg began to implement these new directives. The agency slipped into obscurity again as environmentalists focused on the Alaska park, wildlife, and wilderness issues in the late 1970s. As new policies began to emerge from the agency, ranchers and miners realized they were losing their dominance.

The political response was both predictable and reactionary. By 1979 many ranchers and miners were raising the old battle cry: transfer the federal lands to the western states. The ranchers claimed the BLM was no longer responsive and, with little sense of irony, called the agency "arrogant." In fact the BLM was only trying to follow the new management direction given to it by Congress and the American people.

Once again miners and ranchers created a regional, irrational movement, this time widely termed the "sagebrush rebellion." It was an old refrain, but this time the Marlboro Man image captured the imagination of many urban newspapers and television stations. The "sagebrush rebellion" was portrayed as a new revolutionary force, although in reality it was the same old greed disguised as philosophy.

It had a profound influence on the BLM. Ronald Reagan pronounced himself a sagebrush rebel, and when he was elected he named another rebel, James Watt, as his Secretary of the Interior. Watt in turn named Robert Burford, Colorado's leading sagebrush rebel and a rancher with a history of trespass grazing on public lands, as the director of the BLM. Watt and Burford first intimidated the agency and selectively cut new programs from the budget. Then they began the tedious process of reforming detailed regulations to favor their mining, ranching, and energy-development supporters. Watt appointed some of the most selfish and best-known exploiters of the public domain to the national public-land advisory board. Not one respected conservationist could be found in Watt's appointees, but sagebrush rebels were there. Key positions in the agency were taken over by people with an industry orientation, and people who did not share this view were fired or forced out, or else they resigned with their integrity intact. The stockraisers were back in the saddle on the western public lands.

Within a year livestock grazing fees had been lowered twice. Fees to adopt wild horses were substantially raised to encourage using wild horses as dog food. Predator control was encouraged and wildlife programs reduced. Regulations were adopted to support the miner, the rancher, and economic activities at public expense. The BLM launched an energy-leasing program that proved to be the largest transfer of public wealth in history.

The land may not be able to recover. A hundred years of overgrazing have severely degraded the plants and soil. When ground cover is lost and the plant environment is simplified, the soil is lost, and the plant community cannot be restored. In the extreme case the area becomes a desert; this is desertification, the creation of desert. Widespread areas of the arid western rangelands, some 225 million acres or 10 percent of the United States, are now in the process of becoming desert. An area twice that size is threatened. According to a report by the Council on Environmental Quality, the basic underlying cause of desertification is overgrazing by domestic livestock. With desertification both plants and animals disappear, and the land becomes unable to produce. It is a net loss to the entire nation and to future generations.

Despite scientific reports and obvious evidence, the ranchers and their political allies continue to oppose badly needed rangeland reforms. The reason is short-term economic gain. Cooperating in degrading this public resource are range managers, biased researchers from land-grant colleges, the Bureau of Land Management, and western politicians. All efforts to stop spreading desertification ground to a halt with Watt's administration. Future generations will pay the price.

The problems of the western rangelands and the Bureau of Land Management are intertwined to a large extent, but not entirely. The solutions are political and institutional. Stock raisers have remarkable political power, considering they grow less than 3 percent of the country's beef. Completely removing them from the market would not cause a ripple. Their overgrazing is profitable because it is subsidized on the public lands. The subsidy encourages overgrazing, the loss of soil, and desertification. It also generates political pressure to continue the process. The ranchers' livestock have been and still are on a destructive federal welfare program. One simple solution is to end livestock subsidies on the public lands.

A just public solution would raise the grazing fees to a fair, competitive market value. For each permit term, grazing levels should be scientifically established. Once safe and conservative grazing levels are established, permits to graze should be sold at a public auction to the highest bidder. The State of California uses this process on some of its lands. Grazing fees are ten to fifteen times higher than the BLM's. These are public lands and the grass and forage belong to all the people. If the ranchers do not pay a fair market price, they are cheating every American.

The second fundamental change needed is to assure that true multiple-use management is practiced. Today the public rangelands are managed for a single use. But using the public rangeland is a privilege, and the first priority should be public benefits: water, wildlife, wild horses, and recreation. Only the surplus should go to private consumption. Any developments on the rangeland should be selected with a priority for those that do not use resources as commodities. All commodity-oriented changes should be clearly profitable for the public. The basic concern for every land manager should be first for the land, then for the national public and future generations. The last concern and obligation should be to the economic special interests. Today that orientation is reversed.

In an institutional sense, a fundamental problem is that the Bureau of Land Management, as a regional agency, is dominated by rural western values and policies. In fact, the agency manages a national resource. An institutional structure must be developed to provide a national and future-oriented perspective for the management of these public lands. The era of ignoring urban and suburban taxpayers should come to an end. If necessary, the Bureau of Land Management should be reorganized and combined with another national multiple-use agency such as the Forest Service. A major structural change is needed to end the domination of the BLM by western stockraisers and miners.

Another problem is that many recent members of the BLM's advisory boards have served only their own narrow interests. Service on such boards should require both a conservation and public-service orientation. People with an economic interest in exploiting public resources should be banned; the conflict of interest is obvious.

The education of land managers should focus on the fundamentals of multiple-use management and the integration of uses to keep the land renewed. Training should provide a foundation for a true national perspective. Leadership positions should be reserved for people with a broad and professional background. Grants for academic study and research should be directed to biologists, soil scientists, and ecologists who are true scientists, not advocates for a particular type of commodity use.

The standards for the use of the public rangelands should be simple. The plant, animal, and soil communities must be protected for future generations. In all areas where these resources are threatened, the land must be rehabilitated and restored, regardless of the expense. The test of a land use should be the number of people served. Recreation and non-consumptive activities should have the highest priority. Activities requiring renewable resources, such as livestock grazing, should be permitted only when they clearly do not compete with wild horses and burros on reservations or with native wildlife. Mining and other destructive activities that use nonrenewable resources should be tightly controlled and permitted only when land reclamation is feasible.

Finally, the only right that anyone should hold in the use of the great western rangelands is one—the right to pass the lands undamaged on to the next generation.

Antelope Hunt

II

Wildlife and Commerce

Some years ago I was a smoke-jumper on a large fire near Alaska's Yukon River and the Canadian border. An island in the river provided an excellent helicopter site to ferry equipment to the fire a few miles away. One afternoon, during a lull in the fire, I ended up on the island and decided to hike around it. The river was wide and swift, and the island's interior was dark and foreboding. On the far side of the island, I crossed the fresh tracks of a pair of wolves, clear and sharp in the muddy shore. I was excited by the prospect of spotting the animals. The entire island took on a new meaning; the woods held a promise of the legendary wolf. The rest of the hike I simmered with anticipation. Although I never saw the animals, even the tracks stirred a powerful vision. The wolf's spirit consecrated the island.

A few weeks later I parachuted to a forest fire on the Porcupine River north of the Yukon. The small fire was easily controlled, and my partner and I set up camp early in the evening. It was late summer; soon the evening grew dark and the sky cloudy. We were many miles from the nearest cabin or village. Deep in the wilderness a campfire takes on special meaning; by its warmth and light the two of us were quietly preparing our rations as the day faded. Suddenly, close by, a wolf howled. The instant the long and eloquent howl began, my hackles rose, and instinctively I drew closer to the fire. Several more times the primeval sound swept our little camp. With a mix of eagerness and anxiety, we searched the woods in vain for the creature. The next morning we looked for tracks or a glimpse of the animal, but we found nothing. Years later, the memory of both wolf howl and wolf tracks remain two of my finest wilderness experiences. In neither case did I see the animal; its mere presence was a priceless experience, a lifelong memory.

Wild creatures are part of the land, dependent on it for existence and renewal. But wildlife is more than the earth's bounty; it is precious to many people. Wildlife on the nation's public domain is part of the wealth of the land. The sight of a desert bighorn sheep, a glimpse of a bobcat at a desert spring, the sound of an elk bugling or a wolf howling is a reward from the American land. Wild animals have thrilled the human race for a millenium.

These creatures are also symbols of the freedom of wilderness. Thoreau said it well: "We need the tonic of wilderness, to wade sometimes in marshes where the bittern and the meadowhen lurk, and hear the booming of the snipe; to smell the whispering sedge where only some wilder and more solitary fowl builds her nest, and the mink crawls with its belly close to the ground."

But wildlife also represents a deep-seated conflict between the aristocratic and democratic uses of land. The conflict continues on our public lands today.

In the Roman legal tradition, animals in their wild state were like the oceans or the air, belonging to everyone and no one. When an animal was captured, it was the property of the hunter. The Saxon invasion reversed the tradition in England. William the Conqueror greatly expanded the royal forests. Commoners were excluded; only the royalty could hunt. The cost to the average person was great; during lean times families suffered from hunger. French historian Nonnemere wrote, "The death of a hare was a hanging matter, the murder of a plover a capital crime." In this environment the romantic legend of the twelfth century outlaw, Robin Hood, grew. He poached the King's deer, a deadly serious sport but a cherished exploit during times of famine.

English wildlife law slowly became more democratic. The Magna Charta in 1215 protected public fisheries in tidal waters. Later, control over certain wildlife was granted to Parliament, and it became legal for the public to hunt. The American revolutionary government essentially adopted the English system. The concept of a public trust in wildlife rose from the foundation of Roman and English law, and from the earliest days in our history wildlife was viewed as a common resource belonging to everyone. However, responsibility for it was neither clear nor simple.

On public lands there was no question initially about legal status. The abundant fish and other wildlife were a generous gift of nature for everyone to enjoy. In the face of such profusion, waste was a reflex. The decimation of North American wildlife staggers the imagination two hundred years after it began. Passenger pigeons darkened the skies, broke oak trees with their weight, and fed thousands of people. Their feathers packed mattresses and pillows. They are all gone now. Only their dry husks stare out at us from museum cases. Every generation since the last sterile bird died in 1914 in the Cincinnati Zoo has been deprived of its heritage.

The buffalo were like a living ocean; there were tens of millions of them on the Great Plains. They fed, clothed, and sheltered a thousand generations of Indians. They fell silently from the bullet's bite, first one, then a thousand, then by the millions. It was like draining the sea. Only the lone bone hunters gleaned the last crop of fertilizer from the ghost herds.

Now the buffalo are gone except for the ones in zoos or parks, or those grazing with domestic cattle. They remind us of what was lost and of the national sin of indulgence whose effects all live with.

The passenger pigeon and the buffalo are only two of the best-known examples of wasted wildlife. No one will ever see the great auk swimming along the eastern shore, migrating north with the spring; the last one's skull was smashed by a sailor in pursuit of profit. The heath hen is gone. The last old male was seen on Martha's Vineyard on March 11, 1932. The last California grizzly bear waves at the Sierra from the state flag. Gone are the Carolina parakeet, the Eskimo curlew, the Labrador duck, and many other creatures. The toll continues. Wildlife, which should be a renewable and perpetual resource, faces extinction because of humans' reckless land-use practices.

Clearing and opening land disrupted and changed environments native wildlife depended on. The impact was fatal. Opening wild land simplified the ecology. Often hazards were introduced. During the Revolution, Hessian troops were said to have brought a new insect to the continent, a fly appropriately named

Cedicomyia destructrix and popularly called the Hessian fly, which preyed on wheat and grain crops. Other creatures were imported on purpose to remind European settlers of their native wildlife and fish. The German carp, English sparrow, and starling found wide-open ecological niches.

On the public domain, the majority of the most productive wildlife lands went to state, corporate, or private ownership. Wetlands, marshes, tidelands, and riparian areas are highly productive and diverse. Wetlands are critical habitat for a myriad of birds and mammals. Many species cannot breed or live anywhere else. However, as national policy, the United States set out to transfer such lands to state and private ownership and to drain wetlands, indirectly destroying wildlife by destroying its home. Under the terms of the Swampland Acts of 1848, 1850, and 1860, some 65 million acres of the most productive wildlife habitat in the nation were transferred from public ownership.

Land Commissioner Justin Butterfield began supervising the Swampland Act and led the General Land Office into a morass of lawsuits. Inefficiency and corruption haunted the first two acts. Decades later, courts were still trying to sort out the mistakes and problems the Butterfield administration created.

The Swampland Acts granted land to states, which usually passed it quickly to corporate or private ownership. The administration was so inept that states received desert, farmlands, and timberland under the guise of swampland. One report charged that tracts "situated amongst and embracing portions of the Ozark Mountains" were part of Arkansas's swampland grants. Surveyors had found the tracts to be "too mountainous and hilly for cultivation." The acts eventually transferred an area larger than Oregon. Small grants were made into the 1960s, continuing the drain on habitat. The wildlife population has not recovered from the loss of wetlands.

Other key parcels of wildlife habitat passed to private ownership or were severely degraded by developers. The Desert Land Act permitted ranchers and farmers to claim irregular tracts adjacent to streams and watercourses in the arid West. As a result, most wet meadows passed from public ownership and were devoted to intensive livestock grazing and irrigated crops. In the western rangeland such riparian zones are the most important habitats, supporting the largest variety and number of wildlife.

The few riparian areas in western mountains and deserts that remain in public ownership are severely affected each summer by livestock, which is attracted to the same shade, moisture, and diverse plant community that makes the areas productive for wildlife. Even a handful of cattle on a large range will concentrate on wet meadows and along streams. Regardless of range conditions, riparian areas are the livestock's first target and are nearly always severely overgrazed. The domestic stock destroy plant cover, shade, and the soil's protection. Water tables are often lowered by increased erosion, and dryland shrubs invade lush meadows. Stream banks are broken down, and a grim sequence of impacts that began with livestock overgrazing depletes native wildlife and fisheries.

From sage grouse to song birds, and from raptors to trout, the entire spectrum of wildlife is disrupted and degraded. The problem is often exacerbated when stock raisers place salt blocks on the meadows, further concentrating livestock. Ironically, range-managers still boast of livestock as a wildlife management "tool." Sportspeople, generally tolerant of the stock, do not realize most big-game wildlife species in the West have been reduced to less than 5 percent of their historic numbers on public lands. A major cause of the decline is domestic livestock and how it changes the habitat.

On public lands, conservation and protection of wildlife has been split between federal agencies and states. Many early national parks, including Yellowstone, were established to protect wildlife. The Grand Canyon was protected not only for its scenery, but for the Kaibab deer herd. Early rangers, under the false assumption that predators were "bad" for wildlife, set out to eliminate mountain lions from many parks. They did rid Yellowstone of the wolf and shot other predators, such as mountain lions and coyotes, when possible. Although protecting wildlife was not the only reason for their establishment, many parks, as a byproduct, conserved wildlife.

Private individuals and organizations made the earliest attempts at direct wildlife conservation. One group, the American Ornithologists Union, began studying bird migration in 1885. Soon the little organization was overwhelmed by itinerant birds and asked Congress to establish a Bureau of Economic Ornithology. Typical of early wildlife conservation efforts, the program stressed the economic aspects, not the aesthetics, of wildlife. William T. Hornaday, the redoubtable wildlife conservationist, frequently lectured on the practical benefits of wildlife and birds in controlling insects, pests, and other undesirable critters. Wildlife had to be economically useful to justify widespread public concern.

The protection of wildlife at the federal level evolved into the Bureau of Biological Survey in the pragmatic U.S. Department of Agriculture. The agency acquired the mission of controlling predators and other threats to livestock and agricultural production. The Biological Survey was transferred to the Department of Interior in 1939 and became the U.S. Fish and Wildlife Service. It emerged as the manager of federal wildlife refuges and director of interstate and international wildlife programs.

The evolution was slow. Public land was first reserved for the sole purpose of protecting wildlife in 1903, when President Teddy Roosevelt started the federal wildlife refuge system with Pelican Island, a small spit off the coast of Florida. It was a modest beginning—only a three-acre refuge. Still, the island set aside to save egrets and pelicans from plume hunters was an important precedent. Most refuges since then have been established by the president, and beginning in 1947 by the secretary of the interior.

From the modest beginning at Pelican Island, both the wildlife agency and the refuge system grew. First the agency tackled interstate and international wildlife issues. In the 1930s, Congress imposed an excise tax on hunting equipment and earmarked revenues for wildlife research and refuges. Despite problems and contradictions in its basic mission, the Fish and Wildlife Service grew into a professional organization.

By the late 1970s the national refuge system, largely carved out of the public domain, covered more than 30 million acres, equal to the national park system. Then because of the environmental movement, scores of conservation organizations, and Cecil Andrus, an outstanding secretary of the interior, the refuge system made its greatest progress. First President Carter added 12 million acres to it by executive order in 1978. He established the Becharof Refuge in Alaska, one of the state's finest brown bear habitats, and the Yukon Flats Refuge, an outstanding waterfowl area.

Then late in 1980, after years of debate and the longest hearings of any public-land law, the Alaska National Interest Lands

Act passed Congress. The bill created some of the largest national parks, wilderness areas, and wildlife refuges in the world. The refuge system was nearly doubled: 42.9 million acres of lands were added in Alaska, largely transferred from the Bureau of Land Management to the Fish and Wildlife Service. Nine new wildlife refuges were established and more than 20 million acres added to existing refuges. Unfortunately, more than 35 million acres planned for protection were left out of the final act on behalf of development-minded senators.

At the close of the Carter administration, the national wildlife refuge system totalled more than 87 million acres and 400 units. The spirit Teddy Roosevelt gave to wildlife conservation was alive.

The refuge system is now one of the world's finest, yet the public does not know the lands. Most people are aware of Everglades National Park but not Florida's Loxahatchee National Wildlife Refuge. Westerners may know Montana's Charles M. Russell Refuge, but not War Horse or Lamesteer. Arizona's million-acre Cabeza Prieta Refuge is an isolated and wild area visited mostly by illegal aliens, the border patrol, and federal narcotics agents pursuing contraband. People who visit the refuge realize it would make an outstanding national park.

But establishing refuges does not ensure good management. One fundamental problem is the Fish and Wildlife Service's lack of a clear statutory mission. Congress has passed "organic acts" to guide the Forest Service, Park Service, and Bureau of Land Management, but the mission and direction of the Fish and Wildlife Service have yet to be defined. The agency lacks a vision.

The division of responsibilities between the federal government and states also muddies refuge policy. Historically states manage resident wildlife and set hunting regulations; the federal government manages habitat on federal lands, migratory wildlife, and more recently, endangered species. But the division between roles is not clear. For one thing, the courts have eroded the states' claim to manage wildlife on federal lands. Second, in the absence of state action, the federal agency has established game refuges to protect resident wildlife as well as migratory species.

Intergovernmental conflicts over wildlife issues materialize occasionally. The Alaska lands issue produced a major conflict between the state of Alaska and federal agencies over lands and wildlife. In addition, agencies often disagree among themselves over the management of wildlife lands. In Wyoming's National Elk Refuge, conflicting priorities of a nearby national park, sportspeople, and responsible land management have produced hostilities. Montana's Charles M. Russell Refuge has been the focus of conflicts over livestock and wildlife.

During the Eisenhower administration, Secretary of the Interior Douglas McKay, a former car dealer from Oregon, set out to abolish eleven Fish and Wildlife Service areas and to transfer the large Desert Game Range in Nevada to the Nevada Fish and Game Department. Based on past tradition, this would have been the first step toward converting federal refuge land into the personal estate of a Nevada political family. Aroused conservationists nicknamed the interior secretary "Give-it-Away" McKay and defeated his plans.

During the 1930s, President Franklin Roosevelt established several game ranges in the West: the Kofa and Cabeza Prieta in Arizona, the Desert and Charles Sheldon in Nevada, and the Charles M. Russell in Montana. Unfortunately, the wildlife-oriented Fish and Wildlife Services had to share administration with the livestock-oriented Bureau of Land Management. There were almost daily conflicts over the direction of management— for wildlife or for cattle. After nearly forty years the two agencies had failed to solve their differences except on the Desert Game Range, which had been physically divided between the two agencies. To resolve the competition, in 1975 Secretary of the Interior Rogers C.B. Morton transferred the isolated Cabeza Prieta Range, with no livestock grazing, to the Fish and Wildlife Service. Kofa, Sheldon, and Russell game ranges went to the Bureau of Land Management.

At that point an intelligent and tenacious conservationist was already planning a strategy to protect federal refuges for generations to come. He was Harry Crandell; he had been raised on western refuges, educated in wildlife management, and had enjoyed a successful career as an FWS refuge manager. Harry had seen desert sunsets, cattle's impacts on the desert bighorn sheep, and the frustration of working with a BLM staff intent on accommodating stockraisers. Most conservation movements involve dozens of organizations and hundreds of volunteers, but Harry Crandell was the center of a national movement. From his office in The Wilderness Society, he orchestrated the simple, direct, and immediate reactions of a coalition of major national conservation groups in a dramatic campaign to rescue the game ranges.

Conservationists' angry letters poured into Washington. Morton's transfer was considered not only a threat to every wildlife refuge, but a blow to conservationists' plans for major park and refuge additions in Alaska. Those new parks and wildlife refuges were to be carved from Bureau of Land Management territory because the BLM could not be trusted to manage wildlife refuges; its long illicit relationship with western stockraisers tainted its reputation. Harry Crandell and conservationists routed the BLM and its few supporters. First the transfer was stopped in the courts; then a year later Congress not only reversed the transfer, but gave exclusive jurisdiction over all four game ranges to the Fish and Wildlife Service.

Conservationists also secured one more vitally important element in the rescue. Harry Crandell shrewdly anticipated further threats to refuges in the future, so he arranged a provision to be inserted in the game-range bill abolishing the power of the secretary of the interior to transfer such lands without congressional approval. Congress passed it easily. The interior secretary was free to create refuges but not to destroy them. When James Watt came into office he, like "Give-it-Away McKay," considered abolishing wildlife refuges. Then he tried to transfer refuges to states. But he couldn't. Harry realized the likes of James Watt would always appear on the Washington scene, eager to sell out part of the national heritage.

The wildlife refuges enjoy strong public support, but the Fish and Wildlife Service—clearly the most conservation-minded and professional of the major federal land agencies—has never developed the staff needed to protect both land and resources nor mustered strong citizen support and political ties. Within the agency the refuge program has been a low priority. Only about one employee out of five actually works on a wildlife refuge. The remainder provide support to other agencies, provide administrative services, or work on non-refuge programs.

A product of the low priority and lack of congressional direction for refuges is conflicting programs within the agency. Wildlife refuges, which the public thinks are sanctuaries for wild creatures, are in a state of discord. More than 180 are open to hunting. While refuges are important to endangered species, they are often sprayed with pesticides and herbicides. More than 200 refuges are protected as natural areas, and parts of over 50 managed for wilderness, but, on more than 100, crops are raised both for wildlife and for cooperating farmers; they include not just grain, which benefits wildlife, but tomatoes, peanuts, potatoes, and mung beans. More than 50 other important refuges are open to oil and gas development. Some are open to timber harvesting, and nearly 100 have livestock competing with wildlife.

The agency that has brought the whooping crane back from the brink of extinction wipes out millions of birds annually. The same outfit that is clearly the federal government's strongest defender of wildlife measures its annual application of pesticides to refuge lands in the hundreds of tons. Charged with protecting endangered species, the Fish and Wildlife Service, under the Watt administration, began spending more money to kill wildlife than to protect it. The staff are highly educated and very professional, but the Watt administration repeatedly attempted to wipe out the agency's research programs despite their national reputation for excellence.

More seriously, in 1982 a memo was circulated to all refuge managers calling for new commercial activities. The goal for refuges was to be private profit, not public benefit.

The agency itself cannot be blamed for all the inconsistency. It has been the victim of congressional neglect and of callous interior secretaries such as McKay and Watt, who care more for developers than for wildlife conservation. Congress has added to the agency's responsibilities without providing the staff and appropriations to carry out the mission and has also given the agency some management contradictions.

The oldest and one of the most controversial of these contradictions is the predator-control program. Congress first appropriated funds for predator control in 1915. Since then killing western predators has become an established form of western rangeland welfare. Predator control is built into the federal budgets, institutionalized within the bureaucracy, and regarded not as a subsidy, but as a right of the livestock industry. The Fish and Wildlife Service oversees this program and carries out the operation not only on federal lands, but on state and private land as well through cooperative agreements.

The program involves shooting, trapping, drowning, burning, and poisoning hundreds of thousands of predators annually. In fifteen western states, the federal agents during any decade will kill a few hundred mountain lions, several thousand bears, tens of thousands of bobcats, and hundreds of thousands of coyotes. Periodically evaluated for its unscientific approach to wildlife management, the predator program has grown highly sensitive about its public profile and a few years ago dropped all reference to predators; officially the agency's work is now termed "Animal Damage Control", and the trappers and hunters became "District Field Assistants." Whatever their name, their purpose is to nurture not wildlife, but domestic livestock.

The agency has also developed some impressive techniques for reducing blackbird populations. It sprays roosting flocks with a detergent to remove oil from feathers. On a cold, rainy night, the birds die by the millions from hypothermia.

On the positive side, the same Fish and Wildlife Service operates nearly a hundred fish hatcheries, providing millions of fish for sport, and rears threatened and endangered species, providing additional protection for dwindling creatures.

But the problems facing wildlife are not confined to the federal wildlife refuges and the Fish and Wildlife Service. Other federal land management agencies lack enough professional fishery and wildlife managers. In the BLM, the emphasis is on range managers; in the Park Service, law enforcement is stressed; in the Forest Service, the foresters are everywhere; in all three, the role of wildlife management in public-land administration is minimal. As a result many land-management schemes, especially in the Forest Service and Bureau of Land Management, are highly destructive to wildlife.

In many areas on public lands throughout the nation, the major factor endangering birds and some other forms of wildlife is the use of chemicals and pesticides. Both the Forest Service and Bureau of Land Management have widely used the defoliants 2,4-D and 2,4,5-T, which, when combined, make Agent Orange and a highly toxic by-product, dioxin. There have been widespread impacts on a broad range of both plant and animal species, yet every year various federal agencies spray hundreds of thousands of acres with exotic chemicals to serve commercial interests. Some applications have contaminated groundwater and drinking water with exotic chemicals, some of which are suspected to cause cancer or birth defects. The application of chemicals for the purpose of increasing livestock feed or to encourage a monoculture is not multiple-use management and does not serve the public interest. As long as land managers chauvinistically believe they know best in all areas and do not include professional biologists and wildlife managers in decisions, wildlife on the public land will suffer.

Not even national parks are immune from foresters protecting trees at the expense of the rest of the biological community. During the 1960s, the National Park Service spent millions in Grand Teton National Park attempting to control the Black Hills bark beetle, which infected and often killed mature lodgepole pines. In the process, the forest floor was opened and land became more productive for many types of wildlife. To a forester the dead trees were unattractive; no one bothered to consider what woodpeckers and other wildlife preferred.

The Park Service foresters prevailed for many years. Miles of string were draped throughout the park's forests. Trees were tagged with bright identification marks. Each tree was sprayed by hand with a pesticide in a diesel-oil base. On a hot summer day, a hiker in the park would be rewarded with the reeking of diesel fuel. Finally a distinguished former park scientist and one of the foremost naturalists of his era, Dr. Adolph Murie, exposed the false assumptions of the program. He pointed out that parks were for nature's natural processes to work, not to be frustrated by chemical warfare. The spraying program quietly died. Yet every year chemical manipulation programs are hatched by various foresters and range managers, not for the sake of wildlife, but to assist people who profit from public land.

Almost every environmentally damaging process on the public lands subsidizes one special interest group or another. A simple example is the barbed-wire fence. Hundreds of thousands of miles of fence lace the public lands, virtually all to control domestic livestock. Many were built with taxpayers' money or from the small users' fees. Many of these fences hurt wildlife, especially antelope and big-game animals. It is possible to build and locate fences to minimize impacts on wildlife. However, stockraisers often complain about escaping calves, so strong and tight fences are built that trap pronghorn antelope in winter storms and that catch deer as they leap the wire. The wild animals then starve for the sake of domestic stock.

Another program in widespread use on several million acres of public land is "habitat conversion," a euphemism for converting a natural environment to one more suited to domestic livestock. It has devastating impacts on native wildlife. In some cases range managers spray large areas with herbicides to kill brush and other undesirable plants, then reseed the range with exotic plants. In the process the native wildlife habitat is destroyed, the chemicals pollute the water, and a rash of secondary effects appears.

In other cases the rangelands are plowed and reseeded with alien plants. Such mechanical techniques may be necessary at times to restore badly overgrazed and degraded rangelands, but the objective is rarely to benefit native animals. In many cases, the land could be reseeded with native species and done to support wildlife. Most commonly, however, the intent is to help a local stockraiser increase the grazing that is already heavily subsidized at considerable expense to the public and environment.

Another conversion involves the hardy piñon pine, which grows throughout much of the arid intermountain West. It is a small tree that was vital to the Indian culture once occupying this harsh land. The tree is also a linchpin in the ecology of the Great Basin and the Southwest. However, in the 1950s both the Forest Service and the Bureau of Land Management began a massive program to clear the tree. Hundreds of thousands of acres have been cleared in some years. The procedure, called "chaining," involves dragging a ship's anchor-chain between two Caterpillar tractors. The trees are ripped up, and the soil is plowed and exposed to the elements. Hundreds of long-forgotten Indian ruins and archaeological sites have been devastated. The purpose is simple—to convert nature's woodland to cow pasture on public land, at public expense.

A scholarly but feisty scientist at Utah State University, Ronald Lanner, has been one of the most effective speakers against this practice. Lanner researched the practice and found that more than 3 million acres of public piñon land had been converted to cow pasture. In several articles on the subject, he exposed the environmental problems and the futility of a federal land practice that destroys, on a large scale, not just the native environment, but also prehistoric sites protected by federal law.

Despite the scientific evidence, each year hundreds of square miles of public land are chained.

Water developments are yet another major disruption of wildlife habitat on public as well as private land in the West. Building federal and private dams in the West has drastically reduced anadromous fishing along the West Coast and in some cases has eliminated annual fish runs altogether, because fish cannot reach the upstream spots they need for spawning.

In other areas, the rivers through meadowland flood with the fluctuating level of a reservoir, damaging wildlife habitat and migratory routes. On a small scale, the Department of Agriculture's Soil Conservation Service helps build thousands of dams each year. Water developments constructed by the Forest Service and Bureau of Land Management for domestic livestock are even smaller but very damaging to wildlife. Although they can provide benefits to wildlife, often the agency staff or the stockraisers operate them only for livestock and neglect them when the domestic stock are moved off the range. Wildlife grows dependent on the water and does not move elsewhere, so it loses its water supply.

There are many problems related to wildlife on public land. Virtually every action that benefits mining, logging, livestock, and water development hurts the native wildlife. The result has been degraded habitat and a reduced population of animals, now a small percentage of their original numbers. The destruction of the habitat will continue unless the priorities of managing public lands are reordered. It will take a drastic land reform.

Healthy wildlife indicates a healthy environment. Wild creatures inspire and delight millions of people. Surveys have shown that the vast majority of the public enjoy wildlife. Piecemeal attempts at mitigating habitat loss from water developments and other damaging projects are not enough to protect habitat and biological diversity. Managers of the federal lands should give first priority to protecting and enhancing the native wildlife community.

Public-land wildlife policy needs a major reorientation. Too much diversity has been lost and too many species reduced in numbers and range. Many plant and animal species are threatened with extinction and face not only declining habitat, but fading support from the agencies charged with protecting them. The reason is simple. The economically oriented public-land managers have stressed domestic and consumptive uses of the land. Wildlife has been last. The priorities should be reversed. Wildlife has an inherent and fundamental place on the public lands.

The cornerstone of a comprehensive and future-oriented approach to wildlife management would be to give first priority to protecting, maintaining, and restoring habitat. Economic uses of the land would be permitted, but only when they do not irrevocably harm native wildlife. Non-game wildlife would become more important.

Consumptive uses of wildlife such as hunting or fishing would also be put in perspective. When such activities conflict with protecting endangered species, with non-consumptive use of wildlife such as birdwatching and photographing, or when they reduce diversity and stability, the priority would shift toward protection.

Too much has been lost already, but what has been degraded can be restored with careful protection and management by professional wildlife specialists. Their administrative role must be enlarged, and they should have a decisive part in all types of development on the public lands. They are better trained than most range and forestland managers in science and ecologically-sound management, so they should have more decision-making responsibility than they now hold, in recognition of their skills and their holistic perspective.

The role and responsibility of the U.S. Fish and Wildlife Service should be greatly expanded, also. The small, competent research arm of the FWS was severely restricted during the Watt administration because it had effectively documented the problems wildlife faced with commerce. Such research should be greatly enlarged and adequately funded. More important, the FWS's role in authorizing developments on public lands should increase from consultation to direct responsibility in decision-making. Such authority is especially needed on the lands administered by the Forest Service and Bureau of Land Management.

The importance of wildlife in our society can hardly be overstated. Wildlife indicate the health of our environment, like the miner's canary. Entire species now die at the alarming rate of one per day, a clear warning to the human race.

To protect endangered species the Fish and Wildlife Service should have more jurisdiction over the management of federal lands. The 1973 Endangered Species Act helped, but no sooner had the Act been applied than commercial groups began to weaken its provisions. During the Watt administration the FWS endangered-species program suffered major setbacks despite the *Global 2000 Report*'s warning that between a half million and two million species would become extinct by the year 2000.

Wildlife refuges, wilderness areas, and national parks play an important role in the protection of endangered species, but few of these areas have been reserved specifically for endangered life. No higher purpose could be found for the public domain. William Beebe, the great naturalist, wrote, "When the last individual of a race of living things breathes no more, another heaven and another earth must pass before such a one can be again."

Watt's free-market mentality toward wildlife refuges and public lands was anticipated by Aldo Leopold, who wrote, "A system of conservation based solely on economic self-interest is hopelessly lopsided. It tends to ignore and, thus, eventually eliminate many elements in the land communities that lack commercial value, but that are (as far as we know) essential to its healthy functioning. It is assumed, falsely, I think, that the economic parts of the biotic clock will function without the uneconomic parts." Wildlife refuges, like national parks, should be protected from exploitive commercial activities. They should be for wildlife.

It is imperative that the public-land wildlife policy reflect an ethic of serving all people. An essential element must be a reorientation toward commercial activities. William T. Hornaday, an avid if stubborn defender of wildlife for many years early in the century, wrote in 1914, "Let it be remembered for all time that no wild species of mammal or bird can withstand systematic slaughter for commercial purposes."

A corollary of Hornaday's view, in light of new evidence on habitat, is this: no wildlife habitat and its dependent species can withstand systematic commercial development. Protecting wildlife habitat should be the dominant use on the public lands, not commercial activity. It should be a keystone in a public land ethic.

Hornaday also wrote, "The wildlife of the world is not ours to dispose of wholly as we please. We hold it in trust for the benefit of ourselves and equal benefit to those who come after us. As honorable guardians we have no right to waste and squander the heritage of our children and grandchildren." But this is exactly what has happened on the public lands.

The Great Geyser

12

National
Park Lands

At Grand Teton National Park
I had spent months compiling and researching the park's complex livestock grazing records. Certain grazing permits had been inherited from the Forest Service when the park was established. These permits had been rightly seen as a temporary political price for establishing the park. But I discovered several permits that were obviously illegal, a result of inept record-keeping, poor administration, and blatant political pressure on the Park Service.

With considerable zeal I focused on these permits and began carefully crafting a series of memos to document their illegalities and reasons for cancellation. The largest permits were especially offensive because Park Service employees actually raised the cattle in the park. In addition, several thousand acres of public land inside the park were being irrigated for a cow pasture. But national park land was sacred space not to be used as a common cow pasture. Removing the livestock would begin the process of ecological healing and would help return wild park spirits to that quiet corner.

Many of my attitudes toward the national parks came from a renowned biologist, Dr. Adolph Murie. He had patiently taught me many things, but what I valued most was his concept that a park was a unique, pristine area where the forces of nature acted on the land without human meddling. To Dr. Murie, parks were imbued with special spirits. After working in six parks and many wilderness areas with his guidance, I developed a keen sense of the "spirit of a national park."

As a park ranger, I patrolled hundreds of miles of back-country trails in mountain and desert parks. I fought forest fires, stayed up all night on "stake-outs," and arrested poachers. I patiently explained the reasons for park regulations to hundreds of visitors—why their dogs could not run loose, why flowers should not be picked, and why wildlife was not hunted. For me a park ranger both educated and protected. Managing national parks was both legally and ethically simple and straightforward.

Finally, my documentation and research complete, I went to the chief ranger with my grazing report. Several cattle ranchers held permits, but one was unique. Wyoming's U.S. Senator Clifford Hansen held, in the Tetons, the largest grazing permit in all the Park Service—for 569 cattle. The permit had originated as trespass grazing in clear violation of federal law years before. The record was clear—the Park Service would have to enforce its own laws and regulations and cancel Hansen's permit and others like it. The cow pasture in the park would be returned to the wildlife. Adhering to law was the bedrock of national park policy.

The chief ranger was a tall, experienced man who carefully read my memorandum before he called me into his office. He clapped a fatherly hand on my shoulder and looked both concerned and sympathetic. "Young man," he said, "I don't care what you find in those records; as long as Cliff Hansen sits on the Senate Interior Committee, we ain't going to fuck with his cows."

Since 1916 and the passage of the National Park Service Organic Act, the basic purpose of the parks has been guided by federal law. Parks must "conserve the scenery and the natural and historic objects and the wildlife therein" and "provide for the enjoyment of the same in such a manner and by such means as will leave them unimpaired for the enjoyment of future generations." In my youthful idealism, I thought these words were not only inspiring but carried with them the best of land traditions. In contrast the BLM's emphasis on mining and ranching and the Forest Service's fixation with logging seemed grubby. But the politics of parks and the Park Service bureaucrats' compromises altered the ideal.

The vision of the national parks and the ideal land model they hold for public trust is important. However, for the reality even to approach the ideal, some drastic changes must be made in both public policy and administration.

Part of the problem is the agency, the National Park Service. It is charged with managing the many types of park areas and is also the leading outdoor recreation agency at the federal level. The public thinks of it only as the protector of parks, but a congressional hearing a few years ago demonstrated how far afield it had gone. Congressmen questioned high-ranking park officials about how they rid the White House of mice. (They used a mouse trap.)

The Park Service manages a large domain that has expanded greatly in the past two decades in size and complexity. In 1960 there were 187 Park Service areas covering nearly 25 million acres; by 1980 they had grown to 333 areas and 74 million acres, a territory half the size of Texas. Starting in the 1960s many eastern and urban recreation areas were added to serve the growing recreation needs of urban America. In 1978 the Parks and Recreation Act added 50 new areas to the system, most designed to help correct the imbalance in the system, because the largest and best parks were in remote areas of the West. The Alaska Lands Act in 1980 increased the lopsidedness by adding 10 new areas to the system, including the largest, with more territory for three existing Alaska parks. The total area added was more than 30 million acres, nearly doubling the size of the park system.

The Park Service manages the mammoth parks in Alaska such as Denali, Gates of the Arctic, Glacier Bay, and Wrangell-Saint Elias. In the western states it administers and supervises contractor-operators of Yellowstone, Yosemite, Grand Canyon, Rocky Mountain, and many other parks. Its mix of areas includes the Cape Cod Seashore, Ford's Theater, and the White House. Park rangers can be found at Custer Battlefield, the Statue of Liberty, and Sangus Iron Works. Half the areas the Park Service administers are historic sites. The agency has been chided for its inability to catch mice in the White House, for letting the roof leak in the John F. Kennedy Performing Arts Center, for starving elk in Yellowstone, and for poor squirrel management in Washington, D.C.'s, LaFayette Park.

Overall, American land policies have not been original. But there are two exceptions. One was the comprehensive land and water development system the Tennessee Valley Authority used during the Great Depression. The other was our national park system, a paragon of policy that started with Yellowstone, the world's first national park. The ideal of conservation that originated in the high, remote wilderness of Yellowstone spawned more than 1200 national parks and reserves around the world. It is a legacy the Park Service has held up to the public with justifiable pride.

The most idealistic mandate of any federal agency belongs to the Park Service, which has a proud tradition and a record of accomplishment that is the envy of the world's park systems. But a mix of ambitious purpose and expedient politics has tarnished the agency and left it, after an era of rapid growth and development, stagnating and lethargic. It is badly in need of reform.

National parks are established by Congress. Early parks were inexpensive to designate because they were carved out of the public domain or national forests; the costs of acquiring land were low. But because parks began late in the disposal era of public-land history and most eastern land was already privately owned, most of the early parks were found in remote areas of the West. As development pressures grew more intense, every new park proposal became embroiled in controversy and the competition for land. Each new proposal threatened a rancher's grazing, a prospector's mine, or some energy corporation's plans for development. Whenever economic interests were threatened, new park proposals were either shelved or compromised. In recent years the western lands have been managed by competing federal agencies, usually the Forest Service or Bureau of Land Management, which did not want to lose land to the Park Service. Developers had willing accomplices in scuttling park proposals.

But the Park Service has a powerful conservation tool other agencies lack: the Antiquities Act. The act passed during the era of Teddy Roosevelt. Congress delegated to the president the power to create national monuments from public lands that hold historic, cultural, or scientific values. With the help of any itinerant Ph.D., almost any parcel of land can be shown to hold scientific values.

Teddy Roosevelt first used the Antiquities Act to create Devil's Tower National Monument. Although Congress undoubtedly expected monuments to be small, the act established Glacier Bay and Katmai monuments in Alaska, together nearly 3 million acres. President Jimmy Carter, borrowing Teddy

Roosevelt's boldness, used the Antiquities Act to protect 17 national monuments in Alaska totalling 56 million acres because development-oriented Congressmen prevented the passage of strong protective legislation. Carter's monuments were superseded by the Alaska Lands Act in 1980.

Lofty purposes have not always produced good implementation. All too often Congress establishes parks or the president reserves a national monument while failing to provide adequate funding or personnel to protect an area. The very earliest parks were originally protected only by surrounding wilderness. Others were theoretically managed by the toothless General Land Office. Fortunately several early parks were protected during their formative years by the U.S. Cavalry. Some parks, such as Yellowstone, still have the unmistakable signs of a frontier army base. Yellowstone's park headquarters are converted army buildings, barracks, even horse stables. The cavalry built the first roads, trails, and cabins. They patrolled for poachers and fought forest fires. When early tourists were held up by stagecoach robbers, army scouts led the cavalry in pursuit.

Despite the army's success, the nation needed a competent civilian agency to manage the parks. Although development-minded Gifford Pinchot tried to gain the responsibility for the Forest Service, Congress authorized a separate agency in 1916. The following year Steven Mather was named the first director of the National Park Service. Mather was an early and dedicated member of the Sierra Club and was a wealthy and energetic Chicago businessman. He promoted national parks tirelessly during his tenure from 1917 to 1928, and the agency became popular and widely known. Mather's impact on the Park Service lasted far after his term; he was the spiritual father of the agency, a charismatic leader whose ideas dominated the first and second generations of park managers.

The Park Service grew and expanded during the prosperous 1920s as many new parks and other areas were incorporated into the system. Mather and his followers generated political support for parks and national monuments by promising tourism and economic growth for the rural areas of the West.

The complexity of management grew as the Park Service expanded. Originally its focus was on protecting natural areas. Recreation and tourism produced only modest impacts, and there were few serious demands on the wild-land resource. In

1935 the NPS was given responsibility over historic sites, battlefields, and even certain military cemeteries. The agency was granted the historic sites, many of which had been protected by the military, because of its innovative educational programs in the parks.

At the same time the management of national monuments was consolidated. Several early monuments that had been protected by the Forest Service were transferred to the Park Service.

Overall the Park Service grew slowly during the Depression and World War II. However, after the war American lifestyles changed rapidly, the interstate highway system was built, and more people had more leisure time and money. The result was an explosion of impacts on parks and recreation areas. As one response in the mid-1950s, the Park Service launched its now infamous Mission 66 program for construction and brought large, modern facilities to the parks and eventually even cloverleaf highways to Yellowstone.

With the explosion in outdoor recreation, Congress added a wide variety of new areas to the park system. Cape Cod National Seashore was added in 1961, then other seashores on all the coasts. Most new areas near urban regions required expensive purchases of private lands. In 1964 the Land and Water Conservation Fund made several hundred million dollars available each year from federal oil-lease revenues to purchase park and recreation areas, but most went on a matching basis to states, counties, cities, and to other federal land agencies.

By the late 1960s and early 1970s other urban-oriented recreation areas were being planned and developed. Point Reyes National Seashore north of San Francisco was followed by the Golden Gate National Recreation Area in and around San Francisco. New recreation areas were created in Ohio's Cuyahoga Valley in 1973, and in Georgia's Chattahoochee River and Los Angeles' Santa Monica Mountains in 1978. However, all of the new urban-oriented areas were expensive to acquire and presented the Park Service with difficult management problems. Old and experienced rangers who could saddle a horse, ride all day, and then fight a wilderness forest fire were not about to transfer to an urban park and face blight, pollution, and crime.

Outside the urban areas many other recreation areas were developing. Many Corps of Engineers and Bureau of Reclamation reservoirs were popular. The lands around many of these areas, such as Lake Mead, Glen Canyon, Shasta-Trinity, and Bighorn Canyon were administered as national recreation areas. Some were managed by the Forest Service, further complicating the federal land-management system. All required new recreation policies and construction projects as well as new personnel suited for law enforcement and mass recreation areas, not wilderness parks.

Most of the more than 100 areas added to the Park Service organization since the 1960s have been recreation and historic areas, not national parks. The management emphasis in the Park Service shifted from traditional natural-area protection to recreation and multiple-use policies. It was a seductive process, the result of political pressure. It began with compromise. At no place was political compromise more obvious than in Grand Teton Park.

A small Grand Teton National Park was originally established in 1929, but it encompassed only the Teton Range. Conservationists wanted a park that included the Jackson Hole Valley and Jackson Lake. Local residents did not want any park. The Park Service director persuaded John D. Rockefeller, Jr., to purchase more than 30,000 acres of private land and donate it to the Park Service. The Wyoming congressional delegation still opposed a park. After years of debate, in March 1943 President Franklin Roosevelt declared part of Jackson Hole a national monument. Congress retaliated by cutting off appropriations for the Tetons; the Park Service could not enforce its laws or protect the land. People hunted and camped as they pleased for years. Local ranchers, led by a rising young county commissioner, Clifford Hansen, moved cattle onto the park and grazed in trespass without permits.

In 1950, after years of impasse, a compromise was reached. Congress combined the old park and monument into one national park now known as Grand Teton National Park. The political price was that Grand Teton became the first park to allow hunting. Every fall hunters gather in the Tetons, sign a simple form, and become "deputy park rangers," permitting them to hunt in the shadow of the Grand Teton Mountains. When I lived and worked in the park as a ranger, the contrast of the hunt with the park was more than dramatic; it was painful.

All summer an old moose awkwardly graced one of the park's pothole bogs within sight of the main highway. His homely face and sedate feeding were both a surprise and contrast to the elegant beauty of the Tetons. Secure in the marshy haven, he let his wild image be captured by thousands of cameras as he grew tolerant of people in his last days. Soon after the park's hunting season opened, I walked carefully onto the newly-frozen marsh on a bitterly cold morning. The excited ravens and magpies were my efficient scouts. I knew what I would find. The old moose's dark hide was full of bloody bullet holes enlarged by scavengers' beaks. His body had served as target practice for elk hunters. The mountains still loomed behind the body, now oddly graceful in death, and the marsh was strangely empty without the rude presence of the old patriarch. The next spring I often chatted with tourists about the wonderful view of the Tetons above the willow-lined bog, but I never could tell them about the magic that hunters had, in only a moment, reduced to a pile of wet bones.

In the fall patrols looked for the black ravens in the morning frost where wounded elk had slowly bled, sickened, and died, to be found by the efficient scavenger patrol. Crippled elk, some with legs shot off, were a daily sight. Even the coyotes, commonly seen in summer as they pounced on unsuspecting meadow mice, were changed. Hunters saw them feeding on elk carcasses and mistakenly regarded them as competitors. The coyotes, tails between their legs, loped fast for the nearest forest haven or patch of brush. They learned fast or were dead.

Despite the problems and conflicts with hunting in national parks, more and more new areas have provided hunting seasons and even trapping.

My mentor and friend Ade Murie taught me about the spirit of a park, which is expressed so well by D. H. Lawrence: "But the spirit of Place is a great reality. Yet one day the demons of America must be placated, the ghosts must be appeased, the spirit of Place atoned for.

"Then the true passionate love for American Soil will appear. As yet, there is too much menace in the landscape." That menace must be purged first from the national parks.

Another Grand Teton compromise permitted within park boundaries a large reservoir that fluctuates each summer according to irrigation's demands, providing a model for many recreation areas to follow. The central purpose of an area may now be to develop water for commercial irrigation; secondary benefits are multiple-use recreation and establishing a project managed by the Park Service.

The final concession in the Tetons included accepting not only Clifford Hansen's livestock grazing, but eventually having the Park Service rehabilitate park land and operate the area as a private ranch for Hansen and his cattle raising friends. The livestock are still there every summer eating public grass, protected by park employees, fattening at public expense.

For the Park Service the lesson of the Grand Tetons was clear: establishing large national parks has grown controversial. Other large parks such as Washington's North Cascades and the Redwoods National Park in California made major concessions to industry. Still other national parks, such as the Sawtooths in Idaho and Nevada's Great Basin, have not materialized so far. In those cases the Forest Service has successfully headed off the threat of a park by political maneuvers and by managing its land for outdoor recreation. The purity of the original parks was diluted by the promise of something for everyone. Relaxing park principles did not end the threats to parks; instead, the problems of parks and monuments were only beginning.

The simple mission of protecting park lands grew more and more complicated. Originally an area was protected from hunters, livestock, insects, fires, and the impacts of people. Fires were fought and suppressed, insects were sprayed, and even predators were hunted. Evolving park management came to regard natural communities as dynamic, not static. Fire was considered beneficial to some plant and animal species, insect outbreaks were understood as natural cycles, and changes in the land were seen as part of the earth's normal processes.

Unfortunately, however, Park Service policy toward change is often not based on scientific data. The agency lacks the research arm enjoyed by the Forest Service, and trained Park Service scientists are few and poorly financed. The lack of research capacity grew into a major handicap in recent years; when the agency shifted policy, it was often only following an ecological fad or a politically expedient trend.

All federal agencies are political, but resource professionals consider the Park Service the most subservient to Washington politics. The agency's record in the Grand Tetons and elsewhere shows how easily the Park Service capitulates to political pressure. While some Park Service directors have been promoted from the ranks, many top administrators have been blatantly political. President Nixon appointed White House advance man Ron Walker to the top position, demoralizing many career staff. During the pro-development administration of James Watt, many people regarded the appointment of pliable career man Russ Dickenson to the top position as clear evidence of his willingness to compromise. The submissiveness of top Park Service officials has tarnished the agency's reputation. An ideal land management agency requires a principled director, not one with facile political skills.

In the area of commercial operations in parks, the agency has grown notorious for cooperating with park concessioners. After congressional hearings on companies that provide lodging and other services in parks, Congressman Henry Reuss said, "Our investigations thus far suggest that the concessions, not the National Park Service, are running the National Parks." When the first Yosemite National Park master plan was developed, it had been practically written by the concessioner, Music Corporation of America. A howl of citizen protests sent the agency back to the drawing boards.

Park Service political influence includes a set of VIP houses. Jimmy Carter and James Watt have used Grand Teton's Brinkerhoff Cabin. Shenandoah National Park has Camp Hoover, Cape Hatteras has the Pink House, and Rocky Mountain National Park has the Hofmeister House. The VIP houses attract congressmen and other influential visitors, and a peaceful park setting becomes an opportune place to present the Park Service viewpoint on budgets and policies.

The behavior of the agency in the face of tough decisions has also damaged its record. Most permits for Grand Canyon boaters have been earmarked for influential commercial operators, not the public at large. Environmentally damaging grazing has been continued and defended not only in the Grand Tetons, but in many other parks as well.

In some areas, the agency has closed out small landowners while ignoring the largest, most influential property owners. In Grand Teton, small and politically weak stockraisers were forced out of the park. But Senator Hansen's permits were defended and records were altered to support his subsidized operation. Small landowners in the Tetons were threatened with condemnation for their private parcels, but the Rockefeller family quietly held more than a thousand acres, one of the largest private inholdings in any park. (The Rockefellers gave away 30,000 acres, but a family organization operates the Grand Teton Park concessions.) In many other parks the agency has capitulated to commercial interests at the expense of the public trust.

In part the problem of managing national parks rests with educating and training NPS employees. In other agencies such as the Fish and Wildlife Service, employees have a common educational background and common resource-management principles. The Forest Service has taken this commonality to an extreme and turned an advantage into a disadvantage, much as it turns a forest into a tree farm. Requiring employees to have standard professional training is nevertheless a good idea. The Fish and Wildlife Service employee's first impulse on a federal refuge is to protect wildlife, although this purpose may be modified by political influence. The Park Service staff, on the other hand, lack uniform professional training and experience or a standard of professional park management. As a result, their management is amateurish and political.

A study I made of federal land-agency managers revealed some striking contrasts between the Park Service and other agencies. For example, virtually all Forest Service managers held degrees in natural resources, usually forestry. But more Park Service managers were trained in liberal arts, education, or even police science than in natural resources or park management.

In addition, professional involvement is a good method of continuing education. Almost every profession encourages its members to keep abreast of changes in the discipline. Foresters and wildlife staff belonged to such organizations as the Society of American Foresters—which is less than perfect but does have merits and is the only available professional organization—or The Wildlife Society. Approximately 95 percent of Forest Service managers and 75 percent of Fish and Wildlife Service managers belonged to a professional organization; fewer than 20 percent of Park Service managers did.

Another problem facing the Park Service is that its staff is isolated from conservation groups, which have been its strongest supporters. While 75 percent of Fish and Wildlife Service employees belonged to conservation groups, less than 40 percent of Park Service employees did. Only the Bureau of Land Management was less involved with sympathetic conservation organizations. Part of the Forest Service's success in maintaining its independence has been its ability to develop support from professionals and conservationists outside the organization. The Park Service has failed to do so.

Physical isolation has also hindered the Park Service in adapting to changes. Both the BLM and Forest Service integrate their employees into the nearby communities. The employees are part of the community and understand local concerns and values. In contrast the Park Service has developed its own communities within the parks. Moose and Mammoth, Wyoming, and many other park headquarters are essentially company towns whose social life is tied to the agency. As a result, interaction with outsiders is minimized, and the staff often develops a fortress mentality. In the early 1960s Assistant Interior Secretary John Carver, Jr., accused Park Service employees of "being wrapped up in their own mysticism." Carver's remarks created a storm of controversy within the service because they hit close to the truth.

With the passing years, the insularity and mysticism Carver described have become more obvious and have generated confusion. With the emergence of historic areas, urban parks, and national recreation areas, what was once a clear and concise protection policy has become a hodgepodge of conflicting policies.

For example, one park may shoot exotic animals to restore the natural environment; another park may tolerate them. The Grand Canyon has aggressively removed feral burros, which are exceedingly destructive of the habitat native wildlife needs. Yet at Death Valley National Monument, burros have overgrazed, trampled, and polluted every spring and waterhole in the backcountry. Wild pigs in the Great Smokies National Park are undoubtedly damaging the land, but politics prevents their removal.

The Park Service also remains aloof from other organizations and land-management agencies. In many parks rangers share more information with the Federal Bureau of Investigation than with the Forest Service and prefer discussing their revolvers with border patrolmen to talking about resource management with BLM employees.

After the anti-war demonstrations of the 1960s, the Park Service trained and staffed its own SWAT team. Yosemite National Park had experienced a riot in reaction to its strong-arm tactics against youthful visitors, so in response the park developed a riot plan and trained both rangers and patrol horses how to cope with riots. Tough mountain ponies were traded for sleek riot-control horses. Yosemite also spent nearly $100,000 on a new jail.

A new type of park ranger emerged, trained in law enforcement, not ecology. The new rangers were more interested in firearms than flowers, more oriented toward hand-to-hand combat than mountain-climbing or hiking. They wanted more training in drug enforcement than in interpretation techniques and were more likely to read the latest law-enforcement equipment bulletin than an L.L. Bean catalog. Instead of protecting people from the park's environment and the environment from people, the new rangers concentrated on conflicts among people. They were more suited to be urban police than resource managers or conservation officers.

Other federal land agencies found alternatives to law-enforcement training and arming. The Forest Service, with many recreation areas near urban areas, contracted with local law-enforcement officials for patrols of its campgrounds. Other agencies used a handful of law-enforcement specialists and relied on federal police agencies in a crisis. But the Park Service trained all field staff in law enforcement and lost its focus on protecting the natural environment. The park environments suffered.

The public thinks the park ranger is a skilled outdoorsperson capable of wilderness rescue and outdoor activities. In the past many rangers, especially in western parks, were trained mountain climbers, scuba divers, and fire fighters as well as skilled naturalists capable of identifying wildlife and natural features. Much of that orientation was lost in the 1970s as new rangers were hired largely for their police skills and ability to handle firearms.

The rangers also changed with the acquisition of urban parks. Rangers with outdoor skills who wanted a career in resource management were reluctant to accept transfers to new urban parks or to administrative positions in Washington. As a result many of the most talented rangers now prefer to stay at lower grades while ambitious but unskilled people rise to supervisory levels. A type of selective promotion takes place, creating an agency schizophrenia. Top bureaucrats often have little field experience and minimal affection for wild areas. Lower-level field personnel hold the most cherished values of the agency but are overruled for political expediency. Park administration at regional or national levels is notably unimpressive.

Recently even Congress has lost its patience with the Park Service. A congressional staff report blasted the administration of National Park Service planning programs. "The investigation staff believes any program resulting from a process as disrespected, as untrustworthy as the NPS planning process obviously lacks reliability for congressional use in the appropriations process.... The NPS should take immediate steps to improve the quality of its management at all levels." The combination of political expediency, fuzzy principles, and inadequate training makes that directive difficult to achieve.

However, not all the Park Service's problems are internal. Outside environmental impacts threaten many of the finest parks, and local park officials are legally powerless to do anything about them—such as air-pollution, clearcutting, subdivisions, coal mines, and power plants adjacent to their parks.

Many of the most spectacular parks, such as Bryce Canyon and Grand Canyon, will be seriously affected by air pollution in the years ahead. Under the administration of James Watt, new parks were opened to snowmobiles, although the field staff protested and worked to scuttle the plans. After years of struggling with local political forces bent on opening Grand Teton's airport to jet aircraft, park officials thought the entire air operation would be phased out. Then Watt took over and gave the local Chamber of Commerce assurances that the park would be open to jets.

Commerce inside parks is a problem, too. Park planners struggled for years with the problem of motorboats on Grand Canyon's Colorado River. They drafted plans and measured public opinion, which—on the whole—opposed motors in the Canyon. Conservation organizations supported phasing out motorboats and increasing the general public share of river use. Planners agreed. But Utah's Senator Orrin Hatch, whose campaign coffers were enriched by commercial users of the public lands, attached a rider to the Interior appropriation bill to keep the motors. For his part, James Watt boated down the Canyon and supported motors, even helicopters, to tour the area. The Grand Canyon bored him.

Watt brought enemies of the parks into his administration. He appointed to the National Park Service Advisory Board Charles Cushman, a landholder in a park who was widely known for opposing professional park management, for attempting to block park acquisition, and for holding the parks for ransom. Watt urged park concessioners and businesspeople to come to him if they had a problem with the park managers; he would take care of business. He cut off funds for all new areas, then blamed Democrats for ruining the parks.

Watt has not been the parks' only antagonist. Other agencies, especially the Forest Service, often block park officials' efforts to expand parks or to protect the public resources. For example Lassen Volcanic National Park has several hot springs and geothermal features that are important public resources, and in other places geothermal development has affected geothermal features miles away, but Forest Service managers overruled park concerns, public opinion, and protests from the State of California and leased surrounding forest lands for geothermal development. The Forest Service planned to lease geothermal areas next to Yellowstone Park until it was blocked by congressional protests.

Not all forces are obstructionist. The Park Service has a vast reservoir of public support it can mobilize at any time to protect parks and recreation areas. The agency itself is popular. Its management of historic and cultural sites, primarily in the East, is outstanding. Its innovative living history and interpretive programs are not only popular but set the highest professional standards. Its preservation and protection of historic sites have been the model for states and other federal agencies. In some parks, innovative mass transit systems, bicycle paths, and recycling facilities are projects the nation can be proud of.

This popular agency is in charge of national Parks, the best-known examples of the public-land trust, which the vast majority of the public supports and uses. Nearly every American regards the parks as his or her personal share of the public wealth. Every person who visits one of the great parks understands first-hand the inner power and sense of pride they stimulate. Few citizens are in favor of exploiting them economically or diminishing their character.

The concept of maintaining some wild land and some historic areas for future generations remains a noble democratic experiment. The problems of a sprawling and diverse federal agency chasing the squirrels of political favor can be overcome. Even difficult solutions will be possible as long as the public believes that some lands should be beyond the laws of economics and the consumptive grasp of any one generation.

Finding a solution to the question of recreation on the public lands will require a vision that goes beyond the parks. All public lands hold some type of recreational value. The other federal agencies, especially the Forest Service and BLM, boast of the recreation opportunities on their lands, but they virtually always rank recreation secondary to commercial activities. In the case of Corps of Engineers and Bureau of Reclamation projects, recreation is by force of law secondary to the commercial use of water.

But because they deplete few resources, benefit so many people, and threaten no wildlife, non-economic recreational activities such as camping, hiking, or just sightseeing should have a very high priority with land-management agencies. Just the opposite has been the historic pattern. The Forest Service and Bureau of Land Management have hired recreation staffs last and fired them first during times of lean budgets. Recreationists are disorganized, and their influence is diffused.

Recreation suffers in many ways. Federal water reservoirs that are heavily used by outdoor recreationists are often drained to provide subsidized water for potatoes and alfalfa. In other areas streams below dams are dangerous to fishermen because they fluctuate rapidly to provide peaking power for private power companies. The Forest Service clearcuts and harvests timber despite the impacts on recreation, aesthetics, wildlife, watersheds, and other public resources. Livestock on BLM land require fences and concentrate along streams, in aspen groves, and in the very places the public prefers for camping. The public-land camper has to cope with flies, pollution, a deteriorated environment, and with countless fences and barriers usually built at public expense.

Public-land reform would give outdoor recreation and other

non-consumptive activities a very high priority for the public domain, along with restoring wildlife; the two goals are compatible.

In the case of the national parks a more complex set of reforms would be needed. First, urban recreation areas and multiple-use recreation areas should be administered by an agency prepared for this type of resource management. The Park Service should concentrate on protecting natural areas and historic sites, where it traditionally has been most qualified. Multiple-use management requires one type of professional manager; protecting natural environments requires different training and experience.

To support this management and protection the Park Service should develop a professional staff of trained land managers who, by education and orientation, are skilled in protecting natural environments. Areas with law-enforcement problems should have specialists and outsiders under contract to handle the enforcement.

It is time to curb the park concessions. They have a well-earned reputation for poor service and high prices, they have been feared by park managers, and they have been sources of many internal park problems. They must be firmly under public control, not directing the management of the public parks. The Park Service must not sell them the public trust.

Park managers should be supported by a professional research organization. Studying complex problems brought on by past adverse land uses demands technical research skills. The goal of the agency and its research arm would be to restore the park lands to their natural condition and to keep the areas in such condition for future generations. Every other activity on park lands should be secondary to that foremost objective.

Part of the reform of park lands would be to establish new park boundaries to encompass ecological units and entire biological habitats. The piecemeal politically derived boundaries that have haunted the Park Service and made management difficult would give way to nature's boundaries. As part of this reform, private inholdings and other adverse development such as mining and grazing would be bought out or otherwise stopped quickly. These activities only damage the park land and prevent the use of the area for today's public and future generations.

Exotic plant and animal species would be removed where possible. Conflicts and problems with adjoining lands managed by other agencies, as well as development problems, would be resolved with priority given to protecting park resources and the future generations' stake in the park lands. Economic activities outside parks would be permitted only when it could be shown that they would not harm the park. Such an orientation would require not only stronger laws, but a more principled management staff and the acceptance of a park land ethic.

Park lands and open wild lands are the premier class of public lands, a nation's most tangible expression of freedom. Protecting and enjoying them is a high purpose. Their wealth is an example to all people of resources shared, of a sacred trust in land and the future. National park lands are more than wild laboratories or priceless historic and cultural sites; they are part of the power of our nation, as great a contributor to national strength as steel mills and armies. Park lands are the best of our nation. We as a people and as a country are enlarged by their protection.

Monument Rock—Echo Canyon

13

Our Last
Wilderness

Stooped and solitary, Henry David Thoreau began, "I wish to speak a word for Nature, for absolute freedom and wilderness. . . ." The Concord audience listened in April 1854 as the speaker contrasted wilderness with civilization. Thoreau spoke eloquently with almost a mystical reverence for wild land. Concluding, he declared, "In wildness is the preservation of the world." With his words the American wilderness movement was launched; conservationists had a battle cry. It was more than 100 years before Congress protected the first wilderness area, but the retiring Thoreau linked civilization to the wonder of wilderness and changed the public lands forever.

"Wilderness"—the word is magical. It can trigger more memories, scenes, images, and senses than almost any other word. Memories flow to far-off mountains, cool woods, or perhaps a green and flowering meadow. Buffalo, Indians, trappers, and voyageurs march through wild niches in our dreams. "Wilderness" may conjure up the call of a loon, the raucous cry of a sandhill crane, or the howl of a coyote. All stir a primal vision. It was Thoreau who ignored the pace and strife of civilization long enough to capture the primordial power of wilderness in a lovely net of words.

If "wilderness" is a magical term, the place is a personal perception. The lands belong to everyone, but the experience is perplexing to share or even to translate. It bridges conflicting impulses in the national subconscious. As a resource of the public land, wilderness is seized for private development to serve the market while the public loses wealth, power, and freedom. Yet for many people wilderness as it exists is a source of strength.

Wilderness is more than wild public land; it is the raw material from which the nation was carved and, particularly in a nuclear age, is a powerful symbol, the only living reference point we have to show us where we began. Wilderness is both the most controversial classification of federal land and the land embodying the most hopes, dreams, and history. It has inspired artists, poets, visionaries, and writers. It is a frontier standing in splendid contrast to a nuclear age. It is the heart of the public domain and of the nation.

Seeing wilderness as the heart of the American land helps to explain its political controversy and complexity. The debate over wilderness policy has involved, more than territory, the nation's perceptions of its own history and culture. Along with national parks, wilderness has the strongest, most pervasive spiritual dimension of any land.

Contrasted with the strong spirituality of wilderness, forest and rangeland policy have generated mere political and monetary conflicts. Wilderness debates involve not only trade-offs of resources, but the conviction of foresters, range managers, and many other resource professionals that reserving wilderness is a heresy. There has been a holy war in the West against wilderness that began with the first settler. Its first opponent was Thoreau; the first victory of his philosophy took nearly one hundred years.

For every acre now classified by Congress as wilderness, at least two other acres are under asphalt and concrete. We as a nation have allocated more land to machines, automobiles, and trucks than to the wilderness, which covers about 3 percent of the United States. Most lands designated for wilderness have survived intact because they were, through the years, considered economically unsuited for logging or mining. Many economic practices nevertheless continue within wilderness lands, such as livestock grazing, water developments, and even some mines.

Despite the fact that wilderness areas are being used to produce commodities, some people consider the classification the antithesis of economic land use, the opposite of what America stands for. To them America is progress, development, and growth. Land is to be subdued and used for production. Wilderness is seen as stagnation or, worse, the worship of nature, the ranking of wildland over civilization.

But for others, wilderness is part of America and its history, the last and only frontier this generation will know. Frederick Jackson Turner said, in his famous 1893 essay, *The Significance of the Frontier in American History*, that the frontier was a major force in the evolution of the United States and western democracy, and understanding it was essential to appreciating the history of the country, because Americans and their institutions were forged there. Nations without frontiers were less innovative and less idealistic, so to Turner the loss of the frontier was a major landmark in American history.

But the frontier was not lost, and Americans did not close it; we institutionalized it. With both the national parks and the Wilderness Act, the United States developed a unique institution, a system of lands forever wild. Congress established a tangible alternative to the original frontier—a formalized frontier, a historic link to the past. As a nation, we refused to give up that dream.

Seeing wilderness as a symbol of the frontier helps explain the strong support and sympathy for preserving it. A designated frontier cannot be the same as the original in magnitude, but it can be potent in influencing individuals. Aldo Leopold, in his classic *A Sand County Almanac,* gave three important reasons for wilderness: recreation, science, and wildlife. Each is valid, but collectively they fail to explain fully wilderness's power and natural appeal, which, to people who go there with either their feet or imaginations, transcend its physical resources.

Recreation is important to individual strength. Millions of backpackers will migrate to the wildlands this year escaping from urban life, looking for a physical challenge, or looking for the spirit of the wilderness. This recreation is in some cases a simple diversion. In others, it is a re-creation of self, a renewal of spirit at a fundamental level and in an intimate connection with the natural world that was the beginning and is still the foundation of our country. Many Americans understand the values of the wildlands and develop an appreciation of the pioneers through their outdoor activities. They also develop an increased sense of self-reliance and self-worth. But recreation alone has not justified wilderness.

A second argument for wilderness is that science needs a

natural benchmark against which to measure environmental change for scope and seriousness. This is a valid and important argument, although little wilderness research has taken place yet. As the world becomes more domesticated, the scientific argument for wilderness will become increasingly important, but meanwhile it has not been a major rationale in wilderness preservation. The science is in its infancy.

A third argument for wilderness is to save wildlife. Wilderness has substantial values for certain species. However, many wildlife professionals argue that they need to manipulate the environment to enhance wildlife. Management personnel often oppose wilderness because the classification removes their opportunities to manage game species. Although wilderness protection benefits some species and is essential for the survival of others, it has not been a major reason for preservation.

The image of certain wild animals has been important, however. Wilderness has widespread support as an idea, as a cultural symbol such as the eagle—wild, untamed, and free. The concept evokes receptive feelings and images deep in the core of the national psyche. As the frontier receded, the image of wilderness evolved for most Americans from being fearsome and hostile territory to being a land of peace and natural harmony. As the nation became urbanized, wilderness became a sanctuary, a place of hope, as contrasted with the Pilgrims' view of a dark, foreboding land.

Today the wilderness system provides a perpetual opportunity for a sacred experience, for personal revival, dreams, and tranquility. This perennial rebirth is essentially and uniquely American, a dramatic difference between this nation and the rest of western civilization. Our monuments are alive.

Thoreau argued that wilderness is not a substitute for civilization, but a contrast. Wildland complemented civilization as the original frontier disappeared. Its remnants have become as essential a national heritage as the Declaration of Independence. Supreme Court Justice William O. Douglas advocated a wilderness bill of rights, in which wildland would be guaranteed. To him, wilderness was as fundamental to democracy as freedom of speech or freedom of religious expression, and the overwhelming political support in Congress is obvious. America has been unwilling to give up all of its lands to development.

Some people have heralded space as the ultimate frontier;

others have spoken of the frontier of knowledge, and some consider science an endless frontier. No doubt there is validity in these frontier surrogates. However, for most people they are nebulous tokens in our modern world, available only to a chosen few. The attraction of wilderness is that it is tangible. The urban dweller miles from the wildland may never actually visit a wilderness except through a Disney movie, a National Geographic special, or pictures on a calendar, but the concept remains alive because the place exists. It is democratically available to everyone, not just to a few elite astronauts or researchers. Tangible existence is also important to the person who challenges the frontier with muscle and skill.

Open land, another uniquely American ingredient, was an essential element on the frontier. Open and free land, public land, still attracts the wilderness user. The lack of fences, signs, and restrictions characterizes the wilderness experience. Other recreation experiences in zoos, urban parks, and commercial outdoor recreation areas are restricted.

Primeval land and public use are two essential ingredients of both wilderness and frontiers. Private land, in contrast, is the most elitist type of land use, available only to a landed class. Historically private land has segregated people, not united them. The concept of American national parks dramatically contrasts with the parks for royalty in Europe. Americans gave parks to all people to enjoy forever. The wilderness system is another example of democratic policies, the first public-land program to require public hearings. Like homesteading and national parks, it originated in America as a product of the wild land and a nation wealthy enough to provide a frontier dream for all the people. Wilderness is a human institution of hope, an experiment in living history, a national policy of restraint in a world of overdevelopment.

But at the foundation of the symbol and the cultural heritage is the personal experience. To gain a sense of the drama of history and a sense of place, and to develop the spirit of the frontier, a visitor can stand in the wilderness and conjure up images from history. In the Sierra, one can envision forty-niners struggling over into the gold fields of California. On the wild Missouri in eastern Montana, one can picture the Lewis and Clark expedition pulling upriver, followed rapidly by fur trappers, then steamboats loaded with miners bound for the gold fields. Later blue-suited troopers headed upriver to fight Chief Joseph.

Wilderness, like the frontier, also fosters personal growth and development, a chance for renewal to anyone willing to face it. A person entering the wilderness looks inside first and can learn to value himself or herself in a crowded and impersonal world. In wildlands a person shrinks, and time and life are put into earthly perspective. The experience is humbling. One sees what the essentials of life are; the desperate activity of our daily world diminishes, and the person is calmed. By increasing our self-reliance, wilderness teaches us not only respect for the land, but respect for ourselves. As our self-esteem is enhanced, so is our concept of responsibility. We decrease our dependence upon others, including the government. Wilderness outdoor programs have measurably increased the mental health and independence of participants, many of whom leave the wilderness with a strong sense of self-reliance. People change in the wilderness, as they did on the frontier.

Personal ability can flourish under the primal conditions, too. Many people who find their spirit and talent caged in society and urban life can emerge with confidence in the wilderness. Outdoor skills do not depend on education, social status, or position. A glib ability to function in the modern world or to insulate oneself from the earth with machines and walls is impossible in the wildland. Self-esteem thrives with individual effort. It costs only the effort to try the wild experience and strip away the culturally-bound straightjacket of inhibitions.

Wilderness is a great leveler. Status and power mean nothing there. The poorest student or the wealthiest banker may share a trail or a campsite; the rain and winds affect everyone the same; the water is equally cold; the sense of darkness is apprehensive for everyone. In a crisis, people are as equal as their ability to survive alone. Self-reliance becomes infinitely more important than finances. After hardship and pain travelers on the Oregon Trail over a hundred years ago shared a real sense of equality. The frontier measures everyone by strength of will, not by bank accounts or credit ratings.

The thirst for adventure drove some people to the western frontier. That spirit can live on in land that requires travel on foot or horseback. Today the wilderness encourages people to invent, to substitute, to go without, to be creative. People can still pioneer with rough beds and makeshift equipment.

Wilderness is the most romantic symbol of American history, a national symbol of our past and the hope of the future. Idealism can thrive and develop there, and as long as we have it, the essential elements that nourished the American character are with us. Each successive generation can learn and experience the great weather and great power of the land. Anyone can go to the wildlands to be restored and tested by sunlight and storm, to emerge with more self-confidence. Each generation is capable of coming out of the wilderness with its faith in democracy intact and its ability to participate in society reinforced.

This re-creation of past values remains the most important purpose of wilderness. The magic ingredient of the frontier still lives. To protect it as the original frontier vanished, Congress created wilderness institutions.

Establishing Yosemite Park in 1864 prompted the earliest wildland policies in the United States. Initially the concept and management of parks as a natural landscape were poorly developed, but the idea had entered the public imagination. Designated parks were limited to isolated areas set aside by Congress. However, President Theodore Roosevelt made major changes in conservation and public policy by establishing and greatly expanding the forest reserves, initially viewed as a forest-preservation program. On Gifford Pinchot's counsel the concept of reserves was abandoned for the more popular national forests with plural uses, the basis of the present system. At the same time Roosevelt began to establish wildlife refuges, an administrative designation for public lands reserved to protect and enhance wildlife. Some but not all of these wildlife areas evolved into a system of lands protected as natural environments and wilderness.

Roosevelt's zeal to establish forest reserves prompted Congress to repeal the presidential power to do it. But, Congress unknowingly provided another administrative tool to protect wildland when it passed the Antiquities Act in 1906. Although its intent was undoubtedly far different, presidents Teddy Roosevelt and Jimmy Carter used the Antiquities Act to protect wildlands. Once lands are designated as monuments, they are usually managed by the National Park Service as parks and are maintained in a wilderness state.

By the 1920s presidential proclamation had established sev-

eral national monuments, and Congress had created several national parks. Many of these areas were managed by the National
Park Service. The Forest Service was acutely aware of losing
both land and responsibility to the young Park Service, so it
approved the wilderness conservation ideas of Arthur Carhart,
a Forest Service landscape architect, and Aldo Leopold. The
Forest Service established its first wilderness area in 1924. Later
the agency enlarged its administrative protection to include
three roadless-land classifications: wilderness, wild areas, and
primitive areas, totalling 14 million acres. The tactic of designating roadless areas primarily for recreation was designed to prevent scenic lands administered by the Forest Service from being
transferred to the Park Service.

After World War II, the Forest Service began to open previ-
ously-protected areas in the western states to development, and
conservation organizations grew concerned over the loss of
western wildlands. Forests that had been uneconomical to harvest were opened as more productive private lands were cut
over. The Forest Service also reduced the size of some wilderness areas by internal administrative processes. The public was
isolated by the decision-making process. In addition, the wilderness designations of areas on Indian reservations, established by
a paternalistic government, were quietly lifted as American Indian self-determination became the national policy.

From the time the Antiquities Act passed in 1906 until the
early 1950s, most wildland designations had been made administratively, either by presidential proclamation or by Forest Service action. However, conservationists feared the uncertainty of
this procedure. Faced with losing established wildland areas and
buoyed by achievements in water policy, they decided to seek
a more secure system of congressional protection for wildlands.
The National Park Service and the Forest Service opposed the
attempts as a threat to their management authority.

When conservationists shifted from asking for administrative protection to congressional protection of wilderness, they
launched an era of complicated political maneuvers that opened
public lands, for the first time, to public participation in decisions. They subjected wilderness to a democratic system that
was flawed but more open than before.

During eight years of debate, Congress considered many different versions of the Wilderness Act. When the final version

was adopted in 1964, it was the most debated public-land law in American history. The act (P.L. 88-557) applied to three of the four major public-land management agencies in the United States: the Forest Service, the Park Service, and the Fish and Wildlife Service. The largest land-management system, administered by the Bureau of Land Management, was not included. Western congressmen's opposition and the mistaken perception that the arid lands of the Bureau were unsuited for wilderness prevented the BLM from being covered.

The 1964 act initially established a national wilderness preservation system of 9.1 million acres; the Forest Service had previously designated these lands as wilderness. But the size was not final. The act required an administrative review of all roadless areas with 5000 or more contiguous acres in the national parks and wildlife refuges. Forest Service lands previously protected as "wild" or "primitive" were also to be reviewed. After review and study the agencies were to report to Congress, which held the authority to designate public lands as wilderness. Congress was careful not to delegate this authority to the agencies after its experience with the Antiquities Act and the proliferation of national monuments.

The Wilderness Act was a compromise. It left the wilderness system open to continual dispute, particularly because Congress overlooked two very important classes of land. First were the Forest Service's undesignated roadless lands. Although the other two agencies were to review all substantial roadless areas, only a small part of the Forest Service's lands were covered. The exact acreage in the roadless category is unknown, but it undoubtedly exceeded 60 million acres, or more than one-third of the national forests. The second category of lands were the Bureau of Land Management holdings, vast desert areas in the West and still larger lands in Alaska. Again the exact acreage is not known, but the initial agency inventory in 1979 identified 57 million acres of roadless lands in the western states outside Alaska.

The agency reviews continued for ten years after the act passed. Sporadically Congress added to the system, which had grown by 10 million acres by the end of 1978. The Park Service had nearly 3 million acres in 25 different units, while the Fish and Wildlife Service had 52 different parcels totalling less than 1 million acres. The remainder of the additions had been on the national forest lands. Although designated wilderness occupied less than 1 percent of the total land in the United States and only about 2.5 percent of the total federal lands, wilderness policy was very controversial in 1979 and 1980 because the system was on the verge of its largest additions.

The policy of wilderness allocation had expanded from the originally authorized ten-year review to include three other major programs. Developers and other opponents of wilderness realized that potential additions might double and redouble the size of wilderness areas at the same time energy and minerals exploration on public lands were greatly expanding. Pro-development organizations mounted large anti-wilderness campaigns that put the conservation organizations on the defensive for the first time in years.

The controversy started years before with one of the Forest Service's administrative programs. Several areas overlooked by the Wilderness Act aroused conservation organizations' interest, and the Forest Service found itself debating development plans, so in 1967 the agency began reviewing these remaining roadless lands. The process was termed the Roadless Area Review and Evaluation (RARE) program. During the first step, the inventory, the agency found 1449 areas totalling 56 million acres that met the minimum requirements for wilderness classification. But the second step of the program used a flawed evaluation process reflecting a Forest Service bias against wilderness. At its conclusion, 12 million acres had been selected for consideration as wilderness. At this point in 1972, the agency hoped its role in wilderness review would soon be over. But controversy surrounded the program, which was abandoned because pro-wilderness groups threatened judicial action. The land was closed to most development until the local plans were complete; the slow planning process continued.

In 1977 Assistant Secretary of Agriculture M. Rupert Cutler ordered a new roadless area review, RARE II. The second inventory with new standards identified 2919 roadless areas totalling 62 million acres. After a short evaluation period, again widely challenged for poor data, questionable methodology, and inadequate public involvement, the RARE II results were announced in 1979. The Forest Service recommended 15 million acres to be classified as wilderness, 10.8 million acres to be studied further, and 36 million acres to be released for non-wilderness classification.

Although less than satisfied with the outcome of RARE II, most wilderness organizations chose not to oppose the Forest Service's recommendations. During the RARE II study, corporations using the public land had strongly opposed more wilderness. The environmental movement, strong in the early part of the decade, had declined as a political force. Therefore, fearing an environmental backlash from pro-development forces, wilderness organizations generally accepted the results.

But California's Resources Secretary Huey Johnson insisted that wilderness in his state had not been fairly studied, and he initiated a lawsuit against the RARE II study. Ironically, the leaders of pro-wilderness groups met with Johnson to persuade him not to take legal action against the Forest Service, although he wanted substantial wilderness expansion. The state of California won the lawsuit on much the same grounds that the original RARE program was discredited. The decision was strongly upheld on appeal to the next highest court.

The issue of the Forest Service's *de facto* wilderness was once again stalemated. After two attempts the agency had failed to develop an evaluation program that met the requirements of both a rational planning process and the law. The agency's bias against wilderness had been clearly exposed in the courts, and its case had lost.

John Crowell, President Reagan's assistant secretary of agriculture, who had previously been chief counsel for Louisiana-Pacific, ordered still another wilderness review—RARE III. It opened all roadless areas previously recommended for non-wilderness and began scrutinizing proposed wilderness areas for development. Once again the evaluation was strongly biased against wilderness.

The Forest Service was not the only agency facing problems over wilderness policy. In 1976 the Federal Land Policy and Management Act (P.L. 94-579) gave the Bureau of Land Management (BLM) its first comprehensive multiple-use management direction, and it also required a wilderness review process for the BLM roadless lands. Congress also established a policy of retaining these lands in federal ownership—the first time this was required by law. After a slow start the BLM began to identify the potential wilderness lands under its jurisdiction and established management guidance for them. Although Congress will not classify the selected lands for many years, for all practical purposes the study areas the BLM selects are major additions to the wilderness system.

But the BLM's wilderness inventories generated hostile reactions in some communities of the West. In 1979, because of opposition to wilderness and other BLM programs, the "sagebrush rebellion" began. Starting in Nevada early in 1979, the "rebellion" advocated transferring the BLM's lands to state and private ownership. This political gambit had an impact on land-management practices, especially environmental and wilderness programs. The BLM began to backslide not only on its wilderness inventory, but on its protection program as well. Within two years congressional hearings were held that raised serious questions as to the validity of the BLM wilderness review. During the Reagan administration hundreds of BLM roadless areas were opened to various development activities. Wilderness studies became sharply biased toward opening lands to economic uses.

The third federal land program that polarized wilderness as a policy issue late in the 1970s was Alaska land legislation. Before statehood nearly all land in Alaska was federally owned, but the statehood bill granted nearly a third of it—a record amount —to the state. The state land was then sold or transferred to private ownership. In a complex series of events the Indians and Eskimos gained legislation in 1972 that transferred part of the federal domain to them to satisfy their long-standing claims. This legislation required interim protection and study for land envisioned as several large national parks and wildlife refuges. These proposals became the major focus of pro-wilderness organizations late in the decade. The final Alaska National Interest Lands Conservation Act signed into law on December 2, 1980, covered 104 million acres and established large national parks, wildlife refuges, and wilderness areas that will keep nearly 100 million acres of Alaska in a wildland state. The Alaska bill doubled the size of the wilderness system.

Development organizations strongly opposed all three wilderness programs, and their reaction increased the polarization of wilderness allocation in the United States. During the past twenty years most wilderness-policy issues have concerned the allocation process and have centered around three major groups: the wilderness supporters, through organizations such as The Wilderness Society and the Sierra Club; the mining, logging, and other commercial organizations; and the agencies themselves, which have played a central role in evaluating areas. However, Congress has the authority to classify the land.

To understand the congressional role in wilderness classification it is best to ignore the theoretical processes of democracy and look to the flawed operation of the United States Congress and its committee structure. As the agencies have completed their studies and evaluations, Congress has blocked classification of wilderness. Nationally, wilderness appears to be a popular land-management concept; it has deep roots in history, literature, and art, and no wilderness bill has ever failed to pass once the full Congress had a chance to vote on it. But wilderness support tends to be strongest in urban areas and weakest in rural regions near the wildlands, while the congressional committee structure concentrates power in western congressmen from rural regions. They have preferred commercial development on the public lands, not wilderness protection. Wilderness supporters have had to overwhelm this institutional bias against conservation.

An outgrowth of the legislative process is the erratic distribution of established wilderness areas. Montana has had pro-wilderness congressmen and has numerous large wilderness areas. States such as Nevada and Utah, both with large blocks of outstanding scenic, isolated roadless lands, have only very small amounts of congressionally-designated wilderness. It is a truism of conservation policy that an area cannot be designated wilderness over the opposition of the local member of Congress. The congressional territorial imperative is strong, and members will seldom vote against a local congressman on local issues, even federal land matters. This flawed tradition and the concentration of western congressmen on important interior committees frustrate the national interest.

All four major land-management agencies now have the authority to manage wilderness areas. Wilderness classification is a management and policy veneer over the existing land-management regulations. In some cases, such as in national parks, monuments, and wildlife refuges, this overlay is more symbolic than actual, since the agencies already have authority to manage the lands with more restrictions than the Wilderness Act provides. The major restrictions of wilderness policy concern timber harvesting and the private use of motorized vehicles. Wilderness is not the most restrictive form of public land classification, but it is the most controversial.

The Wilderness Act provides a large measure of management flexibility, so the supervision of such areas has not been a major problem. In the future, as the allocation questions are settled, public groups' attention will likely turn to management issues. Some concern has been expressed over the limitation of use in wilderness areas, over the use of fire-management techniques, and over the handling of some wildlife. These issues may become dominant in the future.

The lack of controversy over management is a result of the act clearly permitting several private uses. Although constraints are placed on the private operator, livestock may graze, including sheep, cattle, and horses. Limitations are placed on fencing, developing water for the stock, and introducing exotic plant species.

Existing water developments and livestock operations continue within a wilderness, and their maintenance and rehabilitation are assured. As a result, some wilderness boundaries include reservoirs, dams, even power plants. Many wilderness areas have non-federal land, such as state or private land, within their boundaries, and access to it—even by bulldozers and mechanized transportation—is assured. Wilderness is in reality a multiple-use area, not a single-use sanctuary.

Other uses are also allowed in some areas under wilderness classification, such as the private use of aircraft, power transmission lines and transmitter stations, patrol cabins, restrooms, and other administrative structures. Mechanized equipment required for emergency uses such as fire control and rescue operations is permitted. Hunting and fishing also continues, subject to the normal regulations and seasons.

The provision that is potentially the most controversial involves mining operations. There are two key points of wilderness mining: first, prospecting for minerals under the 1872 Mining Law continued in established wilderness areas for nearly twenty years after the Wilderness Act passed in 1964. Unlimited claims can be marked; the claimant has partial title to that parcel, can exclude trespassers, and has the right to sell the prop-

nug Corner Cove—Prince William Sound

erty. Tens of thousands of parcels have been claimed in areas that have been classified for wilderness or that are under study.

The second important aspect of the 1964 act is that although the deadline for prospecting passed on December 31, 1983, established mining claims may be developed indefinitely. Therefore a miner can work a claim, even with mechanized equipment, and exclude the public. Today approximately a dozen wilderness areas have operating mines within their boundaries, and fifty areas have claims. In some wilderness areas there are a thousand or more claims, the result of increased prospecting as the deadline approached. These claims and the activities associated with them will scar and haunt wilderness areas for many years to come.

The mining issue will continue to impede congressional action and will further bog down the process of allocating wilderness. Congressional committees have held up some wilderness proposals for more than a decade, and some states' delegations will let another decade or more pass before any action is taken. Most wildlands today are managed as wilderness without the formal classification. Other lands will remain roadless but will not be used to produce commodities for simple economic reasons. Such public land will have value for recreation, research, watershed protection, and other purposes.

The federal administration needs to develop and apply a uniform, interagency system of roadless alternatives to break the congressional stalemate. The additional roadless system should be easier to apply than the present classification arrangement, yet it should be tough enough to prohibit roadbuilding and mechanized development. An administrative alternative, developed with full public participation, and prohibiting declassification during pro-development administrations, would help end the controversy and bring more progressive management to these lands.

Wallace Stegner, in his essay "The Gift of Wilderness," eloquently writes of the value of wildland. He notes that the loss of wilderness has happened so rapidly that we are astonished and "look around us like Plains Indians wondering where the buffalo have gone. There has been some magic; they have disappeared into the ground." He says, "For the preservation of the remnants of natural America ... offers America a physically and spiritually better future than the immediate cashing of our assets would. . . . We need to learn to listen to the land, hear what it says, understand what it can and can't do over the long haul; what, especially in the West, it should not be asked to do."

If wilderness is to have a future on American public land, some drastic policy changes must be made. James Watt helped revitalize the environmental movement by his anti-wilderness attitude. He also clearly demonstrated how vulnerable wilderness is under existing law. Although existing and prospective wilderness areas held but a small fraction of the country's potential oil and gas, they were targets of feverish energy exploration. In May 1981 Watt advocated opening wilderness areas to oil, gas, and other energy development. Within a few months big oil companies had applied for energy leases in more than 150 existing and proposed wilderness areas. They filed dozens of oil, gas, and geothermal lease applications. For the first time since the Wilderness Act passed nearly twenty years earlier, widespread energy development threatened the public trust in wildland.

The solution to threats from not only oil and gas leasing, but also existing mining claims, potential water developments, and other projects, must be unequivocal. First, all development activities in public-land roadless areas must be frozen. Then a new interagency wilderness review must be launched for all federal lands. Obviously it cannot be honestly and professionally administered by either the Forest Service or the Bureau of Land Management, which have distorted and biased earlier studies. Instead a new, independent review office must carefully and honestly investigate the potential wilderness lands. Such an objective study should have a simple and direct goal: every possible roadless area that remains in America must be protected if at all feasible.

Once the new professional review is launched, then congressional wilderness land reform should begin. First of all, the Aspinall heritage of mining and development loopholes must be closed. The protection should accomplish what was intended and should not be subject to the whims of a zealous developer such as Interior Secretary James Watt. Congress must also comprehensively protect the areas now stuck in the legislative logjam. A lone congressman from a sparsely-populated western state should not frustrate the public trust in wilderness land. The democratic process must be allowed to work; the public will has been blocked too long by commercial interests.

As a final reform, once a
as wilderness, land manage
est Service and Bureau of L
their hostility toward wilde
tion, and instinct these ag
tion and have reluctantly s
ness. Until these agenc
wilderness agency should t
derness, or otherwise natur
and deserves a fresh begin

During the 1960s I parac
abandoned mining town of
the fire and the poor weath
Flat had boomed late in the
We wandered among the d
ins and came upon a huge g
Once manned by a crew of
repaired by a lone miner so
through gravel and debris
To young smokejumpers
venture of fighting wilder
seemed like a dull, quixotic j
and suspicious, but proud
waited impatiently for the
miner talked of gold minin
tion of interior Alaska. "So
and valuable," he declared
time I was not sure if he ref
surrounding wilderness. Y
eral land had been transfer
I understood the old miner.
The howl of a wolf in the

As a final reform, once available roadless areas are protected as wilderness, land management must be transformed. The Forest Service and Bureau of Land Management have demonstrated their hostility toward wilderness. By education, training, tradition, and instinct these agencies subvert wilderness classification and have reluctantly served the public interest in wilderness. Until these agencies reform, a new, independent wilderness agency should take over all areas classified wild, wilderness, or otherwise natural. Wilderness as an institution needs and deserves a fresh beginning.

During the 1960s I parachuted into a large forest fire near an abandoned mining town of Flat, Alaska. A rainstorm beat down the fire and the poor weather left us stranded at the old town. Flat had boomed late in the gold rush at the turn of the century. We wandered among the dozens of abandoned houses and cabins and came upon a huge gold dredge floating on a yellow pond. Once manned by a crew of dozens, the huge machine was kept repaired by a lone miner so it could chew its way back and forth through gravel and debris left from the earlier gold rush.

To young smokejumpers absorbed in the excitement and adventure of fighting wilderness forest fires, the miner's quest seemed like a dull, quixotic job. The old miner was hardworking and suspicious, but proud of his old lumbering dredge. As we waited impatiently for the weather to clear and for a plane, the miner talked of gold mining, wolves, and the wilderness isolation of interior Alaska. "Someday people will find all this rare and valuable," he declared with a casual wave of his hand. At the time I was not sure if he referred to the gold, the wolves, or the surrounding wilderness. Years later Alaska's best federal mineral land had been transferred to state and private ownership. I understood the old miner. All wild land was rare and valuable. The howl of a wolf in the wilderness could be like gold.

Snug Corner Cove—Prince William Sound

14

Alaska,
The Unfinished Battle

My first summer in Alaska, I arrived in a battered Bureau of Land Management DC-3. We had flown from Montana through rain and storm, over glaciers and rugged peaks to our destiny in Fairbanks. Eventually, as a smokejumper, I made nearly fifty parachute jumps into the deep Alaskan wilderness to fight tundra and forest fires.

On many long flights I saw the vast, impressive public domain of Alaska. The first landing on the tundra was a surprise, a soft bounce on the spongy ground as the parachute collapsed overhead like a giant orange poppy. The ferocity of the mosquitos, the long sunlit days, and a midnight bailout in the bright sky are some of my memories of the state. On flights from Eagle to Bettles, from Fork Yukon to Lake Minchumina, and from Bethel to Fairbanks, under me I saw federal lands. From the mouth of the Kuskokwim River to the Yukon flowing out to Canada, and from the Porcupine River to the Kobuk, moose were more common than cabins.

The size of the land dominated everything in Alaska, even the wildland fires we fought. They were huge. Once four of us jumped a fire that seemed manageable at the time, but three days later we had been unable to tame the beast, which had grown into a black tongue thirty miles long tinged with fire. Aerial fire patrols took us over hillsides where thousands of caribou swarmed over gentle slopes like ants. The moose were larger than the ones in the Tetons, the bears twice the size of Yellowstone's. The wolf we saw loping across the tundra was like a strange primeval dog, black, outsized, and mystical.

Once, exhausted from days of firefighting, I slept on a flight to a distant fire. When the plane was circling the fire, the jump-master woke us. I stepped to the door and methodically snapped my static line in place, but instead of checking the jump spot, I stood mesmerized. Denali, nearly four miles high, loomed outside like a giant white Himalayan peak. Its cold mass dwarfed the plane, the fire, and all the surrounding rivers and hills. In the early morning its glaciers were like perfectly etched granite; its white mass reflected light like a huge moon. I stepped from the plane still hypnotized, a puny moth fluttering in the wind, attracted by Denali's beauty and size.

Remote wilderness fires took me far up the Porcupine River nearly into the Yukon Territory. A few days later I sat on scorched tundra on the Seward Peninsula within sight of the Bering Sea. A day might begin far up the Kobuk and end in a seedy Anchorage bar. Camped on a remote stream, I awoke one morning to the last cries of a mallard snatched by a hyperactive mink. Before the day was over, a helicopter deposited my crew at a sterile military base complete with the latest jets on line to intercept an enemy on the backside of the North Pole.

We saw firsthand, during those summers in Alaska, the isolated Eskimo and Indian villages. To them the slaying of a moose was cause for a community celebration. A run of salmon would demand that the Native firefighters return home not for sport, but to feed their families. Fish drying in the midnight sun, hides curing, nets being repaired; every village held a reminder of the people's dependence on the land. Every time a Native came to work at firefighting, we learned of Natives' outdoor skills, their lives close to the land. We didn't guess that the land we worked on and the Native lifestyle would be the causes of a long and bitter debate in Washington.

The searing heat of the fires we fought was a modest force compared to the change that came to Alaska. During the last summer I worked in the state, the Fairbanks paper carried banner news: 9.6 billion barrels of oil had been discovered at Prudhoe Bay. Alaska was about to change. Oil began the largest changes in the Native lifestyle, the biggest shifts in federal land ownership. Public lands and their resources, and conservation and development were at the heart of the turmoil.

Alaska, adapted from an Indian word meaning "great country," was purchased in 1867. It has been at war with its resources

since the last Russian troops left. Conservation was an issue from the area's earliest days in American ownership, even before it was organized as a territory in 1871. Over the protest of local hunters Congress protected the Alaskan fur seal in 1869. Despite the local lust for seals, the federal government managed the Pribilof Islands to protect the fur seals.

Alaskans still harbor the most intense relic views that the frontier exists to be developed, and they also have had the sharpest conflicts with the rest of the nation over resources on the public lands. The state's vast size and wealth of salmon, caribou, bears, and other resources have dwarfed its residents' perspective. The resources only seemed limitless. Its awesome mountains, including Denali, the highest in North America, seemed able to withstand the miners' picks and shovels. The 1200-mile Aleutian Island chain, with its thousands of bird colonies, rookeries, and herds of sea lions, seemed inexhaustible—like the buffalo herds. People willing to plunder the public domain but hindered in the "lower 48" could always migrate to the last frontier. Its Native people were isolated and, like every American Indian tribe, politically weak. They, too, could be robbed of their land.

Stateside conservationists considered Alaska the last frontier and the last hope to protect nature on a grand scale. As with the "lower 48" states, the Forest Service began the conservation efforts. Early in the twentieth century it protected some 16 million acres of virgin rain forest in Alaska's southeastern coastal region. As it was elsewhere, however, the Forest Service was soon at odds with the National Park Service and conservationists over the best means of protecting the land. When the Forest Service was offering Alaskan timber as a "second Norway," the Park Service was at work persuading Congress and the president to reserve lands. The great volcanic eruption at Katmai in 1912 created the "Valley of Ten Thousand Smokes." Soon it was protected as a national monument. The Park Service expanded with Mt. McKinley National Park (now Denali) in 1917. The U.S. Navy claimed 23 million acres of oil land as a national petroleum reserve in the 1920s. Glacier Bay, the site of John Muir's visit, became a national monument in 1925. Before long there were several million acres of wildlife refuges in the state as well.

The Forest Service did not rest when the Park Service invaded its southeastern Alaskan turf. Soon after its establish-

ment, Glacier Bay National Monument was reduced to allow logging. Then, satisfying the prevailing attitude in Alaska, the national monument was opened to mining and prospecting, along with Mt. McKinley National Park.

Alaska had begun a practice of eroding conservation gains. By the late 1930s the state's reputation as the last reservation of the frontier-development mentality was well known. The great Interior Secretary Harold L. Ickes visited the state and summarized the situation:

"Alaskans won't tax themselves or the exportable wealth. They think Uncle Sam ought to build and maintain highways, extend and improve the Alaska Railroad, and supply the territory with public works of all nature while they continue exploring every crack and crevice for precious metal which will make them rich and enable them to go back to the United States to live in luxury."

A few years later, when it was attempting to enter the union, the territory was outraged that the federal government protected part of its vast land holdings. The Alaskan congressional representative proposed a statehood bill in 1948 that would have abolished all the national monuments, parks, wildlife refuges, and other federal reservations in the territory. The bill did not pass Congress, but Alaska did not end its war on the federal lands.

When statehood finally came a decade later, Congress outdid itself in generosity. From the public domain, Congress gave the state 103 million acres, the largest land grant in history in total acreage and as a percentage of the state. The state could even pick and choose its lands. Because of its uncertainty over which were the best mineral lands, the state proceeded carefully with its selections.

There was only one problem. The federal parks, monuments, forests, and refuges, as well as the large state claims, were carved from the traditional hunting and fishing territory of Alaska's Indians and Eskimos. Unlike Natives in the rest of the nation, Alaskan Native Americans had not been delegated reservations. In Uncle Sam's eyes they were squatters, although few people would deny that they had powerful legal and moral claims to the public lands. After years of futile protests to Washington politicians, the Natives reached the right man. Late in 1966 Interior

Secretary Stewart Udall froze state and private land claims until the Native land issue was settled.

Most Alaskans and their politicians were not at all sympathetic to the Native claims. Mining organizations refused to accept the moral obligation to the Natives; to them the wilderness of Alaska was to be subdued and exploited. Opposition to resolving the ethical questions was strong; racism, the object of national attention in the "lower 48," was nowhere more obvious than in Alaska during the 1960s and was highlighted by the great Prudhoe Bay oil strike in 1968. Suddenly the land freeze and Native lawsuits threatened to tie the potential oil boom into legal knots.

Prudhoe Bay, on the northern coast, is ice-bound nine months a year. The bay and the geologically similar north slope of the Brooks Range are rich with oil. Commerce demanded a route from there south through the virgin wilderness to Fairbanks, where it wanted an all-weather seaport. First a winter haul road was punched across the virgin land. The frozen rivers and tundra could support the heaviest equipment during the long winter. Before long plans were underway for a permanent road north from Fairbanks, including bridges across the mighty Yukon and other rivers, all to serve a most impressive oil pipeline forty-eight inches in diameter. All these projects involved construction and operation under extreme weather conditions in a harsh but subtle environment that was easily eroded. Concerned environmentalists were pitted against powerful international corporations. Over all the environmental arguments and the boom atmosphere hung the cloudy threat of long, expensive lawsuits the Natives filed to protect their heritage.

A congressional solution was needed. When the lobbying began the Natives were surprised to find they suddenly had powerful allies, the energy corporations. The reason was simple. No pipeline could be built until the Native claims were settled. For months Senator Ted Stevens of Alaska and Interior Committee Chair Wayne Aspinall of Colorado argued for a minimal settlement for the Natives. Then they received their marching orders in a letter from the oil industry. Oil executives wanted "a prompt and just settlement . . ." for the Alaska Natives. With that, Congress began to move.

For decades the issue of land claims for the Natives had been

frustrated by people who represented special interests. Washington Senator Jackson had attempted to hitch oil-leasing reform to the Alaska land legislation, reasoning that the oil wealth should be offered in competitive bidding. But big oil and its potent representatives, senators Stevens of Alaska and Hansen of Wyoming, helped block any changes in the leasing system.

When the battle for Alaska's wilderness soul began, one oil lobbyist said, "Don't worry about the conservationists, we're playing them like trout." But Earth Day was approaching, with its resurgence in America's conservation ethic.

Behind the scenes the Native leaders, Alaskan politicians, and oil people traded public land, its minerals, and treasury dollars to settle the Native claims. Conservationists wanted land-use planning for the federal lands but were having little success. Finally Arizona's conservation-minded Congressman Morris Udall introduced an amendment to the Native Claims Act to study 50 million acres of federal land for possible designation as national parks and wildlife refuges. Several versions of the amendment were introduced and modified. Slowly support for the concept grew in the collective awareness of Congress. Concern for the environment was waxing.

Initially opposition was strong in the House of Representatives. Natives, oil people, and union representatives all opposed the Udall amendment. More important, dictatorial Wayne Aspinall did not like the idea. When the vote was taken, the amendment lost 217–177.

In the Senate the battle was different. Senators Jackson of Washington and Bible of Nevada fought to let the interior secretary reserve federal land for parks and refuges. After all, Alaska, Natives, and oil companies were getting a piece of the state; so should the American people, since it was their land. The Senate accepted Udall's idea 76–5.

The Alaska Native Claims Settlement Act (ANCSA) went to conference committee—the meeting of selected senators and congressmen that resolves differences between legislation passed by the two houses. In the small committee Congressman Udall carried on the fight for an idea his own legislative body did not accept. The final compromise bill granted the Natives more than 40 million acres of land and gave the state clear title to 26 million selected acres. It established twelve Native Corpo-

rations, organizations that would manage Native land and resources and supported them with nearly a billion dollars to initiate projects for the Indians and Eskimos.

For the American people there was a consolation prize. Udall had carried his idea through. Before the remaining public lands could be opened to development, the Department of the Interior would study the land for possible parks and wildlife refuges. Two small sections, 17(a)1 and 17(d)2, changed the course of public-land history. Wayne Aspinall insisted that no changes be made in the oil subsidy, but the bill permitted the interior secretary to prevent development for five years on land to be studied. On December 18, 1971, the Alaska Native Claims Settlement Act was signed into law by President Richard Nixon. Few people realized how intense a battle over land the act had launched.

The state of Alaska did not like the conservation provisions. Defying Congress, the state attempted to claim 77 million acres of federal lands. It was blocked in court. In March 1972 Secretary of the Interior Rogers C.B. Morton withdrew from development 80 million acres under Section 17(d)2 and 45 million acres under Section 17(d)1. Interior launched its study. Later in the year park and refuge planners, impressed with the great land, proposed 63.8 million acres of parks and refuges and 18.8 million acres of additional national forest.

The following year oil companies ushered through Congress a bill of their own. Environmental concerns had blocked the Trans-Alaska Pipeline. Congress passed a bill giving the oil consortium a right-of-way across the public lands and waiving the requirement for environmental impact statements. Construction began on one of the largest projects in history; the oil boom was underway, but the battle to conserve the land was just beginning.

During the next several years an epic struggle took place between Alaskan developers and people who wanted to protect the land for the future. In the annals of conservation, nothing compares to the effort. Eventually the Alaska Coalition, which led the fight for conservation, included 52 organizations, thousands of volunteers, and dozens of lobbyists. The legislation beat the Wilderness Act's record in environmental testimony and involved more hearings and testimony than any other issue in history except civil rights. The Alaskan congressional delegation and multinational corporations fought for their bottom line and future profits; conservationists fought for the soul of the nation and their heritage.

ANCSA protected lands only until December 18, 1978, so in early 1977 Congressman Udall introduced a bill to set aside 115 million acres in Alaska for various parks and refuges. Many Alaskans and their industrial supporters wanted only 15 million to 25 million acres designated, with much of that loosely-controlled multiple-use areas. Congressman John Sieberling of Ohio joined Udall as a national leader for conservation in the House of Representatives. The bill passed by a decisive 277–31 vote. Because of massive grassroots organizing the bill would have passed the Senate as well, but it never came up for a vote. Led by Alaska's senators Ted Stevens, a master parliamentarian, and the erratic Mike Gravel, supporters of the legislation were tied in knots. At the last minute Gravel launched a filibuster, and the legislation died when Congress adjourned in fall 1978. As the end of the year approached, the protection ANCSA provided was about to expire. Oil companies, miners, and developers had bulldozers ready to open the wilderness.

But President Jimmy Carter stopped the bulldozers with Congressman Lacey's 1906 Antiquities Act. Carter turned 56 million acres of Alaska's public land into seventeen national monuments and directed his secretary of the interior to withdraw 40 million acres for twelve wildlife refuges. He also ordered his secretary of agriculture to protect 11 million acres of existing national forests from the infamous multiple-use abuse that agency is noted for. His purpose was to protect an area the size of California while Congress acted. Alaskan developers and oil companies howled in protest, but on that day Jimmy Carter walked alongside Teddy Roosevelt toward conserving the nation's resources.

In early 1979 Congressman Udall was back at the House of Representatives with an even stronger bill and was joined by more than 100 cosponsors. Alaskan developers offered an alternative weak and watered-down piece of legislation. In the following months the conflict was emotional and often bitter. The Alaska Coalition led thousands of active conservationists from every state, including many from Alaska, to make the dream of great parks and refuges on the last frontier a reality.

In Alaska frustrated political leaders were willing to try anything to stop Congressman Udall. During the field hearings on the legislation, Udall, his staff, and other congressmen visited a remote Alaskan lake to get a sense of the land and their mission. They flew into an isolated lake by amphibious plane for a wilderness cookout. Fishing was excellent. While fishing, Udall and his staff saw two nondescript men passing in a canoe. Shortly afterward the canoe returned. This time the men were dressed in their finest Alaska Fish and Game Department warden uniforms. They marched up to the tall, angular Udall. The senior warden demanded to see Udall's Alaskan fishing license. Everyone in camp was stunned. Representatives of the news media poised in anticipation. Undoubtedly it was an attempt to embarrass the congressional delegation. Udall slowly reached for his wallet, his face serious and concerned. The wardens licked their lips, hoping to bust the foremost conservationist enemy. Then, with a flourish and a broad smile, Udall pulled out his valid Alaskan fishing license. Everyone laughed except the two wardens. Congressman Udall, with a long and honorable career in Arizona and Washington, was not going to be outfoxed by the Alaskan bush league. Later Udall and Congressman Sieberling led the House of Representatives to pass the strongest conservation bill in history.

Unfortunately on the Senate side the forces of development were stronger than ever. With Stevens's stalling tactics and Gravel's random behavior, the bill was delayed late in 1980. After a titanic struggle between the forces of conservation and development, key committee members of the U.S. Senate agreed behind closed doors to a hastily-patched-together Alaska Bill. It protected 104 million acres of federal land, but it included loopholes big enough to drive a bulldozer through.

Udall promised to strengthen the bill in conference. Given his record, everyone was optimistic. Then disaster struck. In 1980 Ronald Reagan was elected president, and several of the strongest conservation-oriented senators were swept out of office. Industry-backed political action committees had taken their toll. Conservation-minded leaders in the key Senate committees were to be replaced with people who were more development-oriented. Even the Department of the Interior was to be turned over to the enemies of the public lands. Udall and Sieberling had only one choice—accept the weak Senate bill.

When Udall took to the floor of the House of Representatives, he knew it would be years before an ideal Alaska conservation bill could be passed. "Political reality dictates that we act promptly on the Senate-passed bill," he said. The House matched the weak Senate version. Despite the disappointment, the Alaska bill was better than what Secretary Morton had proposed seven years before at the start of the process.

Despite the disappointment, it was the best conservation law in history. It added 44 million acres to the national park system and 54 million acres to the national wildlife refuge system. The Yukon Flats National Wildlife Refuge totaled 8.6 million acres. The 7.9-million-acre Gates of the Arctic National Park was more than three times the size of Yellowstone. Nearly 2 million acres in southeastern Alaska were added to the national forest system, and 25 rivers were added to the national wild and scenic rivers system, greatly enlarging it. Wilderness was protected in large blocks—some 18.5 million acres in wildlife refuges, 32.3 million acres in parks, and 5.3 million acres in the national forests.

Nevertheless, the Alaska agenda remains unfinished. Great conservation plans were cut short by the election of Ronald Reagan, who set out to weaken hard-won gains at the expense of the next generation. These parks, wildlife refuges, and wilderness areas are of global importance, but their hearts are being gnawed by Reagan's rodents.

Every Act of Congress is implemented, in the real world of land management, by regulations—the day-to-day marching orders for the rangers, wardens, and managers in the field. The destructive genius James Watt brought massive regulatory change to the public lands. He opened nearly all the public lands to more mining, more logging, more grazing, and more energy development. In the case of Alaska, he even got to write his own rules.

The basic legislation, the Alaska National Interest Lands Conservation Act of 1980, is 186 pages of law. Watt's permissive regulations take hundreds of pages more. The rules threaten both old and new parks, such as Katmai, Glacier Bay, and Denali (formerly Mt. McKinley). These areas, protected by previous administrations for fifty or sixty years in their natural state, are now being opened to aircraft, commercial development, and other forms of exploitation. Some of the regulations are directly related to the last-minute legislative compromise.

Noisy, smoky snowmobiles are allowed; airplanes are the accepted method of travel; ten out of the thirteen new parks include millions of acres called "preserves," which allow business as usual for people who earn a living hunting wildlife. The great parklands are open to trophy hunters who have a congressionally-approved license to kill the continent's largest and most impressive wildlife for sport.

Watt and his pro-hunting staff also supported legislation to open even more areas to sport hunting. The reason is simple: it would generate more profit for a handful of commercial guides.

In the 9-million-acre Arctic Wildlife Refuge, Watt permitted exploration for oil and gas using heavy equipment. If oil fields are located, there is little doubt they will shortly appear on the auction block. Private oil exploration is planned on the sensitive arctic coastal plain, too. On the wildlife refuges, however, the conservation-minded Fish and Wildlife Service hindered Watt; he solved the problem by transferring authority for energy development on the refuges to the industry-oriented U.S. Geological Survey. The Geological Survey has a long history of supporting and working closely with the mining and oil industries; the top USGS positions are staffed by many people who previously worked in the private energy sector and have no experience in land management or conservation. Nevertheless the Interior Department's experts in wildlife have been reduced to an "advisory" role in protecting the nation's wildlife refuges.

The 1980 legislation opened large areas of virgin timber in southeast Alaska to development, openly subsidizing the timber industry in some areas. The trees will be shipped to Japan. *The New York Times* suggested the legislation in this area should be named the "U.S. Borax Company Rescue Act, Japanese Export Subsidy Logging Act or the Public Land Mismanagement Act." U.S. Borax, a London-based corporation with 2500 acres of public-land mining claims originally acquired at no cost, was generously provided with a loophole allowing it to explore for minerals in 150,000 acres or 235 square miles, of the Misty Fjords Wilderness. The cost to the taxpayer is not only the mineral wealth, but the wilderness and water. The Wilson, Blossom, and Keta salmon-spawning rivers will be affected badly by the development. The legislation also let the company build a road into the wilderness without scientific studies or environmental impact analysis and gave the company additional land for mining-waste dump sites, water impoundments, and other facilities.

There are other unacceptable situations on the Alaskan public lands. The state owns 20,000 acres in the middle of Wrangell-St. Elias National Park that it wants to sell to subdividers. Conservationists advocate trading less important Bureau of Land Management lands for the state parcels, but the Reagan administration favored sacrificing other park lands, assuring Alaskan developers that more land would stay under multiple-use management.

In March 1981 James Watt said his approach to Alaska was "common sense" and a "means of defusing the Sagebrush Rebellion." His first budget assisted development and hindered conservation. He ignored congressionally-mandated studies and plans for the new areas and accelerated the transfer of federal lands to the state. He cut funding for the Youth Conservation Corps, which trained unemployed youth in conservation work, while increasing funds for energy exploration and development. He eliminated plans to protect the barren-ground caribou while providing funds to support the development of a copper mine. He spent tens of millions of dollars on oil leasing and development but eliminated a small budget item intended to stop walrus-ivory smuggling.

Watt allowed airplanes and motorboats in national parks and wildlife refuges and encouraged the unsavory practice of aerial wolf hunts, in which wolves are shotgunned from aircraft. Under his regulations people can carry guns in a wildlife refuge, cut down small trees, and do almost anything they want. The undersecretary of the interior boasted that Watt's set of rules "lets you take a D-9 [bulldozer] through a national park." This was to allow residents to "continue the traditional Alaskan lifestyle."

As elsewhere, in Alaska Watt was most generous to the energy companies. Soon after taking office, he opened 63 million acres of BLM and Forest Service wildlands for energy exploration, then offered 56 million acres of national wildlife refuges on a first-come, first-served basis. For the first time in history the 23-million-acre National Petroleum Reserve was opened to development. A few months later the secretary announced he intended to sell all the available energy on a billion acres of outer continental shelf (OCS) lands, 80 percent of it off the coast of Alaska.

Oil development is especially dangerous to birds and animals on the edge of the continent because of the violent weather and fragile conditions of life. Nevertheless Secretary Watt reduced the funds available for environmental studies, scientific research, resource protection, and conservation. Just one of several important areas to be affected is the Bristol Bay, regarded by many as one of the richest and most productive fishing regions in the world.

Despite the outstanding legislative victory in the 1980 Alaska Lands Act, the basic conflict in the state is still whether to conserve Alaska's great resources or to turn the public-land trust into a corporate-welfare program. The final Alaskan legislation was hastily drafted by Senator Stevens, and several of its already-weak sections have been crippled by Secretary Watt. The energy-leasing program alone provides a dramatic example of why the interior secretary's office must be stripped of its overwhelming power. Alaskan parks and refuges should be protected from mining, exploitation, and hunting; instead, Watt and his supporters made plans for several dams within national parks and refuges and planned a maze of roads.

In no other state are the needed reforms for the federal lands more obvious. Alaska was purchased by all Americans, and most of it remains in public ownership despite a hundred years of exploitation. The time has come to manage its great parks, refuges, and wilderness areas for the whole nation and future generations.

In no other state is it more obvious that the power of the secretary of the interior must be curtailed. Congress must write more and better protection for these priceless lands into the law of the land. The resources are too important, too rare to turn over to the grey corporate ledgers. The land must be protected in the laws of the nation the way it is cherished in the hearts of everyone who has seen it—or who dreams of seeing it.

Cliffs of Green River

15

The Nightmare of Privatization

Once I camped at a desert spring at the base of Pilot Peak. The following morning, on a solitary quest, I hiked up the slopes of this isolated BLM mountain west of the Great Salt Lake. As I climbed higher I relished the fall mountain air, the solitude, and the wilderness. But with every glance to the desert valleys, I thought of the "sagebrush rebellion" and the people who wanted to sell the vast land. The words of Henry Wadsworth Longfellow weighted the dry air:

> There are things which I may not speak;
>   There are dreams that cannot die;
>   There are thoughts that make the strong heart weak,
>   And bring a pallor into the cheek,
>   And a mist before the eye.

The mountain is powerful and, like many wild places in the West, is haunted with great memories. It drew me back in time, and I remembered that Joseph Walker, an early fur trapper, stopped at Pilot Peak in 1833. Howard Stansbury used the springs of Pilot Peak as a base camp while mapping and exploring the Great Salt Lake in 1849. Perhaps from the slopes of this mountain he first realized that Salt Lake was a remnant of a great inland sea, seeing, with more insight than anyone before him, the beaches of ancient lake shores at the base of the mountain.

On a high ridge I looked east across the chalky alkali route that John Fremont rode in 1845. En route to California on a secret mission, Fremont pushed Kit Carson and his men across fifty miles of desert, gambling that this mountain would have caught enough winter snow to nurture springs in the desert all summer. The mountain did not fail. Several isolated springs still glimmered like silver below me, just as Fremont, Carson, and other pioneers found them. After looking once over this desert route, I understood more of Fremont's ego than any history book every told. From the ridge on Pilot Peak I felt the power of western history, dry tales when told on paper, but vivid and pulsing with life when remembered on a visit to the great western land.

But western history has its dark side as well. The memory of Lansford Hastings haunts Pilot Peak. Hastings wrote a guidebook to California, based in part on Fremont's reports, that was full of foolishness about how the darkness of the desert would flee before the march of civilization. During the summer of 1846 Hastings convinced several midwestern farm families to abandon the Oregon Trail and travel to California via his untried Hastings Cutoff. The route carried the wagons south of the Great Salt Lake, past Pilot Peak, and eventually down the Humboldt River. September 9–15, 1846, this emigrant party camped at the same spring where I camped after it had lost nearly fifty oxen crossing the Salt Lake Desert. Weak, divided, and very late in the season for an emigrant party, the Eddys, the Reeds, the Murphys, and the Donners pushed past the shadow of this mountain toward their tragic place in history. Hastings led them with promises of independence and easy rewards into the Sierra snow. Half the Donner party perished that winter, and the dreams of those who survived had been shattered by Lansford Hastings.

Hastings could well serve as the historic role model of "sagebrush rebels" and other people who want to sell the federal lands. Freshfaced and earnest, strutting around the western landscape full of promise and hope, he and the "rebels" offered to guide westerners to an independent and prosperous future. Just as the early mountain men were stunned to find anyone taking Hastings's advice, the conservation world was stunned at how seriously the Reagan administration took the "sagebrush rebellion" and supported federal land sales.

At first the "sagebrush rebellion" appeared to be little more than a small army of clichés riding across the West in search of a following, like a grade B parody of the West directed by Mel

Brooks. But then with the 1980 election leading "rebels" became the heads of major federal-resources programs, including the Department of the Interior. "Sagebrush rebellion" supporters emerged on key congressional committees. The "rebellion's" links with the New Right, the Moral Majority, and pro-business, anti-regulation organizations gave the movement a wider political base. Increased financial support enlarged the effectiveness of its communications and helped spread its distorted message.

Then came the "rebellion's" final solution to federal land management—"privatization." The "sagebrush rebellion" became part of a national radical movement advocating fewer governmental controls on business, fewer environmental restrictions on resource development, and a free-market economy so devoid of public-service programs that even national parks, wildlife refuges, and wilderness areas were offered as examples of governmental programs that could be provided better by private corporations. The secretary of the interior and his top staff supported transferring federal lands and resources to states and private developers. Watt and his ilk were the first such industrial appointments since Herbert Hoover's administration. With the "sagebrush rebellion" came the twentieth century's most dangerous threats to conservation and public ownership of the western lands.

The "rebellion" became the West's own regional McCarthyism. Like McCarthyism it gained momentum rapidly with fear and distortion, and it reached a fevered pitch wrapped in the flag. Utah Senator Orrin Hatch called it "the second American Revolution." It appealed to the worst human instincts by encouraging hatred for classes of people—federal employees and conservationists. "Rebels" such as Hatch claimed that federal land managers were waging a "war against the West" and were keeping citizens in "shackles." Conservationists were called "radicals" and "ruthless monsters." The "rebellion's" weapons were hysteria and slander supported neither by history nor by facts, but by a thin tissue of lies. It was fueled by greed. Every "rebel" leader was tied to public-land exploitation.

At a personal level, the "rebellion" used vandalism, persecution, and convincing threats of violence to make its point. Cars with environmentally-oriented bumperstickers often had their tires slashed. One Utah county commissioner, Calvin Black, warned BLM employees to travel in groups or in pairs along back roads, because people might shoot them. Many federal employees feared for their lives. Secretary Watt later named Black to the National Public Lands Advisory Council. Throughout Utah, Nevada, Arizona, Wyoming, Colorado, Montana, and Idaho, the mood was ugly for two years. When four big men accosted Dick Carter, a well-known wilderness leader, on a BLM field trip to the Dirty Devil River and threatened to throw him off a 500-foot-cliff a few feet away, he was convinced they would do it. Upon hearing that story, Utah's Governor Scott Matheson tried to cool things off by establishing a bipartisan commission and taking other calming political measures. But the Utah legislature had already passed the "rebellion's" bill nearly unanimously.

During that period I was Associate Professor of public-land policy at Utah State University's large College of Natural Resources. I spoke out against the "rebellion" and, on request for a local speaking engagement, developed a speech calling the "rebellion" "the new McCarthyism" because of its methods; I had studied McCarthyism and was convinced the parallel was sound. Environmentalists in the audience responded favorably, as did former students of mine who then worked for the BLM, but "rebellion" supporters did not. I gave the speech in various places, on request. Finally the leaders of the "rebellion" such as County Commissioners Calvin Black and Ray Tibbetts and the college responded in classic McCarthyesque style. The "rebels" wrote slanderous letters to newspapers and demanded that I be fired. Although Utah State University is the leading educator of federal land managers, the dean of the natural-resources college expressed his "sympathy" for the "rebellion." He would not publicly defend his alumni, his program, or his outspoken professor's right to free speech. The University president had received a joint letter from the Utah Woolgrowers Association, the Cattlemen's Association, and the Farm Bureau threatening to block funds for the dean's favorite project, a new building. University officials assured the "rebels" I would be leaving very soon. "Rebels" claimed publicly they had "fired" me, while the university officials sat on their hands. The "rebels" and the academics had simply verified the charge of McCarthyism by contributing to the personal persecution.

The Utah State University president went on to censor press

releases from the college concerning not only the "sagebrush rebellion," but the MX missile system. At the same time, the Utah State University College of Agriculture published a report sympathetic to transferring federal lands to the state. The report included dozens of errors and misquotations as well as a distorted view of public-land history. It is an embarrassment to the scientific community, but university officials distributed it widely and gave it publicity. The "rebels" did not complain about the report or about several professors who spoke out in favor of the "rebellion." For two hysterical years, academic leaders throughout the West were silent about the honesty of the movement. Academic institutions that had both the data and the historical perspective to challenge the "rebellion" were silent. Not one leader of natural-resource academics in the West opposed the "rebels."

The "sagebrush rebellion" demonstrated the fallibility of our leaders and institutions. Most responsible and moderate politicians from the West did not oppose the movement when its first selfish rumbles came out of Nevada. Finally Bruce Babbit, Arizona's bright young governor who was well educated in history, began to call the "rebels' " bluff. The son of a prominent ranching family, he exposed the dishonesty of the "rebellion" as "a land grab in thin disguise."

The communications media—newspapers, magazines, radio, and television—failed to probe and impartially present the issues. Instead they reported the "rebels' " outrageous distortions as if they were true and made little effort to present the views of conservationists or public-land officials. Such reporting from the small western newspapers—which Bernard De Voto had accurately called a "surprisingly reactionary press"—was expected. But the larger newspapers and media organizations were also captivated by the colorful side of the "rebellion" and their unbalanced coverage breathed life into the corpse of McCarthyism—reincarnated with a cowboy hat.

McCarthyism was perpetuated by fabrications and dishonesty for many years. The "rebellion" utilized the same approach for its considerable publicity and perpetuated several myths. One was the proposal to "give the lands back to the states." The states did not pay for these lands; the republic of the United States did. People from throughout the nation fought and paid for them. A major part of the "sagebrush rebellion's" geography is in California, Nevada, Utah, New Mexico, and Arizona; Marine Corps troops marched into Mexico City during July 1848 and persuaded the Mexican government to surrender its northern territory. The "rebels" asking for "simple justice" could more logically support giving the lands back to Mexico, or to the Indians the Mexicans took them from, than to the states that have never owned them.

Although the "rebels" have tried to perpetuate a myth that transferring federal land out of public ownership is as righteous as the American Revolution, history shows that the cession of the original thirteen colonies' claims to lands between the Appalachian Crest and the Mississippi River was a major issue in the Continental Congress. Its settlement took months of debate and transferred 233 million acres *from* the original thirteen states *to* the federal government. The founding fathers considered the solution fair and just because these frontier lands were "won with common effort, common purse and blood." The cessions gave unity, power, and much-needed capital to the new nation.

For the "sagebrush rebels" to call their movement a "revolution" was insulting. No more Tory-like "rebels" have ever gracelessly clamored for their own self-interest, offering neither sacrifice nor far-sighted vision.

Another of the myths is that the West is a colony held hostage by the East. This view has several historic roots, partly in the writings of Texas historian Walter Prescott Webb. In the 1930s Webb and others conceived of an East-versus-West conflict in public-land policy issues. In a weak defense of the lawless behavior and traditions of the western livestock industry, Webb maintained the East imposed conservation on the West because most of the population lived in the East. The stock raisers were "forced" to break the land laws not because they wanted to, but because they had no alternative. This theme was central to the "sagebrush rebellion." However, if one goes beyond a middle-school version of civics, the opposite point can be made.

A similar basis for the myth lies in what Gifford Pinchot, the first chief of the Forest Service, thought. He spoke and wrote about the western propensity to waste its resources and squander its heritage, as opposed to the eastern concern for conservation. But Pinchot had a simplistic impression not supported by an analysis of public-land laws and policies.

Both Webb and Pinchot were mistaken. Throughout the twentieth century, the House and Senate interior committees have been the major influence over the public lands, because they decide what legislation receives public hearings and what bills reach the full House and Senate for a vote. They develop legislative specialists and concentrate political power. Throughout the century these public-land committees have been dominated by western congressmen. The chairmen are usually westerners born and bred, and most members have been from the West. The major public-land laws of this century have been guided through both the House and Senate by western representatives.

Various important western representatives have supported conservation. Senator Newlands of Nevada wrote the Reclamation Act of 1902. The Taylor Grazing Act was written by and named after a Colorado congressman. Early in this century, Utah's Senator Reed Smoot served twenty-eight years on the Senate Committee on Public Lands and Surveys; he was chair for several years and was a constant leader on conservation policies. He championed giving the public control of the forests, creating national parks, and discouraging the waste of resources. Other western congressmen of the era supported conserving and reserving federal lands—Francis Warren of Wyoming, Thomas Walsh of Montana, and Key Pittman and Francis Newlands of Nevada.

Recent leaders are also from the West. Senator Lee Metcalf of Montana, Senator Frank Church of Idaho, and Congressman Morris Udall of Arizona made strong conservationist marks on the 1970s. Public-lands legislation is still dominated by westerners, too. Congressman Wayne Aspinall of Colorado held even the Wilderness Act of 1964 hostage until it allowed mining, grazing, and water development. More recently western congressmen passed both the Payment in Lieu of Taxes Act and the Rangeland Improvement Act of 1978, benefiting the western states. For more than sixty years hard-rock miners in the West have successfully resisted attempts to modify the hopelessly outdated 1872 Mining Law. Stock raisers and miners both continue to receive the most favored treatment among the growing number of public-land users. Senator James McClure's amendment to the 1980 Interior appropriations bill exemplifies the worst of western influence on public-land policy. The Idaho senator's efforts limited grazing reductions on BLM lands, encouraged overgrazing, and tied the hands of public-land managers. Even the Wild Horse and Burro Act was a western product, and although many westerners liked to blame it on eastern preservationists, its history reveals the West's strong support for saving wild horses.

During the peak of the "sagebrush rebellion," Nevada's Congressman James Santini, an outspoken "rebel," appeared on national television giving an impassioned, inaccurate description of western problems with the Bureau of Land Management since the passage of the Federal Land Policy and Management Act (FLPMA) of 1976. One reporter asked how such an act could pass Congress, and Congressman Santini answered that thirty western congressmen had been outvoted by more than 400 urban and eastern congressmen.

At the time, Santini had spent years on the House Interior Committee. He understood that a western-dominated Interior Committee produced FLPMA after hard work by its members, such as Montana's John Melcher, Arizona's Morris Udall, and Wyoming's Teno Roncalio. He also knew that the final act included many of his own amendments, which served business interests. But on national television, Santini fueled the dishonest side of the "sagebrush rebellion" and ignored one fact: he voted for the act.

Another "rebel," Utah's Senator Orrin Hatch, traveled around the West calling for "the Second American Revolution" and claiming that the federal government was waging a "war on the West." He said, "We must throw off the shackles in which the federal government now holds the destiny of the West— ownership of the public domain." He said the land-management agencies had been "as oppressive as King George III."

But he focused on federal management, and his opponents could not defend themselves. In the 1930s Congress passed the Hatch Act, named for a senator from New Mexico, that kept federal employees from being involved in political controversies as representatives of the government's agencies. The purpose was to protect employees from political influence, but the present Senator Hatch used the act as a shield. Because the BLM's employees and other public-land managers could not respond, they had to sit back and take the insults, distortions, and half-truths Senator Hatch and other "rebels" used to foment contro-

THE NIGHTMARE OF PRIVATIZATION

versy. James Santini once asked a group of militant miners for "solutions to the Bureau of Land Management short of assassination." He practically invited violence against public servants, knowing they could not respond.

The "sagebrush rebellion," led by miners and stock raisers, emerged from the Nevada legislature early in 1979 as Nevada Statute 633(1979), which claimed to seize all BLM land in the state—some 48 million acres. Riding a wave of attention from the media, the concept of taking over federal lands spread to Utah, Idaho, Alaska, and other western states. Several states appropriated funds to pursue the issue in the courts. In Congress Utah's Senator Hatch and Nevada's Representative Santini led the movement. They introduced bills to transfer all BLM lands and some Forest Service lands to the respective states. Development-oriented law firms, such as the Mountain States Legal Foundation led by James Watt, filed more lawsuits; off-road vehicle groups, western counties, miners, and other groups defied BLM regulations. But the idea of transferring federal land to state and private ownership attracted most of the attention.

A key point the "sagebrush rebels" argue for is that the states have a right to the public domain by virtue of the "equal footing doctrine," which should allow them to have an equal percentage of private lands as eastern states.

But this argument distorts the history of the national policies regarding land. When several of the original states ceded lands to the federal government, they insisted that, as a principle, other states coming into the Union relinquish their public lands, too, to be held in trust for all the people. New territory, such as the Louisiana Purchase, Florida, and the Mexican Cession, was acquired and paid for by all the people.

For more than a hundred years, most of Congress's attention was devoted to the problem of public lands, and for a hundred years the lands were transferred to state, private, and corporate ownership. Although in Thomas Jefferson's eyes any frontier lands should be used to benefit all the people, most lands were intended to be transferred to private ownership eventually. But around the turn of the twentieth century, changing social values brought about the first conservation movement. Large blocks of federal land were reserved from private development for conservation and public purposes. In the same period the frontier movement broke against the West's aridity, and tens of thousands of busted homesteaders let hundreds of thousands of acres revert to public ownership. Roughly half the public lands in the West went undeveloped, and for all practical purposes, disposal of public lands ended by the early 1920s.

Then the third Public Land Review Commission transmitted its report to President Hoover on April 10, 1930. One of its many recommendations was that the federal lands be transferred to the states.

Secretary of the Interior Ray Wilbur concurred, as did President Hoover, but sentiment in the West was mixed. Stock raisers wanted preferential bidding and a very low minimum price before they could be convinced that the transfer would be beneficial. Utah's Governor George Dern testified that he and others did not like the idea at all: "The States already own, in their school land grants, millions of acres of this same kind of land, which they can neither sell nor lease, and which is yielding no income. Why should they want more of this precious heritage of desert?"

By the early 1930s the states and ranchers passed up the opportunity to own the public domain, because it was not considered valuable. Then some laws were passed establishing a system to manage the public land, most important of which was the Taylor Grazing Act of 1934 encompassing most of the remaining public domain. The act established the small Grazing Service to serve the stock raisers, who then had the best of both worlds—subsidized grazing without property taxes. The Grazing Service and the General Land Office became the BLM in 1946, still serving the stock raisers.

Not content to have publicly-supported grazing and free minerals, the stock raisers and miners attempted to gain control of all western lands in the 1940s and 1950s, but with Utah's Bernard De Voto in the lead, conservationists prevailed. During the 1960s and 1970s the rapid growth in outdoor recreation and the environmental movement generated more interest in the millions of acres the Bureau of Land Management managed. After many studies and reports, in 1976 Congress passed the Federal Land Policy and Management Act. The opening words of the act were: "The Congress declares that it is the policy of the United States that the public lands be retained in federal ownership. . . ." While it allowed small tracts to be transferred, this

BLM organic act ended 200 years of public-land disposal. The remaining lands were to be held in public trust. The matter seemed settled.

Bernard De Voto could probably have predicted the hydra-headed monster would emerge again as a "states' rights" issue only three years later. This time it was called the "sagebrush rebellion." The cast had both old characters such as Ronald Reagan and some fresh-scrubbed new faces such as Orrin Hatch, but the intent was just the same. Behind the principled rhetoric was a simple goal—to liquidate the West's mineral and energy resources. "Rebels" thought development was too slow, conservationists were too strong, and the federal restrictions on development were too tight. In a nation noted for public-land fraud, this was the biggest land-grab ever, and the issue even included who would control the public's resources.

The objective of the people—and corporations—behind the "rebellion" was more than just title to the dry sagebrush lands in the West. The rise in prices for energy and minerals stimulated a multifaceted mining boom, and mining companies were prospecting for gold, silver, coal, gas, oil, oil shale, and uranium in many remote but spectacular canyon areas and mountains of the western states. Using and developing these lands was the central issue. The several land-management agencies tried to control and direct this development, in part using the authority of the BLM organic act.

Controls that favored the public's long-term interest stimulated the "rebellion," but "rebels" perpetuated the idea that the issue was environmentalism versus development. Senator Hatch was at the forefront of the fray. He criticized park managers as "land embalmers" and said public-land policy was directed to please "a handful of environmental radicals." He reached a new low in symbology by referring to environmentalists as a "cult of toadstool worshippers."

A constant theme of the "rebels" and their newfound partners of the New Right was that the federal government is a ruthless monster. Responsive government has been difficult to obtain on a local, state, or federal level, but the "rebels" said the Bureau of Land Management was an example of big, unresponsive federal government. The BLM has been and remains a small regional agency, long known for its pliability in the hands of local developers. The "rebels" did not oppose the Forest

Service, Park Service, or Fish and Wildlife Service, all more restrictive in their management, and they did not oppose the Defense Department, which is a large western landowner.

Supporters of right-wing political organizations and the "sagebrush rebellion" said the western states would be more responsible managers, although those same states have long been dominated by corporations and have some of the poorest environmental records, the weakest conservation policies, and the most corrupt histories in the management of public land. Nevada State Senator Cliff Young, a former congressman, summarized one record: "The history of the State of Nevada in land management is one of the sorriest chapters in the history of land management among the western states."

A final argument that many of the "sagebrush rebellion's" supporters make is that somehow Congress has a moral right and the public an obligation to give up these federal lands to the states and to the special interests that use them. This argument is often disguised as a states' rights issue, but it ignores our history and the fact that in the 1920s and before, the states had opportunities to acquire the remaining lands now managed by the Bureau of Land Management. The states and private individuals passed up their opportunity. But now the lands are valuable for their resources, and "states' rights" has become a convenient argument.

It is unlikely the "sagebrush rebellion's" leaders really had states' rights in mind. Some states might manage the lands for a few years, but in the end millions of acres would be transferred to private and corporate ownership. Even a superficial look at the history of state land in Nevada, Utah, New Mexico, or Arizona reveals the abysmal state records. Obviously it is easier for Exxon and other energy and mineral corporations to manipulate not the federal government, but Nevada, Utah, Idaho, and other sparsely-populated states.

The leaders of the "sagebrush rebellion" were miners, ranchers, and loggers, but the apparent campaign of the little guy was really financed and planned by large development corporations that have in the past supported not the public interest, but their own private economic interests. They have not advocated multiple-use policies that provide long-term protection of our national resources, but their self-centered commercial interest. Their political spokespeople are noted for short-sightedness, serving their personal and corporate self-interest, not the needs of future generations.

Although its arguments are neither historically nor legally sound, the "rebellion" began for several reasons. First, the lands' resources became more valuable. In addition, people were legitimately frustrated over a tangle of land-management regulations. They began reacting just as new laws began to alter the traditional patterns of land use in the West, responding to national recreation trends and the growth of the conservation movement. For the first time in history traditional public-land users had to share the lands, and land managers were forced to consider the entire public. The "sagebrush rebellion" was a desperate attempt not only to regain past influence, but eventually to gain title to the land itself, with the minerals made available—cheap.

Surely the more rational supporters of the "rebellion" knew their arguments could never hold up in court. The Supreme Court has consistently ruled the federal government can set its own policies on the federal lands; the constitutional authority is clear. There was also little hope of gaining immediate control through legislation. But the "rebels" could terrorize and intimidate the BLM through spokespeople such as Senator Hatch and Congressman Santini. They were successful at that. During the Reagan administration the Interior Department's agencies have been ruled by fear. The clock has been turned back, so the BLM can again be called the Bureau of Livestock and Mining. It has been a reign of terror for professional land managers.

The Sagebrush Rebellion was little more than a regional political movement riding on mythology, but the myths are not so frightening as the reality. Other attempts to transfer the federal lands to the states failed during the 1920s, '30s, '40s, and '50s, largely because the lands were considered worthless. Today more than 65 percent of the nation's remaining energy reserves are found under western public lands. Oil, gas, tar sands, oil shale, coal, geothermal fields, and uranium resources are all there. It was no coincidence that ranchers, miners, energy companies, and right-wing organizations and foundations suddenly joined together to express a newly-found philosophical concern over public-land management. The motivation was money, big money, the mother's milk of American politics.

John L. Mathews, an early muckraker, wrote in *Hampton's*

Magazine in December 1909 about Secretary of the Interior Ballinger granting rights of way on public lands to railroad corporations. Mathews quoted Secretary Ballinger as saying, "You chaps who are in favor of this conservation program are all wrong. You are hindering the development of the West. In my opinion, the proper course to take with regard to this (public domain) is to divide it up among the big corporations and the people who know how to make money out of it and let the people at large get the benefits of the circulation of the money." Ballinger's statement was a classic "trickle down" theory of resource development.

Mathews' analysis of Ballinger easily fits former Interior Secretary Watt. "It is not probable that he is corrupt in the sense that a direct bribe could induce him to defraud the government. Mr. Ballinger is primarily an attorney who has received his training in representing large business interests, and it is entirely natural that his sympathies should be found on the side of corporations and capitalists when they come into conflict with the interests of the whole people as represented by the government." Mathews summarized by saying, "The Domain should not be a grab bag, but a treasure house in which the nation shall hold a vast store of riches to be developed economically for the public's good."

Interior Secretaries Ballinger and Watt shared the same zealous belief in the economic market, a distrust of the public at large, and a sense of alienation from democratic institutions and government. They demonstrated the economic theory by which the public has continually lost resources, wealth, and freedom to corporations.

But while other interior secretaries have set out to transfer public wealth to private hands, James Watt carried out his program on a scale that even his strongest foes took months to grasp. Environmentalists reacted to specific and often symbolic threats to the public lands, but James Watt focused on the wealth of the entire land.

The Reagan administration's program for the public lands took two fundamental directions. First and most direct, it planned to sell large segments of the public lands under a scheme called "privatization." Less directly but more successfully, Watt leased energy resources. For nearly eighteen months the leasing program proceeded virtually unchallenged until two of the nation's largest newspapers, *The New York Times* and *Los Angeles Times*, focused on it. Watt was busy transferring to corporate ownership the largest share of the public wealth ever released in the history of the federal lands. It was a trillion-dollar leasing program. Watt's leases made Albert Fall's Teapot Dome leases look like a child robbing a piggy bank.

The program directly served the economic interests of the world's largest energy corporations. They gained control over the public's vast energy resources, and Watt's new development regulations also gave them near-total control over the resource development. It was patronage for corporations whose interests were not merely national, but international in scope. Teddy Roosevelt often spoke of a nation being only as strong as its resources. Watt, while raising the issue of national security and calling for energy independence, was undermining the very foundation of the nation.

Watt launched his leasing program soon after he took office. He understood that most of the wealth of the federal lands was in energy resources. The rush to develop energy had left private lands exhausted; approximately two-thirds of the remaining fossil and other reserves in the United States were believed to be under public lands and the outer continental shelf. The secretary of the interior had wide-ranging powers granted by Congress to dispose of such resources.

The leases were probably legal. They were essentially sales—contracts. In some cases the contracts will last forty or fifty years or more, at which time the corporations will return the drained lands to the public. The contracts cannot be cancelled without due process and just compensation to the corporations.

The leases may have been legal, but they were also immoral. They violated the idea that protecting resources is a moral obligation to future generations—a sacred trust.

Nevertheless Secretary Watt set out to lease *all* energy resources on the public lands during his term. He scheduled all western geothermal areas, a small but developing energy resource, to be leased during 1982. Only a few were not leased. Geothermal areas adjacent to national parks, wildlife refuges, and wilderness areas were put on the auction block without determining whether development would damage the protected areas. Other geothermal areas were leased in sensitive areas where development would definitely threaten wildlife and water resources. In most cases the agency responsible for leasing prepared only the most superficial assessment of environmental impacts. The price was low, too. On tens of thousands of acres, the non-competitive leasing system earned the public a dollar an acre. Virtually all of the geothermal leasing was done quietly without allowing public comment. Some states such as California protested the size, scope, and speed of the program, but staff were overwhelmed by the process, and they examined only the most critical areas in detail. Only a few areas, in wilderness areas, were blocked.

Watt also leased other forms of energy rapidly. Although oil-shale leases had been offered before and had brought only a small fraction of their potential value, Watt began leasing more oil shale as well as tar sands. Exxon and other energy corporations received billion-dollar federal grants to develop synthetic fuels and were then allowed to buy cheap oil shale on the public lands. But the technology for oil-shale development was not yet developed, so the sensible and conservative approach would have been to save the resource for the future. Being genuinely conservative, however, had no place in Watt's rush to develop the public's energy resources.

Similarly, before Watt's administration federal coal-leasing had been halted for a decade because far more coal had already been leased than could be efficiently developed. More than 16.5 billion tons had been transferred to corporate hands in more than 500 leases covering nearly a million acres of public land. Already-leased federal coal would not be exhausted at current rates of mining for a hundred years. Watt was not impressed. First he loosened the coal-development regulations, then in spring 1982 offered the largest coal lease in history—for the Powder River Basin in Montana.

He sold a billion and a half tons of public coal, worth $20 to $25 a ton at the mine mouth, for an average price of $0.035 per ton. In one sale the public lost resources worth more than $30 billion. By the time the coal is developed in the twenty-first century, it will be worth several times that amount. Coal sold by the federal government a decade before the energy crisis had earned the public more than ten times Watt's per-ton fee; angry American Indians had gone to court to seek relief from scandalous coal leases of the 1960s that had earned them only $0.15 a ton.

But Watt was not stopped by these arguments, nor did he rest. After the massive Powder River sale, he scheduled another 5 billion tons of coal to be sold.

Onshore oil and gas resources followed. In 1981 and 1982 Secretary Watt opened vast areas to development—a hundred million acres in Alaska alone. Several million acres of Alaska's wildlife refuges were opened for the first time to oil and gas leasing. Military bases conserved and protected for decades were offered. Alaska's massive petroleum reserve, considered a wartime reserve since 1923, was released in the largest oil lease in history. Watt allowed California's Elk Hills petroleum reserve, protected since 1912 even from the corruption of Interior Secretary Albert Fall, to be pumped at record rates; it was scheduled for exhaustion by the late 1980s.

Oil companies stampeded to develop oil and gas in the nation's wilderness. Within months they claimed millions of acres in fifty designated wilderness areas. An outraged public in Montana, Wyoming, and throughout the West blocked Watt's plans in designated wilderness. Still the rush for leases went on. In California the BLM sold more than 2500 leases covering more than 3 million acres in only a few weeks. All the leases were non-competitive and were sold for a dollar an acre. Most were sold with a one-page checklist of environmental impacts.

The public that owned the land was oblivious to the massive program. State agencies and conservation organizations could not even discover the size and scope of the program, because it proceeded so rapidly and on such a wide scale. When Watt's orgy of onshore leasing finally abated, *every* possible acre with oil and gas potential had been transferred to private ownership, most under long-term, non-competitive leases.

Watt's largest leasing program, however, involved a billion acres of outer-continental shelf (OCS), where most known oil and gas was to be found. At 1982 prices the estimated potential reserves were worth $1.4 trillion.

In nearly thirty years of OCS oil leasing fewer than 40 million acres had been sold. During his first year in office Watt sold more than 44 million acres. At the same time he prepared a schedule to sell a billion acres; the entire outer-continental shelf was to be sold in five years. As planned, it would be the largest single transfer of public wealth to private hands in the history of the United States. This time Watt met widespread opposition from coastal states, counties, and cities. Undaunted, he finalized the program in the face of lawsuits and public outcry. A few areas were blocked by Congress and legal action, but most proceeded as scheduled.

Watt's energy-leasing program was deceptively simple but will have massive economic consequences for decades. The price the public earned for selling its resources was minimal. At the same time Watt gave more control to the energy companies, which are now free to develop the resources when the prices are highest. As a result resources purchased at a fraction of their current value will not be developed for twenty years or more. By the end of the twentieth century, together they will be worth $36,000 for every American citizen. As a final gift to industry and price for the people, hundreds of regulations designed to protect the environment on public lands were weakened or entirely eliminated.

But if Watt's energy-leasing program was hidden from public view, the Reagan administration's second attack on the public lands was straightforward and clear. The solution to public-land problems was to sell the lands.

Public ownership, according to the Reagan administration's free-market economic theorists, was fatally flawed because of inherently "inefficient" management. Public ownership could not match private ownership in "efficiency" because public servants were improperly motivated. The solution to "inefficient" management was simple: sell—or even give—the lands to private business, which would earn a profit, thus assuring that the lands were properly managed. Not only did this theory ignore all of human history, but at its core it claimed that greed would protect the land.

Early in 1982 the Reagan administration revealed its plans to "privatize" federal lands. The president set up a cabinet-level Property Review Board, which set out to take an inventory of all federal lands and identify those available for sale. The plan was to sell $17 billion's worth of federal lands in five years, ostensibly in part to help reduce the national debt. In reality it was one more attempt to plunder the lands.

Historically more than a billion acres of federal lands had been sold and transferred to private ownership; but almost every public-land law in the twentieth century was designed to conserve and protect federal lands and to keep them in the public trust. Fortunately in the late 1970s Congress protected the national forests and wildlife refuges from arbitrary sale or transfer by an anti-conservation administration. Some congressional limitations protected BLM lands, but they were an incomplete program. Public lands administered by the Corps of Engineers, the Bureau of Reclamation, and other agencies could be offered up for sale.

Free-market economists like Steve Hanke and conservative "think tanks" like the Heritage Foundation began advancing their myopic vision of a nation without any public lands. They decided that all public-land services were flawed, ignoring fifty years of progress in the science and conservation of federal lands. In their tidy vision all public lands, even national parks and wilderness areas, would be sold to private organizations and protected by the willingness of people to pay. They rejected the concept of common land and a public-land trust. The market was their dream, replacing the age-old love of land in the human heart.

Interestingly, the free-market theorists often enjoyed profitable contracts with business-oriented "institutes." The market rewarded many people who were selling the "privatization" concept.

But the market alone cannot reward the people or the land managers or protect the land. Although free-market economists consider the land-managing organizations as boxes on charts, the Forest Service, the Park Service, and other agencies are staffed by humans who spend many hours each day close to the land they are charged with managing. Their stewardship becomes part of their lives. However misguided agencies' policies—and top-level personnel—may be, the field rangers are no heartless bureaucrats, but are people who love the land with a passion equal to the farmers', the ranchers', or the loggers'. It is peoples' love for the land that links the public's property with the organizations that protect it and its resources. This passion cannot be duplicated or substituted for in facile market theories, and it is crucial to good care of the earth.

It may be true that the land managers are not performing at their peak. Many of them are frustrated, and one big reason is that people with economic self-interest in mind encourage the breaking of laws designed to conserve resources. Special-interest legislation and gross subsidies of mining, livestock grazing, and water development on the national commons have defeated federal land-managers' attempts to protect much of the land. But simply blaming the institutions and selling the land will not work. The fault lies with politicians who pass legislation encouraging the waste of resources, and with a system of ethics that tolerates stealing public resources for private gain.

To solve these problems, free-market economists propose more selfishness at public expense. They ignore a hundred years of history in the shrunken perspective of their simplistic economic theory.

The last hundred years of public policy have encouraged conservation, which implies not only land laws, but a land ethic, a moral obligation each generation has to the future. Privatization negates that idea. Carried to its logical conclusion, privatization would ultimately grant to private corporations our finest, most treasured lands—not just the national parks and wildlife refuges, but our shrines and battlefields. Yosemite might be sold to Music Corporation of America, the Grand Canyon to Trans World Airlines, and Gettysburg and the Lincoln Monument to the highest bidder. If a people were to place its lands and sacred places on the auction block, when would the sale end?

The Reagan administration's plans for privatization are a first step toward liquidating the public lands. The emphasis on the initial land sales, which covered several areas and a few thousand acres, was to sell high-value urban lands, even though for two decades it has clearly been the Interior Department's policy to acquire lands near urban areas to correct the imbalanced distribution of public lands. The Reagan administration's privatization program set out to reverse that trend and, with each acre sold, to remove tangible assets from the American people.

The legacy of the Reagan-Watt administration is massive wealth taken stealthily from this and future generations. To sell such a treasure to reduce the national debt is like selling the family farm to support a drug habit. To cut off the people from their historic ties to wilderness land would eventually weaken the heart and soul of the nation. It would mark the rise of land barons and reduce the collective strength of the people.

President Reagan's economists who promote the privatization program often speak of the wonders and freedom found in a free-market economy, but their "freedom" contains only the single dimension of monetary freedom. The public lands offer a multi-dimensional freedom that cannot be found in cities, on highways, or anywhere else in a modern world. Common land, open and free public land, is a place for the heart and the human spirit to be bound not by walls or fences, but by the strength of one's legs and the span of one's vision. Each acre sold costs the heritage of the next generation and diminishes freedom in this nation.

Land has always been more than a commodity, and the ethic of caring for it for the good of future generations represents one of humanity's most fundamental hopes. It is both a vision and an obligation, which sets humans apart from the other animals and civilization from barbarism. Free-market economists want to replace altruism and concern for the future with a grubby struggle to buy and sell every scrap of earth. It is a dreary view, an insult to the beauty in the human spirit and the earth.

Summit of the Sierras

16

Land Reform For
the Future

Sagebrush valleys and rugged desert mountains made strong impressions on Wovoka as he grew up during the middle of the nineteenth century. He was a youth during the western Indians' eclipse, and the heroic tales he heard from the old people in the tribe contrasted sharply with the daily insults to both land and Indian that he witnessed. The foundation of Native American life was being systematically purged, and Indian people were persecuted, robbed, even casually shot.

The desert sun conspired with the winter storm and ancient dreams to build an exalted vision. Wovoka imagined the ghost dance. From Walker Lake, Nevada, his vision caught the wistful dreams of a thousand humbled warriors from dozens of diverse western tribes. The vision was so powerful and the dance so bedazzling that age-old enemies whose territories had been mapped by combat dreamed and danced together. The ghost dance would bring back the buffalo, warm and vibrant, from the blood-soaked soil that had swallowed their power. Generations of warriors who had fought lifetimes of enemies would rise up, drive the white people out of the West, and save the earth. According to Wovoka, warriors purified by dance and dreams would be impervious to the white peoples' bullets.

Wovoka was mistaken. But the western sun has fired more than one mystical frenzy; the vision of public lands' inexhaustible abundance mesmerized a corporate attorney, James Watt. When he became secretary of the interior he envisioned that not warriors or buffalo, but oil rigs and bulldozers would spring forth from the arid lands. Watt's dream was a mirage of coal, oil, and gas, a cornucopia of resources to feed the voracious appetite of industry. In his vision, under his leadership the public-land resources would "restore America's greatness." As old warriors' hearts were stirred by dreams of buffalo thunder on the land, so were the warriors of Wall Street stirred by Watt's dream of unleashing the machinery of industry on the public lands.

The ghost dance fantasy died at the Battle of Wounded Knee, the last Indian uprising. Wovoka lived quietly near Walker Lake, Nevada, a fallen messiah until his death in 1932. Watt's oil derricks are just beginning to rise.

We have had a federal land system for two hundred years. It united the nation and provided freedom to choose a national destiny, power to guide the choice, and wealth to pay the price. Land was a public treasure, a national commons, and a community of life that was intertwined with the emergence of a democratic society.

Selling federal land financed the Louisiana Purchase, Jefferson's great bargain with the French. But the freedom of open land did more than just attract settlers. Land powered the march to the northwest territory, and was the essence of manifest destiny. The American land guided our history and still holds its boldest lessons and its brightest dreams.

But the history of the public lands is a tale of waste and corruption. America squandered its lands, giving far more to railroads and corporations than it ever gave to schools and colleges. The history is a story of broken promises to war veterans, to Indians, to the poor and landless of the nation. In the West stock raisers subverted the settlement acts and homestead laws to control large blocks of grazing lands. Many homesteaders ended up losing their lands to eastern trusts or land barons.

The wave of the frontier washed across the plains and into the Rockies and the Great Basin, but it broke against the aridity of the West and settled into hundreds of valleys, where sparse water could nurture the agrarian dream. The highlands and dry lands remained public domain.

The geography of the land, combined with the finest altruistic instincts, generated a major national land reform nearly a hundred years ago when a major social movement called conservation was launched. Conservation and aridity left most of the West, from the Rocky Mountain front range to the west slope of the Sierra, in public ownership. Mountain islands and desert plateaus were left wild and open.

The history of these lands, particularly in the twentieth century, has some noble aspects. The United States set some lands aside to save as part of our history, the heart of a great biological and natural heritage. The United States pioneered the concept of national parks, a democratic ideal of land management that has spread throughout the world. The nation now has the world's finest systems of parks, wildernesses, and wildlife refuges. Finally, the United States originated a theoretically good (if badly implemented) conservation effort by using public lands for multiple purposes to serve not only the demand for resources today, but the needs of future generations as well. The record of conservation on public lands helps to redeem the greed and selfishness that dominated the first hundred years of American history.

The redemption came by way of a complex system of laws designed to protect the public land while providing for its use and development. Changing priorities over the last hundred years from disposal and private use to conservation and public use was a major shift in federal policy that was built on the bedrock of national moral values. However, implementing the conservation gains depended on the good faith and judgment of one person, the secretary of the interior. Congress delegated that cabinet position almost unlimited discretionary power over the public trust; the underlying assumption was that the position would be held by people committed to conserving the heritage for future generations, not by someone like James Watt.

The conservation agenda remains unfinished because the public lands do not yet fully serve the American people; they serve special interests. Reforms that began as conservation a hundred years ago were never completed. While the federal lands remain in public ownership, their valuable products have largely become privately-controlled commodities. Grass, timber, water, and minerals including oil and gas are still controlled by a handful of people. This problem is aggravated by federal subsidies for every commercial product removed from the public lands. Private enterprise has used the political process to control the market and prevent the owners of the federal lands from earning an honest profit from their resources. Inefficiency, wasted resources, overuse of the land, and unfair competition are a few of the byproducts. The American taxpayer, whose land and wealth are harvested by private developers, is still cheated by every oil well, every mine, and every dam.

Public lands are the source of the largest welfare program in America. Laws subsidize livestock grazing and timber harvesting, in turn encouraging overgrazing and overcutting. Federally financed and built water projects obliterate fishing, wildlife habitat, freeflowing rivers, and community resources for the profit of a few people or agribusinesses. Under mining and mineral-leasing laws, national mineral resources are transferred into the hands of a few people with negligible benefit to the public. The American people have been losing not only their wealth, but the freedom to use the land.

That direction is opposite from what was intended by the social reform called conservation, which aimed to maintain the wealth of the national land as a public good using a democratic model of public-land use. Conservation was designed to end the aristocratic system by which only a few people benefited from public resources. Recent land laws have mandated more cooperation, more democracy, and more public hearings and involvement in guiding the use of the public domain. Benefits have rippled out to more people as outdoor recreationists have flocked to use the federal lands, which are a tangible source of freedom for many urban people.

But democratizing public lands threatened the old landed aristocracy, who rose up in protest. Development corporations and aristocratic land users promoted the "sagebrush rebellion" and related efforts to sell federal lands. Their power was magnified by their large political contributions, sympathetic people on congressional committees, and public indifference.

The "sagebrush rebellion" pointed out a fundamental weakness in how the public lands had been protected. The federal land agencies were unable to safeguard democratic and authentic multiple-use management. Most environmental organizations were eastern-oriented and largely neglected public-land issues. The shrillness of the small but sharply-focused minority, the "rebels," outweighed a commendable but unfocused obligation to future generations. The "sagebrush rebels" repeated the lie of "returning" federal lands to the states and were not refuted by the agencies, challenged by the media, or corrected by the academics. The agencies were afraid to respond, and the media focused on shallow and diffuse issues. The academic community in natural resources was captured by the "rebels." As the one faculty member in any western college of natural resources—at Utah State University—who did speak out, I was encouraged to leave my position. The "rebels" used most of the tactics of McCarthyism, including persecuting individuals and suppressing freedom of speech.

A conservationist's perspective on national interest, public-land history, and honesty were lost. What took their place was the rhetoric of the pioneers, innocent of the benefits of hindsight. To the pioneers, the vast oak and hardwood forests seemed limitless, but the trees fell to the blades of axes. The prairie soil was rich, deep, and tough, but the steel plow rolled the grasses over. Sixty million buffalo thundered across the Great Plains, but they fell one by one before the long reach of the Sharps rifle.

While "sagebrush rebels" talked about abundant resources, many environmentalists believed the vast mountain ranges, mesas, and deserts of the West were protected by the land's harshness. Aridity has been a great conservationist. So has economics. But just as technology made a quantum leap from the Osage bow to the Sharps rifle, some people are leaping in theories today from the ideas of conservation and sustained yield to "privatization," which declares that using land today, not conserving for tomorrow, is the most "efficient" form of management. Privatization insists that private ownership is superior to a public trust. The shift is away from the concepts of multiple-use and sustained yield toward managing land to get the most from a single nonrenewable resource. The leap is from letting livestock graze to letting giant mining shovels forage. Technology on the public lands is moving the equivalent distance from the Sharps rifle to the MX missile.

The "sagebrush rebellion" and the privatization crusade discovered a fault in the bedrock of the conservation movement. The breadth of vision and clarity of purpose were muddled. Conservationists could clearly answer why they wanted a national park, a wildlife refuge, a wild river, or a mountain wilderness. They could not answer as clearly nor as eloquently why half the western United States should remain in public ownership. They had lost sight of their basic principles. They had no arguments as appealing as the outrageous claim of the rebels to "return" their land or the pop-economic theories of the free-market economists. The bulk of the federal lands have bumped along toward protection largely as a result of historic accidents, geographic limits, economics, and a few persistent visionaries. But public lands transcend economic theory and historic accidents. They have a rightful place in the lives of this and future generations.

The Rockefeller family has generously supported conservation of public lands and parks and has purchased parts of several national parks. The Rockefellers bought about 30,000 acres and donated them to the American people to be part of Grand Teton National Park. The Grand Tetons are a great and mythical range. They are visible a hundred miles away and harbor the spirits of pioneer fur trappers and settlers. The highest peak, Grand Teton, breaks to the north in a frozen granite wave attracting snow, lightning, and climbers from around the world. Each year thousands of people climb the mountain and feel its height, breadth of vision, and sense of wellbeing. Millions of other people find similar feelings of pleasure and inspiration by only walking at its foot.

But free-market economists say private land ownership is the best way to prevent "inefficiencies" in land management. Some theorists have advocated giving the public lands away to ensure "efficiency." What would be lost if 30,000 acres of Grand Teton Park were owned by the Rockefellers? The wind, storms, and changing shadows would go on as before, giving pleasure to everyone who paused and looked. But private ownership would steal some precious magic. It would make the appreciating eye a trespasser or a mere recipient of permission to pass and would take away the sense of belonging to the mountain and its history. Today the mountain requires no cash, no permission from a benevolent landowner, no furtive trespass. It belongs to all the people, who have earned the mountain and the western lands through war, taxes, and the right of citizenship. To sell it for any price would cheapen the nation. Disappointment and sadness would accrue to non-owners who viewed the mountain.

West of the hundredth meridian lies this nation's geography of hope. From the eastern foothills of the Rocky Mountains to the western slope of the Sierra, from the Sonoran Desert to the North Cascades, the western land is an inspiration, the wildest and most rugged land. The land is higher and the air dryer, carrying a person's visions and dreams a great distance. It has left a strong mark on the nation's culture, literature, art, music, and history. From Charlie Russell to John Wesley Powell, Black Elk, and Fremont, the western land has spawned artists, heroes, and visionaries. Zane Grey, Walter Van Tilburg Clark, or Edward Abbey could not have created the images and moods of their books anywhere else.

The eastern parks and forests and other public lands have been purchased and were not part of the original public domain. They serve an essential purpose for outdoor recreation and watershed conservation, and they are beautiful. But they have, for the most part, been owned and used. The western land remained in the public domain largely because it was not suited for private ownership. Instead, cooperative and shared use and development of the land evolved. The land remains largely unsuited for a single use or solely economic purpose. Its ecology and interdependent resources require multiple uses and multiple ownership. Bundles of partial ownership have been parceled out to miners, cattle raisers, and recreationists through the political process. It is a myth of the homestead era that the western public lands are suitable for agriculture or specialized economic development. The land's best use is to be retained in shared public ownership. One generation, one political party, or one election does not give a group the right to negate the legal and moral authority to public land ownership.

There are several reasons for keeping the lands public. The arid areas are most suited to well-managed multiple-use. Combining protection and use in good stewardship requires all the intelligence and ability that any generation can muster. In this way the public lands are important demonstration areas for testing and developing conservation and rehabilitation practices that might prove applicable to private lands.

Second, federal lands are a capital resource of enormous magnitude. They are a more visible part of the public wealth than the gold in Fort Knox. Managing them as a trust requires that the public owners earn a fair market income. The federal lands are important sources of forest products, mineral resources, and energy in many forms. They hold large reserves of natural resources whose development should benefit the nation; the federal agencies should be honest representatives in managing and selling these resources.

Third, public lands are more than commodities, they are storehouses of a biological and cultural heritage. The frontier and the dimensions of the pioneers can be felt only on the public lands, which are also vast storehouses of plant and animal species we have only begun to understand. In the future the federal lands will be needed as priceless gene pools of resources that were squandered in the single-minded development of private lands. These lands are not a burden on society, but a sacred responsibility.

Finally, the public lands are worth protecting because they are tangible objects of irreplaceable beauty. They are as valuable in their natural state as the rarest painting, sculpture, or other human artifact. They are a national gallery of wild land, beautiful and inspiring. The federal land has a spiritual dimension that is vital not only to Native Americans, but to millions of other Americans who venture out in search of something larger than themselves.

The freedom to use this land is a cherished right. The spiritual energies available from public lands are not the targets of private enterprise, but they will be lost if the attempts at privatization are successful. We will be like the Indians a century ago who lost their land, and with it their power and their source of inner strength. They looked around, and not only the buffalo were gone, but their land as well. Linda Hogan, a Native American, described the fate: "We're full of bread and gas getting fat on the outside while inside we grow thin. The earth is wounded and will not heal. Night comes down like a blackbird with blue flame that never sleeps and spreads its wings around us."

Unrestrained development of resources can also kill the spirit of the land. Until recently—the Pleistocene epoch—there lived in the West mammoths, mastodons, saber-tooth tigers, two species of bison, camels, horses, and ground sloths twenty feet long. In many of the dry caves in the Great Basin, above the water levels of the Pleistocene lakes, a hiker can still find the scats of giant sloths. Although these great mammals survived several climatic changes, they began to disappear rapidly when the weather dried and warmed 11,000 years ago. Throughout North America many Pleistocene species became extinct shortly after —and probably because of—the arrival of the world's most efficient predator, *Homo sapiens*. Armed with an elegant tool crafted from solid rock, the Folsom spear point, early humans preyed on all the large Pleistocene animals.

The animals' rapid decline began in North America when people arrived who had a simple weapon and the ability to cooperate but little understanding of the consequences of their actions. A common trait of theirs was the limited use of tools with an unrestrained use of resources.

In the nineteenth century George Perkins Marsh described the same pattern through history and linked it to the decline of civilizations. Such an irresponsible view of land and resources should have died with the Pleistocene's great mammals, but it did not. The relic ideas of cave people clung like small remnant glaciers; deep in the reptilian core of the human brain lurked the dark instinct to waste the environment. Today the lands are managed allowing essentially an unlimited use of tools and little restraint on resource use; conservation was a thin veneer of reason on a barbaric brain-pattern reaching back into the eons.

In the early 1980s more energy and more public wealth is being given away than ever before in the history of the public lands. The Reagan administration's radical changes in managing and disposing of the federal lands have, with every major action, diminished the public grip on the lands and favored people and corporations with an economic interest in development. In a long line of interior secretaries, James Watt emerged as the most successful representative of corporate profit at public expense. He used the perspective of a Pleistocene man.

James Watt has shown clearly the necessity for reforming the system that administers public land. As matters now stand the record of interior secretaries guarding the public trust must always remain unbroken; if even one breaks the pattern, the public loses. For example, a dozen interior secretaries may follow Watt for the next fifty or seventy-five years, and each may be deeply committed to protecting the federal lands for future generations. But without reform each will watch as the thousands of oil, gas, geothermal, and other leases Watt virtually gave away are cashed in. At least three generations of Americans might witness his damage.

Congress must seize the power from Interior and condemn the underpriced leases of the Reagan administration. It is possible for Congress to cancel the leases and return the cash invested by the energy corporations. In the future, the leases can be developed when the public is assured a fair and honest return on its heritage. Other leases can be challenged in court and cancelled for legal reasons. But it will take an interior secretary as committed to conservation as Watt was to the corporation. The leadership must come from the owners of the land; then Congress and the Interior Department will follow. As long as the lodes of energy lie beneath the public lands, the leases are merely paper. Paper can be torn up, and the lands and resources can be saved for the next generation—but only if citizens demand it.

The public must rescue the lost lands and ensure they are protected for the future. The first reform is simple: Congress delegated awesome powers to the secretary of the interior and now must remove them. Watt vividly demonstrated the potential for abuse. Congress must regain control over the sale of public land and resources. The interior secretary's powers must be carefully trimmed and circumscribed by Congress, and both the secretary and agency staff must be required by force of law and threat of criminal punishment to completely and honestly represent and protect the interests of the American people, the public interest. They must never represent the corporate sector.

Congress must ensure that the secretary of the interior and top agency professionals are not guilty of collusion with public-land industries. Agency secretaries should be prohibited from recruiting top Interior and Agriculture officials from the industries they are charged with supervising. The test of the suitability of public-land officials should be their past records and commitment to the public interest. The nation's top conservation officer should be an environmentalist by previous experience, not a representative of industry. Public service in the resources field should be an honorable profession and should not be service to economic development.

Still another reform must require that land managers let the economic market operate for the benefit of the owners of the public land. Congress must end the subsidies of special economic groups. All resources taken from public lands must earn a fair return, and there must be an end to long-term leases and resource sales that permit developers to gain windfall profits at public expense.

Two examples of areas needing reform are grazing permits

and water rights. The grass sold from public lands should be auctioned off to the highest bidder; no one should have preference at the expense of competition. Water flowing from the public lands should be by law a public resource, and its highest and best uses should be public ones. Whenever it is diverted to private economic uses, the public must earn a fair and honest profit. Water developed and sold from public projects should earn enough to amortize the cost at prevailing interest rates.

Special economic interests should not by law or tradition have any preferred tenure rights on the public lands. Many early developers gained the use of public lands by fraud or trespass, and these activities should be discontinued when they conflict with public uses and are subsidized by taxpayers. Long-term leases should be shortened to allow reevaluation of their terms and to change their conditions. Such leases only eliminate public benefits.

The federal government should not directly develop public-land resources, but should be an honest broker for the public. Minerals and other resources on the public lands should be developed, but not by the government. The government should sell resources at a fair market price so as not to compete with private development or to subsidize a few fortunate corporations. Public agencies should watchdog the public rights.

The Reagan administration insisted that private enterprise could best manage the lands, but this was only an excuse to give away public-land energy. The lands would be efficiently managed if the market were allowed to operate for the public-land owners—the American people. An end to subsidies would end the unfairness and would allow the resources to be developed more rationally and effectively. Everyone would benefit. Perversions of the market would be erased, the land would be well managed, and the public would earn a fair return on its land.

Congress should establish a perpetual public-lands-investment trust fund with some of the revenues from the public lands, particularly from selling non-renewable resources. A priority objective of the fund would be acquiring lands to serve the public interest. Incomplete national parks, national forests, and wildlife refuges should be completed. Ecological units should be acquired where possible. Parcels that are small and isolated or that are needed for community development should be sold or traded; however, the funds from such transactions would be earmarked for new public-land acquisition.

A large portion of the trust fund would be invested in the productivity of the land by reclaiming mines and damaged lands, replanting clearcut forests, and stabilizing stream banks. Renewable resources such as salmon and wildlife would be restored; soil would be protected and conserved. The trust fund would use money earned from nonrenewable resources to develop renewable resources. In this way the public lands could grow more productive and useful to future generations even as the nonrenewable resources are exhausted. In today's program income subsidizes development or reduces local taxes.

The final point in public-land reform concerns an essential aspect of our nation: democracy. The solution to managing the public lands better is not more private control by economic interests; it is more democracy. Congress must assure that the total public is honestly represented in the management of federal lands. The special interests must be thrown out. They should not have, by tradition or political muscle, any special rights. Hearings, public discussions, and advisory boards should promote open and widespread public expression in management decisions.

Land managers should be required by law to operate openly in the public eye, but also to manage land according to a national perspective, not the local economic interest. The true owners must be served, not those chosen few people who live close to the land. In case of conflicts and doubts the federal land manager should not have the discretion to decide; managers who go to school in, then live in the rural West rarely develop a national perspective. The local influence of friends, church, or habit obscure the national view. Managers should be required to serve the national public first and foremost. Local concerns should be considered only when they do not conflict with national objectives.

If the management choice weighs a non-economic use against an economic option, the public's long-term interest must be served first. Private economic development should proceed only when it does not threaten or reduce national non-economic values. Throughout history the public lands have been torn between democratic uses that benefit a broad population and aristocratic or economic forces with narrow interests. It is time for Congress to choose clearly not just for today's industry, but for future generations as well.

The nation needs a manifesto for the land—a declaration that public lands are to be managed for the long-term public good. This ethic must rest on the legal bedrock of a public trust, recognizing that protecting the lands is the most meaningful expression of public-land law and policy. The details would be complex, but the fundamental standard for using and developing public land must include the following concepts:

1. The public lands are common lands to be managed on behalf of a democratic people and are not to be kept for aristocratic use.
2. The public lands are a national heritage and trust and are not to be used or controlled exclusively by any region, state, or corporation.
3. The public lands are to be managed on behalf of all the public and are not to subsidize limited economic activities at the expense of the public interest. People who use the land for economic profit must be clearly differentiated from people who use it for personal growth and development, and priority must be given to people who do not profit from the land.
4. Revenues earned from the public lands, particularly from nonrenewable resources, must be invested to develop future renewable resources benefiting all Americans.
5. Most important, our public lands must be used and developed with constant consideration for conserving them for the future. Priority must be given to developing renewable resources. Future use of the land must take precedence over the present, especially in the case of nonrenewable resources. The public lands are this nation's gift to the future.

A manifesto for the public land is a manifesto for humans as well. As a nation, we must turn this era of waste and exploitation into a time to discover and articulate the special benefits of the land we all own. We must expose the politics of greed, declare that the land is a unique renewable resource, and insist that it be kept that way. We are personally tied to this land and its strength; we are the freest people on earth, largely because of our public land. We must not forget the land, nor permit anyone to take it or destroy it.

We need a wild land full of promise and hope, its strength and integrity intact. We need a land to challenge new generations, not pamper them, and public lands contain this nation's wildest and most rugged land. We need places to discover the spirit of the earth. Such a challenge can come only from public land—land shared in common with all of our people in this generation and countless generations to come. The public land must be kept as unique as its tradition and as exhilarating as its epic history.

We need a spacious and free land to learn the depth and passion of our history—to touch and feel and smell it. We need to have places haunted with the past and full of promise for the future, not consumed by and for the present.

James Norman Hall once wrote in the *Atlantic Monthly* that the spirit of place is not to be captured in a butterfly net of words. He said the subtle, elusive spirits live in the smallest island, on the greatest continent, on hills and in valleys. Spirits of place rule people by coloring their moods and by arousing their souls. This spirit of place is the essence of the nation.

But people have the power of life and death over these spirits. As a nation we have power over the spirits of the wild that remain only on the vast commons—the federal public-domain lands—where we have kept them alive. We may find them, along with the spirits of humans who knew them well, in a rock hunting blind left by an ancient Paiute at a Nevada spring, or in a tepee ring whose entrance faces the sun above the wild Missouri. Or they may be found in a dark Utah canyon, where we can touch the canyon walls, trace the outline of a petroglyph with our fingers, and find ourselves connected through time to some ancient artist.

Those of us who have felt the spirit of a wilderness know the loss when a wild place is developed. We also know that most of these wild places are found only on the lands we own in common, each with its own feelings and array of stars. Every one of us has a place that is our homeland. No other region will satisfy; no other place feels like home. We are part of the land, and the land is part of us.

The American landscape has never been at one with the white culture that has changed the land's spirit and character everywhere but the places left as the public domain. Our manifesto must maintain a public domain haunted with a great past, a land intact and sustaining. The land must be kept free for us to use together, part of the geography of our frontiers of yesterday and of tomorrow. If we fail we will be like Black Elk, the Sioux visionary, who saw a vision of his land and his people's spirit fail at Wounded Knee. Decades later he told the poet and writer John Neihardt:

"And I, to whom so great a vision was given in my youth, you see now a pitiful old man who has done nothing, for the nation's hoop is broken and scattered. There is no center any longer and the sacred tree is dead."

If we do not reform the way our public land is managed, and if we do not write a strong manifesto for the public land, we will lose our land, our wealth, our power and freedom. We will be like the Indian severed from mother earth. Without the land we will grow ox-like. As a people we will then have only the option of striving for material goods in a human-created world. We will lose touch with the spirit of the earth and be adrift in a sea of materialism. Our love for the great land of America that we own in common as a nation must be more powerful than greed. Our children must have their heritage.

Selected Bibliography

Cameron, Jenks. *The Development of Governmental Forest Control in the United States.* Baltimore: John Hopkins Press, 1928.

Calef, Wesley. *Private Grazing and the Public Lands.* Chicago: University of Chicago Press, 1960.

Culhane, Paul J. *Public Land Politics: Interest Group Influences on the Forest Service and the Bureau of Land Management.* Washington: Resources for the Future, 1981.

Dana, Samuel T., and Sally K. Fairfax. *Forest and Range Management,* second edition. New York: McGraw-Hill, 1980.

Dick, Everett. *The Lure of the Land.* Lincoln: University of Nebraska Press, 1970.

Foss, Phillip. *Politics and Grass.* Seattle: Greenwood Press, 1960.

Fox, Stephen. *John Muir and his Legacy: The American Conservation Movement.* Boston: Little Brown, 1981.

Fradkin, Philip. *A River No More: The Colorado River and the West.* New York: Alfred A. Knopf, 1981.

Frome, Michael. *The Battle for the Wilderness.* New York: Praeger Publishers, 1974.

Gates, Paul Wallace. *History of Public Land Law Development.* Washington: U.S. Government Printing Office, 1968.

Graber, Linda H. *Wilderness as Sacred Space.* Washington: Association of American Geographers, 1976.

Hays, Samuel P. *Conservation and the Gospel of Efficiency.* Cambridge: Harvard University Press, 1959.

Hibbard, Benjamin. *A History of the Public Land Policies.* New York: Macmillan, 1924.

Ise, John. *Our National Park Policy: A Critical History.* Baltimore: Johns Hopkins Press, 1961.

Kaufman, Herbert. *The Forest Ranger: A Study in Administrative Behavior.* Baltimore: Johns Hopkins Press, 1960.

Marsh, George P. *Man and Nature: The Earth as Modified by Human Action.* New York: Scribner, 1874.

Nash, Roderick. *Wilderness and the American Mind*, third edition. New Haven: Yale University Press, 1982.

O'Toole, K. Ross. *The Rape of the Great Plains: Northwest America, Cattle and Coal.* Boston: Little Brown, 1976.

Peffer, E. Louise. *The Closing of the Public Domain.* Stanford: Stanford University Press, 1951.

Powell, John Wesley. *Report on the Lands of the Arid Region of the United States,* edited by Wallace Stegner. Cambridge: Harvard University Press, 1962.

Public Land Law Review Commission. *One Third of the Nation's Land: A Report to the President and the Congress by the Public Land Law Review Commission.* Washington: U.S. Government Printing Office, 1970.

Richardson, Elmo. *Dams, Parks and Politics.* Lexington: University Press of Kentucky, 1973.

Robbins, Roy M. *Our Land Heritage.* Princeton: Princeton University Press, 1962.

Robinson, Glen O. *The Forest Service: A Study in Public Land Management.* Baltimore: Johns Hopkins Press, 1975.

Rogers, Andrew Denny. *Bernhard Eduard Fernow.* Princeton: Princeton University Press, 1951.

Runte, Alfred. *National Parks The American Experience.* Lincoln: University of Nebraska Press, 1979.

Schiff, Ashley. *Fire and Water: Scientific Heresy in the Forest Service.* Cambridge: Harvard University Press, 1962.

Shands, William E., and Robert G. Healy. *The Lands Nobody Wanted.* Washington: The Conservation Foundation, 1972.

Shankland, Robert. *Steve Mather of the National Parks.* New York: Alfred A. Knopf, 1951.

Stegner, Wallace. *Beyond the Hundredth Meridian.* Boston: Houghton Mifflin, 1953.

Thirgood, J.V. *Man and the Mediterranean Forest.* New York: Academic Press, 1981.

Udall, Stewart L. *The Quiet Crisis.* New York: Holt, Rinehart and Winston, 1963.

Voigt, William. *Public Grazing Land: Use and Misuse by Industry and Government.* New Brunswick: Rutgers University Press, 1976.

Webb, Walter Prescott. *The Great Plains.* New York: Grosset and Dunlap, 1931.

Wyant, William K. *Westward in Eden.* Berkeley: University of California Press, 1982.

Index